C72
3
Rau

P9-BZN-200

Rev. A. Ettenhofer

Heath United Methodist Church

W. Richard Waddle, Pastor

1149 Hebron Rd., Heath, Ohio 43056   Church 522-3133   Res. 522-4710

Presented by:

REV. ARNOLD ETTENHOFER

NEW FRONTIERS
OF
CHRISTIANITY

NEW

FRONTIERS

ASSOCIATION PRESS   New York

OF
CHRISTIANITY

edited by
RALPH C. RAUGHLEY, JR.

NEW FRONTIERS OF CHRISTIANITY

Copyright © 1962 by

National Board of Young Men's Christian Associations

Association Press, 291 Broadway, New York 7, N.Y.

All rights reserved, including the right of reproduction in
whole or in part in any form, under the International,
Pan-American, and Universal Copyright Conventions.

Publisher's title stock number: 1479

Library of Congress catalog card number 62-9395

 72

Printed in the United States of America

Introduction

THE purpose of this symposium is to chart, in each of a dozen major areas of contemporary life, some of the new frontiers on which Christianity will find significant problems—and opportunities—in the days and years ahead.

What is said here will ignite vigorous differences of opinion. When dedicated specialists discuss the future of their own fields, they run the risk of being considered visionary and impractical, and sometimes bellicose and inflammatory, or even heretical; leadership always includes being a target. It is informed imaginations such as theirs, however, that nourish the growing edge of Christianity and maintain its strength.

John Bennett's proposals for resolving the dispute over tax aid to parochial schools; Ian Barbour's vision of a hope in modern science for a deeper understanding of the fundamentals of the Christian faith; Roger Hazelton's provocative distinction between a viable theology and a rigid ideology; the possibilities for Christianity to become far more effective in the universities, as seen by J. Edward Dirks; Paul Schilpp's warning of the implications of rational philosophy for our theology and for the semantics of doctrine; the newly urgent problem, as articulated by Joseph Kitagawa, of our stance in confronting other religions in the coming compression of the world's population from numerous, widely scattered redoubts into a single shrinking chamber; the iconoclastic tactics proposed by Graydon McClellan for rescuing the minister from the religious-club chaplaincy to which he is increasingly relegated.... These are just a few samples of the challenges that the participants in this symposium discern in the road ahead.

It is not a book for everyone. The authors have made no attempt to confine their utterances to a mass-circulation level, nor do they avoid sensitive subjects in deference to the artless. They are addressing their peers. For informed and thoughtful Christians—for those who can contemplate new ideas without blinking, even though they may pale a little at times—this discussion should be absorbing and significant.

There are two groups for which this panoply of spiritual and intellectual vigor should have special values.

One consists of those thousands of able, well-educated, zealous clergymen immured in the loneliness of the typical parish ministry. From the exciting seminary atmosphere of growth and vision and understanding and encouragement, they have gone to a milieu which sees them not as prophets but as comforters —not as guides to a new and better world but as resuscitators of a dying one. They go "not in entire forgetfulness, and not in utter nakedness," but mightily lonely, and increasingly uncertain. To the east they see the absorbent-cotton coast of Dr. Peale, and to the west the Birchwood grove of Dr. Fifield; in the newspapers they read that Martin Luther King is arrested again and Malcolm Boyd is tried for heresy and a patent-medicine-Bible type of "evangelist" has added thirty-two more stations to his network program. Imperceptibly the wonder grows as to which is reality, and which dream. The local Council of Ministers is concerned about possible conflicts among the three fund-raising drives scheduled for September. Contacts with more experienced and wiser colleagues usually consist of the hurried visits of bishop or superintendent; and, if the discussion of administration and finance and church school curriculum leaves little time for theology and philosophy, it is no one's fault. The minister needs the backing of pure ideas as the family physician needs the backing of pure research. It is our hope that he may find some here.

The other group, admittedly less likely to be reached, consists of the majority of literate and cultured people outside the ministry who are also, in every meaningful sense, outside the Church—teachers, scientists, doctors and lawyers, writers and artists.... This book would probably affect most of them somewhat like the sight of a dinosaur walking down the street—this demonstration that Christianity is still, as it has been for two millennia, the yeast in the ferment of revolution; a living force in today's terms, and not just a historical fact in yesterday's. Because most churches usually present themselves to the public scrutiny as defenders of the *status quo*, they assume that that is what the Church is. Because so many Christians are illiterate in their theology, infantile in their Christology, superficial in their understanding of the Bible, and inarticulate and insecure in morality and social ethics, those without firsthand knowledge assume that that is what Christianity is. The following chapters might reveal vistas wholly new to them.

Some of such hard-shelled eggheads might, of course, react by saying that the dedication and the spiritual and intellectual integrity of a few outstanding men, though admirable enough, are irrelevant. Can it matter what possibilities a Samuel McCrea Cavert sees in the ecumenical movement when millions of churchgoers interpret "faith of our fathers" as "denomination of *my* father"? Can it matter that a Roger Shinn has a vision of Christianity healing the malignant lesions in our social body when white Christian meets Negro Christian in the narthex and says: "You are not welcome here"?

All our history shows us that it does indeed matter. It matters more than anything else. When Martin Luther rebelled, he was at first alone. Søren Kierkegaard wrote in desperate solitude, and died long before his work showed the first symptoms of long-term viability. In our own times men like Walter Rauschenbusch, Ernest Fremont Tittle, G. Bromley Oxnam, and Harry Emerson Fosdick knew what it was to breast the wave of the contemporary that can so easily overwhelm the individual. But nothing can permanently contain the force of an idea that embodies a truth; the world changes for the better because someone conceives the possibility and has faith in it.

*   *   *   *   *

The editor is grateful for the opportunity to work on this volume because it has conferred the privilege of association with some of the finest men and most acute minds our civilization has produced—men who are the embodiment of the creative spirit that Christianity has done so much to nurture and expand.

A special debt is owed (far beyond the worth of this small gesture to repay) to Dr. Samuel McCrea Cavert, whose generous guidance has been literally indispensable, and whose kindly but incisive criticism of each stage of the project has been an education and a challenge.

R. C. R.

Manhasset, New York

About the Contributors

IAN G. BARBOUR

Ian G. Barbour is chairman of the Department of Religion and associate professor of physics at Carleton College, Northfield, Minnesota. He earned the Ph.D. in physics from the University of Chicago, and the B.D. in theology from Yale. Currently he is on leave from Carleton to teach at Chicago Theological Seminary. He is the author of *Christianity and the Scientist*, he contributed a chapter to *Science Ponders Religion* (edited by Harlow Shapley), and has written many articles for various scientific, philosophical, and theological journals.

REUEL L. HOWE

A pioneer in relating the pastoral ministry to modern psychology, Reuel Howe taught for a score of years at the Philadelphia Divinity School and the Theological Seminary, Alexandria, Virginia, before becoming director of an experimental project, the Institute for Advanced Pastoral Studies, Bloomfield Hills, Michigan, where selected ministers who are interested in better pastoral counseling can secure special training. He is an Episcopalian minister whose latest book, *Herein Is Love*, shows loving and being loved as the heart of the Christian experience.

ROGER L. SHINN

Roger Shinn received his B.D. at Union Theological Seminary in New York, and then entered the army, serving as a major in World War II. He was awarded the Silver Star for gallantry in the Battle of the Bulge. Following his discharge, he was ordained in the Evangelical and Reformed Church and earned

9

his Ph.D. at Columbia University. He is now professor of Applied Christianity at his alma mater, Union Seminary; previously he had been professor of Christian Ethics at Vanderbilt Divinity School, Nashville. He is a member of the editorial board of *Christianity and Crisis* and a frequent contributor to that and other journals. His many books include *Christianity and the Problem of History*.

PAUL H. ELMEN

Paul Elmen has managed to find outlet for two major interests—theology and English literature. His present position as associate professor of moral theology and Christian ethics at Seabury-Western Theological Seminary, Evanston, Illinois, follows nearly a decade of teaching in the English Department at Northwestern University concurrent, for two years, with a post as curate at St. Mark's (Episcopal) Church. He served as an army chaplain in World War II, was wounded in France, and decorated with the Silver and the Bronze Stars for gallantry. Literary and religious journals frequently carry his articles and book reviews, and he is author of *The Restoration of Meaning to Contemporary Life*.

J. EDWARD DIRKS

As Stephen Morrell Clement professor of Christian methods at Yale Divinity School, J. Edward Dirks is responsible for teaching in the field of theology and higher education. Earlier he had served as associate general director of the National Council of Churches' Commission on Christian Higher Education, and before that had been professor of philosophy at Lake Forest College, Illinois. Ordained in the Presbyterian Church, U.S.A., he received his theological training at McCormick Theological Seminary, Yale Divinity School, and Union Seminary (New York); and he has his Ph.D. degree from Columbia University. He is the editor of *The Christian Scholar*.

GRAYDON E. McCLELLAN

A Texan by birth, Graydon McClellan early migrated to California, where he was graduated from the University of

California and then earned his M.A. and B.D. degrees at the San Francisco Theological Seminary. After serving as executive director of the National Council of Churches' department of the ministry, he is now general presbyter of the New York Presbytery, The United Presbyterian Church in the U.S.A., where he has the dual problem of enlisting ministers and insisting on a "tough new breed of servant-minded pastors." A former ecumenical fellow at Union Seminary, New York, he has written articles on varied subjects for several religious periodicals.

NORMAN GOODALL

Norman Goodall, of England, is assistant general secretary of the World Council of Churches, having previously served as secretary of the Joint Committee of the World Council and the International Missionary Council. A minister of the Congregational Church, he received his theological preparation at Mansfield College, Oxford, spending the next twenty years in pastorates and in missionary administration. He is the author of numerous books, the most recent being *The Ecumenical Movement: What It Is and What It Does.*

JOSEPH M. KITAGAWA

Born in Osaka, Japan, Joseph Kitagawa is a naturalized citizen of the United States. He has been teaching the history of religions at the Federated Theological Faculty of the University of Chicago since 1951. He has his B.D. degree from Seabury-Western Theological Seminary, and his Ph.D. from the University of Chicago. Previously he studied at Rikkyo University in Tokyo, and he has also taught at the Buddhist Koyasan University in Japan, and in other Asian universities. A contributor to religious and scholarly magazines, he is the author of the full-length study, *Religions of the East.*

JOHN C. BENNETT

The first to be honored by appointment to the Reinhold Niebuhr Chair of Social Ethics at Union Theological Seminary is John C. Bennett, who has taught there since 1943 and has been dean of the faculty since 1955. Previously he had been professor of Christian theology and philosophy of religion at the Pacific School of Religion, Berkeley. A Congregationalist, he is a frequent lecturer and contributor to various journals, is co-editor of *Christianity and Crisis*, and the author of several books, including *Christians and the State* and *Christianity and Communism Today*.

SAMUEL McCREA CAVERT

One of the chief architects of the World Council of Churches, Samuel McCrea Cavert has been a leader in interchurch cooperation for more than thirty years. He served in the key post of general secretary in the Federal and the National Councils of Churches, and was also executive secretary for the World Council in the U.S.A. A *summa cum laude* graduate of both Union College and Union Theological Seminary, he holds many honorary degrees. He was appointed official historian of the World Council's New Delhi Assembly, December, 1961. In his book, *On the Road to Christian Unity*, he recounts the ecumenical movement's first half-century.

PAUL ARTHUR SCHILPP

Paul A. Schilpp, professor of philosophy at Northwestern University and editor of the Library of Living Philosophers, was born in Dillenburg, Hessen-Nassau, Germany. He came to this country at the age of sixteen and studied at several schools, receiving his B.A. at Baldwin-Wallace College, Berea, Ohio (where he was later awarded an honorary Litt. D.); M.A. at Northwestern University; B.D. at Garrett Biblical Institute; and Ph.D. at Stanford University. Ordained in the Methodist Church, he had several years of parish experience before entering his teaching career. He has held several distinguished lectureships, and represented the State Department at a philosophy congress held in Pakistan in 1956. The many books he has written include *The Quest for Religious Realism*, and among philosophical works his *Kant's Pre-Critical Ethics* is outstanding.

ROGER HAZELTON

Roger Hazelton took up his post as dean of the Graduate School of Theology at Oberlin College in 1960. In the same year his *New Accents in Contemporary Theology* won him recognition as one of the front-rank theologians today. Previously he had taught theology at Andover-Newton Theological School and philosophy and religion at Pomona College. Born in Chicago, he received his formal education at Amherst College, Chicago Theological Seminary, the University of Chicago, and Yale University. He also spent a year at the Sorbonne doing research on Pascal under a Fulbright grant.

Contents

NEW FRONTIERS
OF
CHRISTIANITY

IAN G. BARBOUR

The Natural Sciences

WHAT will the space age do to the world view of Americans? At what points will the growth of technology have theological implications? What new discoveries are likely to be made, and what might be significant Christian responses to them? These are vast and far-reaching questions, and we can only select here some sample developments from three very different aspects of the scientific enterprise: first, from *pure science,* some possible scientific discoveries and their effect on our religious ideas and understanding of the world; second, recent thought about *the methods of science* as it may influence our conceptions of truth and reality; and, third, some examples of the impact which *applied science* or technology will have on our values and on the future of man.

Can we anticipate that future scientific discoveries will have religious implications? I should want to start by urging considerable caution because, in the past, theological conclusions drawn from science have usually been dubious, and have often failed to distinguish genuinely religious questions from scientific ones.

THEISM AND DARWIN'S CENTENNIAL

The Darwin Centennial has redirected attention to the evolution issue. Even today, few laymen understand that most theologians completely dissociate the religious message of Genesis from the views of the natural world current in ancient times.

We still need to underscore the specifically theological meaning of the doctrine of creation, assertions such as the following: The world is good—the biblical view emphasizes the goodness of life in contrast to Hinduism which tends to look on the world as essentially unreal and illusory, or the teachings of Buddha which sometimes refer to matter as evil. The world is orderly—and science itself must assume that nature is law-abiding and intelligible. Creation is purposeful, so existence is not meaningless and accidental. Above all, the world is dependent on God, the source of all that is. These are primarily statements about man's relation to God and the meaning of human existence and nature in the present. Of course, none of these assertions need be abandoned if we say that God's way of creating was by a long, slow process rather than a six-day feat.

But in addition to the mistake of expecting Scripture to answer scientific questions, there has been the reverse error of expecting science to answer theological questions—a temptation for theistic as well as atheistic authors, and one which can be criticized on both scientific and theological grounds. In the classic expression of the argument from design, Paley suggested that if one finds a watch on a desert island, he concludes there must have been a watchmaker; if one observes the intricacy of the human eye, he concludes there must have been an intelligent designer. The analogy is inadequate scientifically, for it assumes that man originated in his present form. The analogy is inadequate theologically, for the image of God as maker is taken too simply from the human craftsman, and the meanings of causality and dependence are not analyzed.

Now some Christian biologists continue today this same error in a modified form by trying to exploit problems about the mechanisms of evolution which are still under debate. Are favorable mutations abundant enough to provide in the time available the variations which natural selection would require? (Laboratory data give no clear answer, for mutations from ionizing radiations appear to be both too rare and too predominantly unfavorable.) How can one account for the elimination of unused organs that are in no way detrimental (for example, the eyes of cave animals), or cases where an advantage would be gained only by the simultaneous occurrence of a large number of modifications, each of which is detrimental by itself (for example, factors in the nesting pattern of the cuckoo bird)? Some biologists consider such instances, for which no clear biological explanation is agreed upon, as evidence of God's intervention. This interpretation can be criticized scientifically, for it discourages the search for further understanding. It can also be criticized theologically as a continuation of the "God of the gaps," a rearguard action invoking God to explain an area of temporary ignorance. As C. A. Coulson puts it: "When we come to the scientifically unknown, our correct policy is not to rejoice because we have found God; it is to become better scientists."

Equally dubious are the opposing efforts to use evolution as evidence for a naturalistic world view. Julian Huxley's address at the Darwin Centennial conveys the impression that naturalism is a conclusion of science rather than a philosophical interpretation. He extends evolutionary categories into cultural and ideological areas as if they were direct deductions from biology, rather than analogies which may be inadequate because of the differences between the situations compared. For example, he uses Teilhard de Chardin's word "noösphere" or "sea of thought" to refer to man's mental environment, by analogy with the "hydrosphere" in which fishes live. "We try," Huxley says, "to use our conscious thought and purposes as organs of psychosocial locomotion and direction through the tangles of our existence." He speaks of religions as "organs of psychosocial man" which are destined to disappear. But does this analogy help us to discriminate among ideas? Is there some law of the survival of the fittest among ideologies, and what is the relation of fitness to truth?

Particularly problematical are the attempts to derive from the evolutionary process ethical norms for man's future evolution which, being subject to conscious choice, is a radically new and distinctive mode of change. In the last century, a picture of "nature red in tooth and claw" was often used to justify competition and social struggle; biological categories, such as survival, dominance, and control of environment, were transformed into social goals. At that time, Thomas Huxley, by contrast, saw man's duty as opposing the principles of previous evolution. Today, when the presence of co-operation and mutual aid in nature is recognized, Huxley the grandson enjoins us to take our ethical norms from evolution. The geneticist Dobzhansky replies: "Human acts and aspirations may be morally right or morally wrong regardless of whether they assist the evolutionary process to proceed in the direction in which it has been going."

If we can thus avoid the temptation to try to use a scientific theory as proof of our ultimate commitments, whether theistic or atheistic, we can see some important though more limited implications in evolution. We must reckon with the relatedness of all forms of life, the mutual interdependence and interaction of the various parts of the total web of life. The interaction of the individual unit and the total environment assumes new importance. There is continuity between different levels of reality, though each level has distinctive aspects transcending those of lower levels and not reducible to them. We have to take seriously the role of time, process, and development. Where classical thought had identified the real as the unchanging, now the dynamic character of existence, the presence of development, novelty, and growth, are seen as fundamental. The influence of evolutionary categories on the philosophies of Bergson, Whitehead, and Dewey may be especially noted.

In more specifically theological terms, evolution can help us to recover the concept of continuing creation, which was part of early church tradition until it was completely subordinated to the idea of instantaneous creation *ex nihilo*. To be sure, Christianity sees the locus of God's activity primarily in the sphere of the personal—the selfhood of the individual, the life of the group, events in history. Yet God's creativity in nature has been affirmed, and can acquire new meaning in relation to the long history of nature. Attention to God's immanence need not lead to pantheism or the denial of transcendence. Evolution does make creation a slow and costly process, accompanied by pain and suffering. But surely Christianity has always maintained that God's involvement in the world is costly, and makes the cross the supreme symbol of the significance of suffering. This is a God who participates in the drama of the world, without being just a part of nature.

This raises the question of the reign of uniform mechanical laws. The deterministic view of scientific law has of course been weakened by the presence of chance (random mutations) in biology, and indeterminacy (see pp. 25-26) in physics. But in any case explanations in terms of scientific law do not necessarily rule out the possibility of purpose. If theologians have been mistaken in arguing that God interferes at discrete points, naturalistic philosophers have been equally mistaken in arguing that an explanation in terms of secondary causes disproves the existence of God. A human action can be described in terms of physiological causes and also in terms of teleological goals; both types of explanation are valid, for man uses law-abiding processes for the expression of his purposes. It is not self-contradictory to say that God works through finite causes. Purpose and design are then expressed not in specific intervention but in the very structure of a universe suited to the emergence of life and mind, and in the requisite chemical and biological laws, which L. J. Henderson referred to as "the fitness of the environment." I have tried to indicate some of the implications of evolution for our concept of God, but a similar approach could be followed in looking at implications for the nature of man.

NEW ATOMS FOR OLD

In the case of the new physics also, it seems to me that many interpreters have claimed too much for philosophical and theological implications, and we must again start with a word of caution. The development of a mechanistic philosophy from classical physics was based on inadequate science, which the revolution of twentieth-century physics has replaced. But it was also dubious philosophically. Following Galileo and Newton, the authors of the French Enlightenment construed reality to be matter in motion. They attributed to reality only those properties—mass and velocity—with which physics had been able to deal successfully. E. A. Burtt refers to this process as "constructing metaphysics out of a method." The categories of physics, which had proved so powerful, were believed to be adequate to describe every aspect of man. All causality was said to lie in the forces between atoms. To explain anything meant to reduce it to its elementary parts. Laplace claimed that if he knew the position and velocity of every particle in the universe, he could predict all their future positions and hence all future events.

Twentieth-century physics has transformed the science on which this mechanistic philosophy was based. At first the new experimental findings—the electron, radioactivity, X rays—were interpreted in essentially mechanical terms. You have all seen this early model of an atom, composed of a nucleus with electrons whirling around it. Enlarged a trillion times, it would have a heavy nucleus the size of a pinhead, with several football-size electrons whirling around it in orbits a hundred yards across. But this model has been replaced by a wave structure described by differential equations—an abstract mathematical representation of fields which can't be visualized at all. If you imagined yourself inside the new atom, you would be surrounded by a pattern of waves filling the whole region in harmonic relationships in space and time, which we might compare with a sort of three-dimensional symphony of musical tones of incredible complexity. The other revolutionary development of modern physics is relativity, in which mass, length, and even time are not unchanging properties of objects in themselves, but properties of relationships; mass is a temporary manifestation of energy, and vice versa.

Now some interpreters see far-reaching significance in these changes. Matter consists not of little particles but of patterns in probability-waves, so Eddington and Jeans acclaim the downfall of materialism and the victory of idealism. But surely there is nothing more mental or spiritual about energy or wave equations than about the older model of the atom which seemed more tangible. It is true that space and time are now relational rather than substantial, and that analysis of systems into their smallest parts is no longer the prototype of valid explanation; but we must not claim too much for this new perspective. Perhaps we should be glad that the concepts of modern physics are difficult for the layman to understand and impossible for him to visualize, so they have led to fewer false inferences than did the ideas of Newton and Darwin. Moreover, quantum mechanics and relativity apply to the domains of the very small and the very large, and hence do not yield for everyday experience any comprehensive explanations or useful images and analogies. With this caveat in mind, however, we can note some interesting but modest implications.

One strange result of the new physics is expressed in the Heisenberg Uncertainty Principle. The quantum atom can only be described by probability distributions, and no exact values of position and velocity can be determined. For example, the time at which a particular radioactive atom will disintegrate, causing a click in a Geiger counter, cannot be calculated, for nuclear theory allows only determination of statistical distributions. A few physicists, including Einstein and Planck, have held that behind these probabilities are more detailed causes

at present unknown; uncertainty would then reflect only the
limitations of our present knowledge. But most physicists believe that the uncertainty is irreducible and implies a break in
detailed causality. This would mean the refutation of Laplace's
claim that the future is in principle predictable.

What is the implication of the Uncertainty Principle for
human freedom? Clearly the determinism of mechanistic philosophy is undermined. A gap in the causal nexus may introduce
the possibility of freedom, but I cannot agree with those who
say the problem is now solved. For within physics, indetermin-
ism is treated as entirely equivalent to chance. To be sure, both
freedom and chance result in unpredictability, yet they have
little else in common. We wouldn't attribute freedom to a
roulette wheel even if in principle it were unpredictable; the
alternatives within physics are cause and chance. In the analysis
of human freedom and the meaning of selfhood the categories
of physics seem to me to have only limited applicability. Responsible choice is not arbitrary and "uncaused" activity, dis-
continuous from any antecedents, but rather acting in accord
with one's own purposes and values. The Uncertainty Principle,
then, has served a valuable theological function in undermining
the reductionistic determinism of earlier thought, but I do not
see that it has supplied useful categories for the discussion of
freedom.

But there is a change brought about by the new physics which
seems to me more fundamental. There has been an important
change in the physicist's understanding of what a scientific
theory is. Previously, scientific knowledge was thought of as a
literal description of reality, an exact reproduction, or at least
a model of nature as it is in itself. Today we recognize that our
theories are much more indirect and symbolic representations
of the particular aspect of nature which we are studying. They
are more like the image of a countryside viewed at night on a
radar screen, in which we have to try to reconstruct the characteristics of the countryside as best we can from the way in

which different parts of it reflect our radar signals. The physicist tries to reconstruct the atomic world from the results of his experimental probings; in the case of the atom, the relation of the scientific representation to the reality represented is particularly indirect. We shall return shortly to this new understanding of the role of a scientific theory.

DISCOVERIES IN SPACE

The distinction between scientific and religious questions, which was stressed in considering evolution, is also important in considering some of the discoveries that may be made in the next few years. Some Christian authors have stated that man can never cross the gap between nonliving matter and living organisms. But year by year this gap is narrowing. Already biochemists have taken apart and put together again virus molecules which can reproduce themselves. Surely no religious principle is at stake if, in the future, living cells can be constructed in the laboratory.

As another example, two theories of the age of the universe are now being debated by astronomers. According to the so-called "steady-state" theory, popularized by Hoyle, time is infinite, and matter is being continuously created throughout time and space. According to the rival theory, sometimes called the "big-bang" theory, for which Gamow has been a spokesman, the universe has a finite age and came into being instantaneously about six billion years ago—though this figure may have to be revised upward in the light of recent findings. At present the scientific evidence is not sufficient to decide between the two theories, and some theologians have taken sides in the debate. But I don't believe Christians need be committed to a finite time-span or a sudden origin for matter, because as I have indicated this is not what the doctrine of creation is all about.

Or consider the question of life on other planets. It seems

probable that the necessary conditions for life exist elsewhere
in the universe. The number of stars is so gigantic—the number
one followed by about twenty zeros—that if even one star in
a million had a suitable planet revolving around it, there would
still be 100,000 suitable planets in our galaxy alone. The same
scientific laws which hold on our earth appear to hold throughout the universe. Dr. Urey and Dr. Miller in their laboratory
in Chicago passed sparks through a mixture of gases similar to
those which might exist on a lifeless planet. They found that
there were formed many of the amino acids, the building-blocks
of life. Of course the only certain way to find out if life exists
elsewhere is by direct investigation. The giant radiotelescope
in West Virginia, trained on other galaxies, has been listening
for possible intelligible signals. Space travel to other planets
would be the conclusive test. It is rather likely, however, that
the nearest inhabitable planet may be too distant for practical
travel. There is an upper limit to possible traveling speed,
namely the velocity of light; to reach a star a thousand light
years away would require at least a thousand years, or thirty
generations in the space ship!

It has sometimes been stated that on theological grounds we
can be sure there are no intelligent beings elsewhere in the
universe. I would reply that as Christians we can await with
great interest whatever exciting new discoveries are in fact made.
True, the existence of other creatures would demote even further our geographical egotism in the cosmos, but would be no
threat to our religious faith, our belief in a universal God. We
can be confident that if there are such beings, God's love
includes them also, though perhaps we shouldn't try to predict
just how this has expressed itself in other worlds, or what
Christ's role there might be. If there are missionaries on our
first space ship, I would hope that they can listen and observe
and learn before they speak too much.

In the unlikely event that we do have cosmic neighbors near
enough to reach, we could speculate about our relation to them.

Of course much would depend on the kind of beings we found. Their intelligence might be considerably greater than ours—or it might be less. One might guess that some of their basic problems would be rather similar to ours. On any planet, for example, there would be the question of the relation of the individual to the group—whatever form of social or political organization existed—and some of the same tensions between love and hate, co-operation and competition. Perhaps they will be highly advanced in scientific knowledge, as science fiction imagines, or perhaps they will have degrees of artistic and musical sensitivity as far beyond us as we are beyond the cave man. Perhaps the depth of their religious experience and understanding of God is more profound than ours. It may be that God has revealed himself in their history in ways we cannot imagine. How will we treat our cosmic neighbors? Our past record in treating people even a little bit different from us—even a difference in skin color—is not too encouraging. We tend to react to strangers with fear instead of love. Will we spread the conflict and discord which has been earth's history into outer space? Today these are only problems for speculation, but within this century they could be questions for responsible decision.

Note, then, the general approach I am suggesting to future problems of scientific knowledge, the content of specific discoveries. It starts by distinguishing scientific from theological questions, and it does not expect science itself to provide a comprehensive view of reality. But it also believes that science makes important contributions to our world view, and that conversation between scientists and theologians can be valuable when each respects the integrity of the work of the other.

THE METHODS OF SCIENCE

We have looked at pure science as specific knowledge. Science is also a method, a way of thinking. To college students this aspect is often the most influential; science seems to them the only reliable path toward knowledge, the only valid approach to truth. This same emphasis appears in C. P. Snow's *Two Cultures and the Scientific Revolution*,[1] which describes the inability of men in the sciences and in the humanities to understand each other. To improve communication, Snow recommends educational curricula requiring deeper acquaintance with areas outside one's specialization. Perhaps analysis of the methods of the scientist can also illuminate similarities as well as differences between fields.

Contrary to the popular impression, scientific discovery is seldom simply a matter of precise observation and accumulation of facts. Human creativity enters because theories require the invention of mental constructs in terms of which the data can be understood and organized. The concepts of valence, entropy, and nucleus were not given to us ready-made by nature, but were interpretations created in order to co-ordinate data. We have mentioned that the new physics is not a literal representation but a symbolic device by which to correlate and predict patterns of experimental relationship. Major advances have usually required new conceptual schemes, new ways of looking at facts, new ideas for the design of apparatus. Here imagination and originality are necessary, and the work of the scientist has much in common with that of the artist. There is even an aesthetic element in the scientist's response to the intellectual beauty of a theory.

In several ways the assumption that science is detached, impersonal, and objective has come under new scrutiny. "Objectivity" cannot mean the simple observation of facts, for creative imagination is necessary for the invention of new concepts. The personality of the scientist and the particular way in which his mind works is especially important in the creation of original and revolutionary theories. Moreover, the scientist is far from

---

[1] Cambridge University Press, 1959.

detached, for he has strong personal motivations in his work; these may vary from curiosity and intellectual satisfaction to economic security and personal ambition.

Some authors have made much of the so-called "involvement of the observer" in his experiment, which several branches of modern physics have disclosed. Atomic uncertainty can often be attributed to the disturbance of the system by the measuring process. In relativity, the mass, size, and even the time scale of objects depend on the frame of reference of the observer. The neat distinction between observer and observed breaks down, and we find that we are always dealing with relationships, not objects in themselves. It should be pointed out, however, that this "involvement of the observer" refers to the effects of the measuring apparatus (which might be an automatic camera) rather than to the scientist's involvement as a person.

A more personal and subjective involvement of the scientist has been stressed by Michael Polanyi in *Personal Knowledge.*[2] He has indicated that there are unavoidable elements of individual judgment in selecting the questions that are considered significant to ask, in weighing the evidence, and in assessing a theory and taking responsibility for its truth. Science is a very human enterprise, not a mechanical operation that infallibly mass-produces results. It is human in that it involves many facets of man. It is also a social enterprise, for the scientific community plays an important role in almost all phases of the work of the individual scientist. And science not only influences but is influenced by the larger cultural matrix and its presuppositions and interests and categories of thought.

Granting all this, I still believe that science does not entail the same sort of personal involvement that is required in religion. The scientist deals with the public world as his object of investigation, and observational techniques are objectively

<hr>

[2] *Personal Knowledge: Toward a postscientific philosophy* (Chicago: University of Chicago Press, 1958).

standardized. Public verification is sought through results re-
peatable by other competent observers, or "intersubjective
testability" within the scientific community. Scientific work,
though inherently private *qua* human experience, can yield
objective data because it deals with the impersonal world and
specifies operations not subject to individual idiosyncrasies.

It is an amazing process of refinement by which the exceedingly human activity that goes on in the laboratory—broken
test tubes, bright ideas, discussions with colleagues—ends up
as a single sentence in a journal: "The reaction was found to
be aided by the addition of 3 per cent NaOH"! We try to
impress this impersonality on our students in the very wording
of reports. The English Department might be delighted to
receive a theme reading: "I took the block and, though I had
a headache, I put it on the scales...." But for us it must be
written impersonally: "The block weighed...." H. D. Smyth
puts it vividly: "We have a paradox in the method of science.
The research man may often think and work like an artist, but
he has to talk like a bookkeeper in terms of facts, figures, and
logical sequences of thought." Thus the results of research are
public, objective, and impersonal.

In contrast, personal involvement is necessary in many areas
of life. In the social sciences the observer cannot stand outside
the social and historical process he is studying, and in the
humanities the attitude of the detached spectator yields only
limited understanding. Participation and response are the
essence of art and literature. The deepest knowledge of another
individual requires involvement in a relationship of trust and
love. Again, though the sciences can investigate significantly
many aspects of human behavior, the full meaning of selfhood
can never be studied externally. Total participation rather than
detached speculation is also a prerequisite of relationship to the
biblical God who acts primarily in the sphere of personal
existence.

tions. The scientist limits himself to sense-data and prefers variables which can be measured and treated by the developed formalism of mathematics. The more abstractive he can be, the more exact will be his results, but the further from ordinary life and from the immediacy, concreteness, and variety of human experience at all its levels.

In any specialized field there is a temptation to identify a partial perspective with the whole of existence. The biologist studies man as a biochemical mechanism, and it is easy for him to go on to say: man is *just* a biochemical mechanism. Reductionism is the interpretation of higher levels of organization exclusively in terms of lower; for example, "Psychology is just biology, biology is essentially chemistry, so atoms alone are real." Whitehead called this "the fallacy of misplaced concreteness," the tendency to attribute reality only to one particular set of abstractions, or to use one type of analysis to the exclusion of other modes of description. The validity of various levels must be upheld—levels related to each other and yet each having distinctive concepts and categories. Today the concept of organism seems to be a more fundamental image of nature than the machine, and there is a greater willingness to grant ontological status to factors occurring in higher levels of life and in human existence.

The assertion "only that with which science deals is real" can be defended only as a philosophical interpretation and not as a conclusion of science; for if the methods of the sciences are inherently selective, it cannot be decided on the basis of science alone whether the scientific description of existence is complete. The point is illustrated in Eddington's delightful parable about the zoologist studying deep-sea life by means of a net of ropes on a two-inch mesh. After repeated expeditions he concluded that there are no fish smaller than two inches in the sea! So also the scientific enterprise selects certain types of variables. Conversation between adherents of naturalism and theism, then, is not an argument between science and theology,

THE LIMITATIONS OF SCIENCE

We have examined in detail one self-imposed lin
science: its inability to deal with personal involvemen
of the requirements of objectivity. A second limitati
impossibility of judging ethical issues on scientific
which has been brought home to physicists by the
of the destructive potential they have unleashed. A thir
tion is the inability of the methods of science to deal
unique event. Scientific understanding aims at a particul
of knowledge, namely reproducible relations expressible i
eral laws. It is interested in individual events only as ins
of general laws.

Consider by contrast what a history teacher means whe
says he wants to help his students understand an event,
the French Revolution. His primary interest is not the form
tion of universal laws, but the analysis of a unique patt
among particular social factors and persons. We might call t
goal "configurational understanding," the attempt to see ho
the parts of an unrepeatable whole are related to each othe
General theories, though they may emerge, are not the primar
concern here. So also confrontation by a work of art, music
or literature is primarily a question of insight into the relations
among its parts. The theologian might add that for each person
the basic religious questions deal with the significance of the
one life each of us experiences from the inside, and its relation
to the singular God who is never one of a class of objects.

A fourth limitation which we must examine arises from the
selective character of any of the sciences. Every discipline develops its own symbolic language in terms of which it replaces
the total complex situation by a model representing those variables in which it is interested. In physics problems, an elephant
on a river bank becomes a mass with a coefficient of friction,
and a Beethoven symphony becomes a set of molecular vibra-

but between two ultimate commitments, two metaphysical interpretations of the nature of existence and the significance of human life.

There is a greater tentativeness regarding both scientific and extrascientific conclusions evident in the pronouncements of most contemporary scientists. At the close of the last century a physicist changed his vocation, stating in his resignation from the U.S. Patent Office that he wanted to get into "a field with a future"; it was widely believed that scientific knowledge was nearly complete, final truth all but achieved. Today the dynamic, relative, and partial character of specialized knowledge is more widely recognized. There is also greater cautiousness, in general, in projecting sweeping claims from scientific findings.

In the positivist movement of the 1930's, this caution took the extreme form of rejecting all metaphysical issues. Logical positivism claimed to be the philosophy which could speak in the name of science, and many scientists were willing for it to do so. It was asserted that the only meaningful statements are those verifiable by sense-experience, or definitions and tautologies. All other statements were considered to be meaningless; all discussions in metaphysics, ethics, and theology were said to be neither true nor false but "pseudo statements" or "purely emotive utterances."

Although logical positivism has been beneficial in encouraging greater clarity in the use of language, and has induced caution about claiming too much for the implications of scientific discoveries, it has been subject to criticism on several grounds. The purported dismissal of metaphysical questions often disguised a naturalistic or phenomenalistic metaphysics. Moral and theological arguments were ruled out arbitrarily in advance, not after considering them. It proved difficult to avoid dealing with the relation of statements to reality, and the attempt to reduce all propositions about the world to propositions about sense-data was unconvincing (for example, the status of other minds, past history, causality, and even ordinary "objects"). Another difficulty centered in the character of the central principle of positivism: "Only verifiable statements and definitions have meaning." This principle is not itself scientifically verifiable by sense-data. But it is not a definition either; branding a proposition "meaningless" derives its force from the usual connotation ("unintelligible," "nonsense," and so on). By its own criteria, then, the principle appears to be merely an emotive statement.

It is significant that most contemporary philosophical analysts have moved beyond positivism to recognize the diversity of purpose and function of different types of language. The new motto is: "Don't ask about the meaning of a statement; ask about its use." J. O. Urmson suggests: "Language has many tasks and many levels; we may not be trying to describe the world, and when we do we may do it in radically different ways not reducible to each other." So philosophers today are more willing to discuss metaphysical and theological propositions, and the role of analogical as well as literal language. We need to use various categories and frames of reference in dealing with different aspects of human experience.

Openness and humility, which have usually characterized the great scientists, are today more common among the philosophers and interpreters of science. The student of today, who will be the scientist of the next generation, must share these qualities, or he will be an easy victim of a positivist "scientism" which will exclude the possibility of religious commitment. Recognition of the limitations as well as the power of the methods of science may be as important a contribution to the future relations of science and religion as any specific developments in applied or pure science.

APPLIED SCIENCE AND CONTEMPORARY VALUES

Having considered pure science as specific knowledge, and scientific method as a way of knowing, we turn finally to applied science. To the man on the street, science means technology: TV sets, jet planes, plastics. It is these applications for which nations around the world are reaching out, and their future will be influenced by the patterns of life which the United States herself creates. One of the factors which will influence the next decade is *automation*. Where 1000 radios were until recently assembled daily by a crew of 200, two persons now run a machine with the same output. The man in the control center of an oil refinery in Oklahoma watches a wall of dials and gauges and a console of switches and buttons, as he presides over acres of pumps and tanks. In many types of industry, machines are already automated to control themselves in performing programed operations. The years ahead will see widespread use of computers to tend machines. How will such developments affect our values and our goals?

The applied scientist—the man who designs this automatic equipment, or develops color TV or guided missiles—experiences a *sense of power*. It is distinguishable from the curiosity and intellectual satisfaction of research in pure science, though the two are seldom separable. Power and exhilaration have long been expressed in the mythology of science-fiction adventures; today they are found within the laboratory. Where earlier generations spoke of understanding nature, we talk of the creation of new civilizations and the conquest of space. The motives of our space program are (1) military and (2) scientific, but also (3) political, in terms of international prestige in relation to Russia, and (4) psychological, as a symbol of the power of modern man. Scientific work is in itself exciting and challenging; here a man may be working in a world ten years ahead of the general public. Though he may have occasional doubts about the future of society, the scientist as an individual finds it almost impossible to share the mood of despair of contemporary existentialism. How could he see the world in Sartre's terms as an irrational and structureless chaos when he is making daily use of laws and structures? How could he see life as meaningless and purposeless, when he is caught up in an exciting project? In such creative achievement he has a purpose in his life and an orientation toward the future.

The new technology will increase per capita productivity which will result in higher living standards. From the biblical perspective, there is surely nothing wrong with technical progress in itself. We should indeed be deeply concerned about the conditions under which people live, for backbreaking scarcity and disease hardly enhance human fulfillment. There is an escapism and irrelevance about some of the proposed Christian answers: withdrawal to the monastery to preserve personal purity, or the rejection of the modern world by the Amish communities, or T. S. Eliot's suggestion that an agricultural civilization is more compatible with Christianity than an industrial one. No, the Church need not withdraw from the coming world, nor, at the opposite extreme, accept it uncritically; she must be involved in that world attempting to transform it.

This would mean welcoming the new technology and the immense benefits it can bring, and yet being aware of its dangers. Biblical religion does not object to material progress, but it does object when possessions become the only source of meaning in life. Unqualified devotion to technology as a total way of life can become a sort of idolatry, ultimate allegiance to something less than God. Even though we were overtly religious, our actual hope, our real faith, would then not be in God, but in the machine, as the source of good. Confidence in the power of man and pride in our know-how make us self-sufficient, and readily distort our attitude toward God. Exclusive preoccupation with technology can warp our values and goals, our picture of what life is for. We are a nation with greater material security than any people in history, and yet anxiety is more widespread. In the frantic pursuit of happiness in external things, we may end by being slaves to our own comforts. Here the values to which the church witnesses can bring men, not to a renunciation of scientific progress, but to a balanced perspective concerning the goals of life.

Another danger which will increase is the tendency for technical attitudes to predominate over man's personal existence. The same external, manipulative approach that is used in science can be projected into personal relationships. The biblical tradition enjoins us to love people and use objects; instead we love objects and use people. Thus it is essential to strengthen the strongholds of personal relationship—the family, the small group, and the local community, all of which are being eroded by our industrial civilization. In a day of depersonalizing forces, the Church is a community of acceptance, forgiveness, and joint search for meaning. Its gospel points to the irreducibly personal character of selfhood and of relationship to God and neighbor. This will be an essential message if the person is not to be submerged in the technological civilization of the future.

The age of automation will challenge the Church in other ways which we can only mention without elaboration. She will need to develop: (1) a theology of work, relevant to a culture in which the machine, not the worker, will be productive, and men as groups, not as individuals, will make decisions about work; (2) a theology of leisure suited to the shorter work-week of the future, in which "spare time" must be seen not as "the sin of idleness," but as creative opportunity for use of what will be the major portion of a man's waking hours; and (3) a theology of consumership which, in the coming economy of abundance, can stand up against the "hidden persuaders" and resist the assumptions about man and the images of success transmitted by the mass media.

SCIENCE AND THE FUTURE

What other developments in science may occur in the years ahead? Discoveries can never be predicted, but certain lines of advance seem probable, first in the biological sciences. Medical knowledge has in a quarter century increased further than in previous recorded history; in the next quarter century we can expect all the major diseases to be conquered. The replacement of defective organs, including hearts, has been predicted. Some scientists have spoken of the improvement of the human species by eugenic selection or, less plausibly, by influencing the chemistry of genes or the production of mutations. "Brainwashing" and subliminal advertising give us hints of what psychology will be able to do; tranquilizers provide a sample of the power of drugs, and lobotomy a glimpse of the use of surgery to change personality. Undoubtedly further understanding of the physiology of mental processes will be achieved, along the lines of experiments already carried out in which various sensations and memories can be stimulated electrically with very small electrodes placed in the brain. Computers capable of carrying out many types of "mental operation" can be anticipated.

There are two aspects of such discoveries which will be of concern to theology. In terms of theoretical knowledge (pure science) we can expect increasing evidence of man's rootedness in nature. Where Darwin showed man's historical dependence on the biological world, future developments are likely to underscore his present dependence on biological processes, from the chemistry of genes to the physiology of brains. Any remaining "gaps," such as those between "living" and "nonliving" or between "mind" and "brain," are likely to be closed. The temptation of reductionism will be great, and there will be those who will claim that a materialistic world view has been vindicated. The valid Christian response will not be the denial of man's fully biological nature, nor the attempt to recover an ontological dualism. But recognition of the continuity of the levels of existence does not mean the denial of the reality of higher levels. Process philosophy in the tradition of Whitehead, as well as the insights of Gestalt psychology on the relation of parts to wholes, provide categories which, it seems to me, will be useful in expressing the distinctive Christian perspective on the uniqueness of human personality without denying its biological basis.

In terms of the applications of knowledge these biological discoveries will create major ethical problems, for they will give greater possibilities of manipulating human personality than have ever existed previously. Under what circumstances would the use of drugs on persons be illegitimate? If individuals can be modified or fashioned genetically to specifications, who is to decide the formula for prefabricated man? By what image of superiority would a "superior species" be planned? Many Christians will believe it sinful to "tamper with God's creation." But we don't consider it sinful to remove a deformity with which a child is born or to improve man's eyesight, health, and intelligence. And few biologists consider man the terminus of "natural" evolutionary change. I can see no clear line as to *degrees* of modification of man beyond which it would in principle be wrong to go, though I can see profound ethical choices as to the *directions* of modification, and major social problems in any program for carrying them out without violating human freedom and dignity. Such an eventuality will be a dramatic instance of a general fact: every increase of knowledge brings greater power, and power can be used for good or evil.

New discoveries in the physical sciences will be particularly interesting at the extremes of the very large and the very small. We may find clear evidence as to whether our universe is finite in either space or in time. Space travel will yield knowledge of conditions on the moon and important clues to the history of our solar system. We may know more about life on other planets, as we have speculated above. Concerning the subatomic world, physicists are at the moment unhappy at the profusion of "elementary particles" following no apparent rhyme or reason, and the high-energy accelerators under construction will probably disclose others. Hopefully the development of new nuclear and particle theories will provide the desired unifying structure; such theories would also have far-reaching experimental and eventually practical implications. Controlled hydrogen fusion has been achieved for a fraction of a second in the laboratory, but there are many technical and theoretical problems which must be solved before a self-sustaining fusion reaction can become a useful source of energy.

The practical consequences of such advances are tremendous. Hydrogen fusion is potentially far more important than atomic energy reactions, for where uranium is scarce and expensive to mine, hydrogen is literally as abundant as the ocean. Such a source of energy may turn the deserts of the world into fertile and habitable lands; with adequate economic and political structures, the industrialization of underdeveloped countries could be greatly speeded. Nuclear technology is in its infancy. New knowledge of the extraordinary properties of metals and semiconductors, of which transistors give us a preview, will yield new materials, processes, and devices. Because scientific development is not just increasing, but increasing at an increasing rate, a few decades will transform the pattern of man's life.

The next decade is likely to be among the turning points of man's long history because of decisive choices about the use of science. The great constructive opportunity lies in technical assistance to underdeveloped countries, whose awakening to national self-consciousness is occurring at the moment when global technological development is for the first time scientifically possible. The overshadowing destructive threat lies, of course, in nuclear war, which for the first time could disrupt the total fabric of global civilization. Analysis of these two momentous issues has been omitted here only because they have been discussed elsewhere in this volume. Used creatively to fulfill the lives of persons, science may help bring in an age of abundance and universal well-being; but in an inadequate social context it will contribute to human degradation and enslavement, or even lead to man's destruction and extinction. The choice remains before us: "I have set before you life and death ... therefore choose life" (Deuteronomy 30:19).

REUEL L. HOWE

The Psychological Sciences

MANY students of the psychological sciences and of theology feel uneasy whenever a dialogue between their two disciplines is attempted. And some of them flatly refuse to consider the possibility of a mutual relation between the two fields of study. The promoter of dialogue is often treated as if he were an adulterer having an affair with an unlawful partner. The critic may even say, "I do not want the purity of the gospel to be adulterated with the humanism of psychology," which represents an attitude so prevailing that the conversations between the meanings of the gospel and the meanings of contemporary life are slowed down tragically.

The potential relation between the psychological sciences and theology is closer than we have yet realized. The psychological sciences are disciplines that help to raise out of human existence the questions for which Christianity is supposed to be an answer. They undertake to describe the nature and manner of man's living, the predicaments in which he finds himself, and the ambiguities with which he is faced. His actual existence stands in sharp contrast to what seem to be his essential potentialities, and raises questions concerning his purpose or destiny. Without such existentialist description as comes from psychology, affirmations about the nature of man's being are idealistic and discussions about his need of salvation remain theoretical.

It would seem, then, that the dialogue between theology and the social sciences cannot remain an option. It is necessary not only to theology, but to psychology as well. Whenever Christianity or any of its theological systems ignores or evades the

existential question by whomever raised, it becomes irresponsible.
One word of caution, however, is needed. *Christian theologi-*
cal thinking needs to beware of abdicating to the disciplines and
authority of psychology. There is much that we can learn from
the psychological sciences and we need their contribution to
our thought and practice. But we must remember that they
have only begun to scratch the surface of the truth about man
that is there to be uncovered, and that they subject what they
have discovered to many confused and contradictory interpretations. *Both the psychological sciences and theology need the*
disciplines and judgment of the other, and we should strive to
maintain the polarity between them. We turn now to a consideration of some of the contributions of the psychological
sciences to theology.

CONTRIBUTIONS

To the Doctrine of Man

The first and most important influence of the psychological
sciences on theology is in relation to the doctrine of man. The
task of formulating a theological interpretation of man must be
tackled afresh by each generation. Contemporary study has produced a deeper understanding of the nature, functioning, and
predicament of man that helps us to see anew in the terms of
descriptive science the insights of Augustine and the Reformation. Protestantism since the Reformation had developed a
weakened concept of the power of sin and the reuniting power
of grace, and combined it with an emphasis on individual and
social morality. So pervasive is this Pelagianism that a high per-
centage of church members believe that their membership in
the Christian fellowship depends upon "keeping the law" and
"doing good." The insights of the various psychological studies
expose how vain is the appeal to free will and how empty of
power is the moralistic approach to human need.

They explore and describe, for example, the nature, source, and pervasive power of man's egocentricity which makes ambivalent his power to respond to love and to love. Their contribution thus helps us to understand the radical alienation that exists between egocentric man and God who is Love. An understanding of the radical nature of the human problem helps us to understand the radical nature of the remedy. Understanding of the questions that come out of human existence prepares us to understand the answer implicit in the gospel. Without the radical question we might hold the gospel answer superficially and complacently. In some ways psychologists take the human questions such as guilt more seriously than do the theologians. At a time when theologians tend to view aberrant human behavior as illness, psychologists are taking seriously their patients' sense of guilt and are beginning to think in terms of sin.[1]

Another influence of the psychological sciences on our doctrine of man comes from the discovery of the psychology of the unconscious which undermines moralism by showing that the emotional forces in human life are too strong to be directed and controlled by rational process. The uncovering of unconscious motivations that operate even through conscious processes makes clear to us that we cannot trust ourselves to do good. We can will the good; but that which we would do, we cannot. Even though we may keep the law in its letter, we shall sin in the spirit. Something is needed to change the spirit of man in order that his behavior may be altered. Legalistic and moralistic religion has imposed upon people standards from above, and in so doing has failed to awaken a sense of personal responsibility. Therefore, life is lived in response to the expectations of

[1] O. Hobart Mowrer represents in his *The Crisis in Psychiatry and Religion* (Princeton, N.J.: D. Van Nostrand Co., 1960), the tension between the interpretation of human behavior as symptom of illness and as sin representing a sense of guilt. In the development of his theme, however, he shows his need of theology's assistance because many of his theological identifications and formulations are inadequate.

some vague "they," which separates man from the possibility of being re-created by a new spirit, the Spirit of Christ, which produces an authentic morality in response to new relationship. The psychological rediscovery of the nature of man and his need in this respect coincides with the theological rediscovery of the work of the Holy Spirit and our dependence upon Him.

A third contribution of the psychological sciences to the religious view of man is that in addition to revealing his existential ambiguity, they help us to see that he does have within himself, and available to him from outside, resources that can heal him. At this point psychology is helping us to understand what is represented by the concept of salvation. Christian interpretations of man have varied from the view of him as being totally depraved to that of being able himself to build the kingdom of God. Neither view is a true one. Implicit in man's sickness is health, and his estrangement and separation speak of a relationship of unity and wholeness. Man's sickness and sin are to be understood not only in terms of morality but in terms of the dynamics of being as well. They are signs of man's attempt to find himself, to actualize himself in relation to all the forces of life that seem to threaten and prevent his self-realization. His struggle for self-actualization points in two directions: first, to that which man essentially is, and second, to what he may become. These insights, which are the contributions of both psychology and theology, were anticipated by our Lord who, in addition to man's existential plight, saw also something else in him on which he could build. He had the power to speak to men through their consciousness and change their unconscious motivations. He called men out of their existential plight and brought them into a creation of new possibilities.

Psychotherapy has demonstrated and explained what Jesus revealed, and has helped to make available to all the power to heal and to restore the quality of wholeness to life. We now know that when we are really present to a distressed person and stand with him in his distress, when we hear him, accept him and his problem, help him accept and use it as his curriculum, and allow the relationship between us to be the school in which the problems of his curriculum can be worked out, we are often able to reach and change the inner dynamics of his living from one of destruction to salvation or wholeness. We can say this because if a man's relationship to man is changed in this way, he is changed and stands in another relationship to God. Are we to conclude, therefore, that psychotherapy is to replace the gospel? No! The power of God works through the relations of men, which would include the therapeutic relationship; but the work of therapy or healing is not to be confined to those whose training and practice are professional.

Unfortunately, however, this full and deep view of the potential of human nature and relationship for healing is not shared by too many ministers. To the degree that their understanding of man is incomplete, their ministry to him does not reach him in the depth of his living and does not bring the human question into dialogical relation to the Divine Answer.

To the Dialogue Between Question and Answer

Since they raise the existential question by describing the nature of man, the social and psychological sciences force us to look for the contemporary relevance of the gospel. Without the polarity between the existential question and theological answer, our understanding of the gospel and its theology can become quite sterile. And it has for those who ignore or evade the question.

The dialogue between the human question and the gospel answer stimulates thinking "livingly" about theology, and theologically about living, which saves us from the deterioration of only thinking theologically about theology. The dialogue between the existential question as raised by such disciplines as psychology and the theological answer implicit in Christianity can result in a psychology with perspective and a theology with

relevance. How tragic it is, then, that the dialogue too often
makes the theologian defensive.

The understanding of man that comes out of existential psychological analysis helps to restore meaning to the words of the
faith that have lost their meaning; such words as "fall," "sin,"
"grace." Protestant ministers almost unanimously affirm that
their greatest problem is the problem of communication. One
of their many frustrations is that the biblical and theological
words and concepts are not congenial to contemporary man
since he neither gives nor receives meaning with them. The
dialogue between psychology and theology helps us at this point
because the study and description of the meaning of man's existence reveals contemporary significances for which the theological word may be a symbol, and, at the same time, a bridge
between the new and the old meanings. An example is to be
found in the word and concept "fall." Traditionally it represents the myth of man's being cast out of paradise because of
his disobedience. The literal meaning of the myth is unacceptable to modern man but may be used to represent the truth to
which the myth has always pointed, namely, the existential
alienation and estrangement from one's self and others so that
God is no longer accessible to us. "Sin" is another word that
is being restored to contemporary use because it is now seen
to represent not the sins and violations of convention, but the
deeper alienations of man from himself, from his neighbor, and
from God. Thus the Holy Words of our faith are freshened as
a result of the dialogue between psychology and theology.

Another problem in communication of which many are unaware is that Protestantism depends almost entirely on rational
activity and sets great value on verbal articulation and formulation. Unfortunately, however, man is able to express his feelings
and meanings only partially through rational verbal processes.
All his deep unconscious, subliminal yearnings and feelings that
psychology has uncovered require a language of symbol for unconscious nonverbal expression. One of the tragedies of the

Reformation was that the ancient symbols that would serve this purpose were relinquished and allowed to be monopolized by Roman Catholics and Anglo-Catholics who kept them tied to a Thomist theology and philosophy. It is to be hoped that the liturgical revival aided by the various pastoral psychology resources will recover for Protestant thought and life the communicating power of symbol. We need to break out of the bareness of the exclusively rational and verbal and find expression through the use of ancient symbols so that contemporary meanings may be completed, purified, and transformed by the meanings of the faith as they meet in symbolic action.

The psychological study of existence raises questions that help us to recover the principle of dialogue as the true principle of communication and therefore of proclamation. Both education and religion lost this view of communication and used, instead, a monological distortion of it. All education to a greater or lesser degree, and religious education to a high degree, has sought through the process of the transmission of ideas to impose new meanings on students. Missionary activity also sought to transmit and impose the meanings and practices of a new religion and its culture on the native culture without regard for its indigenous meanings and values. The results achieved by both education and missionary activity by these methods are not impressive. Monologue only lays a veneer of meaning over meaning. Dialogue, in contrast, brings about a meeting of meaning in which the meanings of both participants are completed and increased. The benefits of dialogue are mutual. From it the teacher derives new understandings of his message and its relevance, and learners receive illumination in relation to meaning and values they already hold. Out of the dialogue comes a new understanding of truth which neither of the participants could produce by himself. Dialogue between the word of man and the Word of God is the way by which each generation may hope to understand Christianity anew and both affirm and add

to the old understandings. Here is a dynamic understanding of
the nature of tradition and its source.

Only dialogical communication of the kind that we have just
been describing has the power to overcome the meaning barriers
that inevitably separate person from person and culture from
culture. Each partner to communication has preoccupations,
anxieties, defenses, images, and purposes that can easily drive
them away from each other. Furthermore, each has to the other,
and to the demand of the truth which confronts them, a deep-
seated ontological resistance that keeps them from meeting.
The psychological sciences have contributed enormously to our
understanding of the nature and working of this meaning bar-
rier that separates man from man. Psychotherapy has made clear
how essential it is for persons to persist in communication with
each other if the blocks to relationship are to be overcome. Each
person must keep in communication with himself, with others,
and through them with the truth that both judges and saves.

We now know that dialogue is to relationship what blood is
to the body; when the flow of blood stops the body dies, and
when dialogue or honest communication stops the relationship
dies. By honest attempt at dialogue men open themselves to
the work of the Holy Spirit which becomes then the miracle-
working power of dialogue. This power is needed for some of
our problems: for recovering the tensions between form and
vitality, for finding an effective form and role for the local
church, for finding an effective relation between the Church
and the world, and for the reunion of the churches. Out of this
interchange the new form of the Church's life and work will
appear. The question is, however, do we have the faith and
courage with which to participate in this kind of dialogue?

One of the areas in which dialogue might renew and empower
the church is in the preparation of people for church membership. Much present practice tends to reduce Christianity to
the dimensions of a religious cult, and many who are presented
for church membership drift away from the church partly be-

cause it seems irrelevant. Of those who remain some maintain only a formal relationship with the church; others have a moralistic understanding of Christianity and think they have to earn their membership by being good instead of depending upon the love and forgiveness of God. Others substitute the local church for the Kingdom and work and pray and give for its success rather than for the Kingdom. Others leave it to the clergy to carry on the church's ministry and in so doing contribute to the disease of clericalism, a disease that overstresses the role of the ordained members and confines the activity of the church's ministry to what they do. A discussion with almost any group of laymen from any church reveals how ignorant they are of the faith they profess and how unable they are to use it in relation to any consequential question. As a result of all these conditions the Church does not influence the world as it might.

There are at least two reasons for the Church's weakness and irrelevance: (1) Many ministers and other religious teachers tend to oversimplify life in their presentations of the relation between religion and life. Laymen complain that they do not find in our teaching a recognition of the complexity and ambiguity that a man encounters in his own life and in the social order in which he has to live. Issues are mixed and confused, data for choice are not fully known or available, decisions are seldom simple black-or-white choices, and men's motivations are hard to unravel. Because of these conditions it is not possible to live without guilt, and not easy to know what one's witness as a Christian should be. Religious teaching that does not deal with these difficulties and the deeper questions that grow out of them seems unauthentic to contemporary man.

A second reason for the Church's reputation for irrelevance is that we turn the teachings of Christianity into abstractions. Love ceases to be the power of God at work in relationships where men hate and resent each other and, instead, becomes mere sentiment. Grace ceases to be the power that accepts the unacceptable, and becomes nothing but kindness. Even God becomes simply an idea for group discussion, instead of the living Spirit who works through and between men to reconcile them. Religious teaching is authentic and influential when it brings together unflinchingly the truth of man and the truth of God.

The influence of the ministry will return when ministers and other religious teachers rise out of their theorizing chairs, participate in the ambiguities of life, and engage in honest dialogue with the people who are not only asking questions out of the tensions of contemporary life, but are also seriously addressing themselves to the answers. Christian teachers do not have a monopoly on the truth. Their understanding of the Word of God can be made fuller and more competent by their listening to the word of man. There is something to be learned from the world that will help us to recognize the power and relevance of the gospel because it was born out of the meeting between God and man. The psychological and social sciences contribute enormously not only to the raising of the question, but to the content of the question and to the process by which the question and answer are to meet in mutual address. This means that clergy must stop being "kibitzing spectators" and become player-coaches. They must expect to learn from those they teach and in so learning discover that God accomplishes reconciling work through the layman as well as the clergyman, and through the world as well as the Church. And if the laity were trained for honest and serious dialogue with the world, local churches might become centers where, in the name of Christ, courageous experiments with individual and social problems might be carried on instead of being, as they so often are, centers where the *status quo* is maintained and problems are evaded. The glories of leadership will not be available to the church until clergymen and laymen are willing to accept the pains of being leaders.

To the Group Significance of the Church

The psychological and social sciences have made another contribution to contemporary church life through a rediscovery of the dynamics of group relationships and their significance for the life and well-being of the individual. The workshops of the National Laboratory of Group Development at Bethel, Maine, and the various church and group life laboratories conducted by the churches have all increased Christian people's sensitivities to the relational side of Christian fellowship. Along with this movement, as well as in response to other emphases, has come a recovery of the meaning of the personal as distinct from the functional. Fruits of these insights are to be found in the rediscovery of the power of family relations, the restoration of the personal in education, the development of concern for persons in business and industry, to name only a few. Theologically we have been helped to see that grace means the acceptance of the unacceptable which gives us the power to accept acceptance.

To the Pastoral Ministry

The psychological and social sciences have made a tremendous contribution to the development of a pastoral psychology that has produced a new pastoral care. These contributions can be indicated only briefly:

• Modern pastoral counseling is born of the union of the church's ancient pastoral concern and the new understandings of psychodynamics and of interpersonal relationships.

• Christian education has benefited from a depth understanding of human growth and development and the fundamental questions it raises about the meaning of relationship for self-actualization. Although the question is raised psychologically, it moves in a theological direction, especially when met by teachers who bring the existential question into dialogue with the theological answer.

• The ministry of the church to people about to be married and to married people whose relationship is strained or broken has been strengthened and deepened by the new understandings of sex and marriage that have come from psychological and clinical study. And the correlations of these with theological understandings of love have opened the church to a new realization of marriage as a means of grace.

• Understanding of the psychosomatic nature of much illness has helped to restore the church's ministry to the sick to a position of major importance. The power of love and trust to reconcile and heal is a matter now of medical as well as of religious affirmation.

Studies of mental and physical illness have also helped us to understand the nature of conflict and its role in life. It is now recognized to be a means by which people try to work out problems in their relationships. Their response to crises may be destructive or constructive. "Mental disorder, for example, is an attempt to deal with an intolerable sense of personal failure and guilt. This attempt may take a number of forms . . . (a) drifting, withdrawal, throwing in the sponge; (b) delusional defense building, transfer of blame; (c) desperate attempt to reorganize." [2] Of these reactions, the third is characterized by an accentuated religious concern and a high recovery rate. Understanding of such phenomena by the church may produce a ministry that will bring means of grace to the aid of the creative and constructive potential in conflict and illness.

• Clinical studies of the aged, of bereavement, and of dying have brought into focus the human questions for which the various traditional ministries to the aging, dying, and bereaved are responsible. The new understanding of grief, for example, unlocks many of the meanings of bereavement so that ministers and others may more knowingly guide, correct, and comfort the grief-stricken.

[2] Anton T. Boisen, "Religious Experience and Psychological Conflict," *Pastoral Psychology*, May, 1961.

Out of these and other developments of pastoral psychology has come a pastoral theology that is itself a correlation of existential question and theological answer as well as a promoter of such correlations.

To Theological Education

One of the great contributions of the psychological sciences is to the training of the church's leaders. Their influence in the field of theological education has been considerable and could be even greater. The theological curriculum had been primarily concerned with a study of theology and its sources, namely, the Bible and church history; but because this study was separated from the stimulus of life and its questions it had become more and more preoccupied with itself and unrelated. The products of this kind of theological education were ill-prepared to minister to people in the contemporary world. As a consequence, many ministers used their theological learning for the formal occasions of preaching and teaching, but developed a "bastard" or indigenous theology for their practice. They acquired a knowledge *about* God but nothing *about* man and society. And because the emphasis of theological study was on subject matter abstracted from encounter, they *knew* neither God nor man, and their ministry lacked the authenticity that comes from personal participation in the encounters between God and man. This kind of education caused many students to lose the religion they brought with them to their seminary training but failed to help them find a new one to take its place.

The theological curriculum lacked two essential elements: polarity and integration. The lack of polarity was seen in the preoccupation of the curriculum, faculty, and students, with religion abstracted and isolated from life. And the lack of integration was seen in the multiplication of practical courses in all sorts of things in an attempt to adapt a theoretical approach to religion to the exigencies of the ministry in the world. Not only did the curriculum become encumbered with a multitude of courses, but the chasm between the practical and the theological became greater.

Forty years ago, however, a reform in this matter began to occur. The study of man and his experiences in life began to be introduced into the curriculum, not only as another subject but as directed participation in the living of others. There appeared on the scene, for example, the resource known as clinical pastoral training which provided theological students with the opportunity to study in face-to-face relationships, under the supervision of trained chaplains, what it means to minister to others in the context of our contemporary cultural situation and out of the resources of the Church and gospel. Clinical training took place in a therapeutic context that drew on the insights of the psychological and social sciences. It became a resource for the study of human relationships in the context of theological understanding, for the training of ministers for their work with people, and for theological education generally. The resistance of theological educators to clinical pastoral training and other comparable resources has lessened considerably, but the number of seminary graduates who are still sent into their ministries with only a theoretical understanding of the relation of faith to life is appalling.

Teachers of the theological disciplines must recognize that students need experiences of ministering to men and women who are passing through a crisis, and that out of this experience they will raise questions that make their disciplines more, rather than less, important and relevant. And teachers in the field of pastoral psychology need to realize that their understandings of man, formulated out of psychological insights, call for completion by the understandings of theology. Out of this meeting between the disciplines of theology and the psychological sciences emerges a dialogue which will become increasingly beneficial to all concerned.

The curricular polarity thus achieved will eliminate the need for many technique courses because students who have an understanding of the dynamics that lie behind the ministry are able, with a minimum of suggestion of how things are done, to "create" methods in response to the demands of each situation. With a decrease in so-called "practical" courses, which suggests that other courses have a right to be impractical, and an increase of courses that stress the relation of faith and life, the chasm that separated the pastoral from the theological will close to their mutual benefit and to the real edification of the church. To the degree that this occurs the whole faculty, regardless of the discipline for which each is responsible, will have a contribution to make to the training of ministers for their work in the Church and in the world.

The correlation between the insights of the psychological sciences and theological study has helped also to eliminate the necessity for pastoral specialization such as counseling as a way of finding a significant ministry. As long as theology and pastoral work seemed to be irrelevant to the existential question, it became necessary for people who wanted a really useful ministry to turn to specialties such as pastoral counseling, education, social service, and others. And the training necessary for competence in such a specialty was often given over against the theological education and unrelated to it. The correlations between the two fields, however, helped to make it possible for the average pastor not only to employ the special techniques of pastoral counseling and use it in the context of the church's total ministry, but to find opportunities for relevance in his other ministries of general pastoral care, education, preaching, visitation of the sick.

One of the unfortunate effects of the emphasis on the contributions of psychotherapy, especially when uncorrelated with theology, is the intimidation of many pastors in the carrying out of their pastoral function. Many of them have mistakenly thought that because of the special knowledge and skills that are now available in the care of human ills, one needs either to be a psychiatrist or to refer troubled persons to psychiatric care. In order that pastors may recover from this intimidation, it is imperative that theological schools develop curricula that train men for the full exercise of their responsibilities as pastors, teachers, preachers, and administrators, and further prepare them to collaborate with the other disciplines that exercise a care and concern for people.

Another responsibility of theological education in response to the contributions of the psychological sciences is to train men to think theologically about life. Unfortunately, however, many graduates of seminaries are afraid to think theologically, partly because they are afraid of being heretical, and partly because theology has become institutionalized to the point that both clergy and laity drift into the attitude that theological thinking is for the specialist only. Somehow or other we need to rediscover that theological thinking is human thinking about ultimate meanings and that one can think theologically in two ways. One can move from the theological formulation to the human situation for which it is intended, or one can begin with the human situation, find its meaning, and then look for the ultimate meaning to which it points. Ministers who would lead the Church in its dialogue with the world should be capable of both kinds of theological thinking and capable of training their laity in engaging in it too. Because every man is a theologian of sorts, it is quite possible to train him in his theological thinking. If he does it anyhow, let us help him to do it creatively and constructively.

One of the more common complaints of seminary graduates is that their teachers did their theological thinking for them instead of teaching them to do it for themselves. Now that they are in the ministry they do not know how to use the resources they are supposed to have; they do not know how to use their theological understandings to interpret the life around them. This is a serious incapacity for spiritual leaders and suggests that theological teachers might benefit from a study of how learning occurs so that they might employ the knowledge in

their teaching. Too many seminaries are filled with teachers
whose only qualification is some mastery of a part of the curriculum but who are ignorant about or inept in the teaching-
learning process itself. Many so-called teachers even brag that
they know nothing about education, an arrogance that has done
the Church and its ministry a lasting disservice.

A knowledge and employment of the art and science of education would not only produce better-trained ministers, but they
in their turn would be better able to train the laity for the
Church's ministry in the world. A pastor's fundamental responsibilities are preaching the gospel, administering the Sacraments,
pastoral care, and the coaching and training of his lay men and
women in their responsibilities as Christians in every area of
life, not just within the structure of the church. The latter is
one of the great lacks in seminary training. Seminary graduates
do not know how to work with people and bring out in them
through teaching and training a real sense of responsibility and
commitment. Ministers are very open in their admission of this
inability. They are not able to awaken and train committed
church members because they do not know how to communicate. Furthermore, their concept of communication is inadequate to the task of communication, a concept which they
acquired by watching their teachers. The misconception is that
communication is accomplished by telling people what they
ought to know. That it does not work that way is attested by
the frustrations experienced by the clergy in response to their
attempts to communicate.

The true concept of communication is that of dialogue in
which meeting occurs between the meanings students bring to
the educational encounter and the meanings responsibly presented by the teacher. In seminary this would call for dialogue
between the meanings (questions, affirmations, values) of the
student and the truths of the subject matter or discipline being
studied. The teacher would function as director and resource
to the dialogue in which, of course, he would also be a partic-

ipant. This concept of the teacher stands in sharp contrast to the monological one that so widely prevails and that enfeebles the church. The student would then be a responsible participant in his own education and, in addition, would be able to use the same process in the teaching of his laymen so that they too would become informed, committed churchmen. The polarity of theological education provided through the dialogue between existential question and the theological answer would renew the church through the renewal of its leadership, both ordained and lay.

Psychiatric examination and treatment, personality tests, vocational guidance and other similar resources can contribute much to the selection, training, and maintaining of men for their ministries. Some churches already require psychiatric examination of all candidates for the ministry. Some seminaries employ psychiatrists as either part- or full-time members of their staffs who not only care for the students but in some instances participate in the teaching. The usefulness of these resources cannot be disputed if the training of men for the ministry has any depth at all. The work of the ministry calls for tremendous personal strength and capacity for relationship, but the relational milieu out of which men must come produces in them conditions that inhibit and incapacitate them. A careful use of psychiatric consultation and treatment can often release men for their work both during seminary training and later during the years of ministry when pressures and demands may become more than they can stand.

Something now needs to be said on the other side. Great care should be exercised in the use of psychiatric resources. It does not follow that because a man is a psychiatrist he is competent and responsible. Ministry of any kind to the personality is a serious business, and should be undertaken only with reverence for the human soul and a knowledge of what one is doing. I would thoroughly disagree that psychoanalysis should be required of all candidates for the ministry. Nor do I believe that every candidate should undergo some kind of short-term psychiatric treatment. I do think, however, that seminaries should have someone on the faculty competent to discern when students might need help, and to co-operate with any treatment given. Such a man could also help the faculty to understand that problems calling for treatment are not reasons for eliminating a student, but may become, in response to treatment, a source of strength for the ministry.

CONCLUSION

A discussion of the kind that we are now concluding may easily give the impression that Christianity is an impoverished beneficiary of the munificence of the psychological. To guard against this interpretation we need to remember that the relation between the psychological and the theological should be dialogical. Each needs the benefits of the other.

We live in a time when the forces of tyranny and terrorism threaten even life itself. The issue is one in which the choice is between terrorism or dialogue. Whenever anyone holds whatever truth he has dogmatically, cloistered from contact with other possible truths, he is participating in tyranny and turning his back on dialogue. The church, clergymen and laymen, theologians and scientists, theological educators and their students, must choose. If they choose dialogue, and thereby open themselves to the working of God, they will accept the responsibility to make the proclamation of the gospel faithful to the meaning of the gospel, and help the hearing of the gospel to be faithful to the meaning of life. In other words, the word of man must be in dialogue with the Word of God in order to be judged, purified, and transformed. And the Word of God must be in dialogue with the word of man in order to know itself as the Word for man.

Dialogue renews the power of the word by reuniting the person to the word, so that the word becomes the servant of the person rather than being a substitute for the person. Dialogue therefore enables the word and its meaning to become incarnate in the person. Out of this should come great courage and capacity for living.

Though our age is one of great achievements, we have not achieved greatness of character. Let us look at this observation from the point of view of psychology and theology. The effect of psychological thought has been to produce in us a concern for adjustment and normality. Although clinical study reveals the potential in persons for variety and versatility, we seek uniformity and conformity. The need to be comfortable by being faceless and voiceless binds us to mediocrity.

Much that calls itself religious seems to produce in men preoccupations with petty concerns, meanness of spirit, and a fervent devotion to the *status quo* that tear congregations apart and keep them from being heroic servants of the Spirit. So obvious are these results that many people will have nothing to do with religion and the Church.

These responses to psychiatry and to religion are due in part, at least, to their isolation. We have been saying that they need each other to complete their respective meanings. Religion without the existential question becomes mere religious observance expressed at best by commitment to the trivial; and the question without faith becomes more than man can bear, so he seeks to hide in uniformity, conformity, and mediocrity. Let us, therefore, commit ourselves to a life of dialogue in order that the greatness of truth may be incarnate in persons and that great persons may be developed to serve the truth.

ROGER L. SHINN

Social Ethics

THE twentieth century has been both momentous and troublesome for Christian social ethics. Vast political movements—fascist, Nazi, and Communist—have abused the Church and persecuted leaders who dared to speak the Christian social message. Protagonists in the world ideological struggles have used religion irreverently as a weapon in their own causes. New terrors and possibilities of destruction threaten humanity, and new ethical problems call for decisions in areas where there are no Christian precedents. Hence churchmen may be baffled by the ethical problems they must face.

Yet this century has seen examples of Christian social witness as dramatic as any since New Testament times. And within the Church is emerging a way of thinking about social ethics that is both biblical and contemporary, both sensitive and realistic. We cannot yet tell how effective it will be in meeting the gigantic problems of our time. But we can discern the situation in which it works and the directions of its development.

SOCIETY AND RELIGION

Every society would like to capture religion, domesticate it, and put it to some use. If the vitalities of religion can be channeled to work for the aims of the society, men can feel contented and secure. Religion then supports the society in its dogmatisms and its fights with its enemies.

A second best goal is to trivialize religion. If it will not sustain

63

a society, religion can decorate it. Then men can enjoy the ceremonies and comforts of religion without letting it disturb them.

In either case, the world is likely to treat religion rather well, as men are accustomed to provide for machines that serve them and pets that entertain them. The official representatives of religion can accept the praise and patronage of a grateful society.

But—what if someone really believes in God?

Faith in a righteous God introduces an element of discord. Neither religion nor society can peacefully go its way if a living God demands that men serve him faithfully and meet all other human beings in responsible love.

Hence biblical faith through the centuries has struggled with the social forces that wanted a docile religion. Moses, descending from Mount Sinai, destroyed the golden calf fashioned by the people and their priest. Elijah challenged the corrupt power of King Ahab, who sought to avoid the "troubler of Israel." Amos, announcing God's judgment upon social injustice, found an opponent in the priest Amaziah, who sought to chase Amos out of Bethel, "a temple of the kingdom."

"Unless the Lord watches over the city, the watchman stays awake in vain" (Psalm 127:1). The Lord watches over the city in love, but as he watches, he sees much that offends him. He has a quarrel with the people whom he would save. The people in turn often see the God of love as a threat to their interests.

Thus men turned against Jesus Christ and crucified him. His apostles went to jail as agitators and trouble makers. In Thessalonica they faced accusations as "men who have turned the world upside down" (Acts 17:6). They disturbed economic interests in Ephesus (Acts 19:23ff.).

The social impact of Christianity has continued through the centuries. Empires have both persecuted and wooed Christianity. The Church in turn has sometimes contributed legitimately to the morality and morale of a society. Too often it has modified its message to court the support of powerful interests. But, unlike ancient Assyrian religion or modern Shinto, Christianity has a built-in resistance to becoming the ideology of empire. Its heritage has recalled it repeatedly to a mission of protest and transformation.

Recent history has made that mission a costly one. The vast ideological conflicts of our time have brought intense pressures upon the churches to warp or subdue their social message. By persecution and flattery the powers that be have made the two-pronged effort to capture the Church for their purposes or to trivialize it.

Hitler brought pressure on the Church to modify its theology and ethics so as to support the Nazi movement. He gained some successes among the party of "German Christians." Where he was unsuccessful, he tried the second technique of relegating the Church to insignificance. He had no quarrel with a religion of ceremony and spirituality, provided it did not meddle in social criticism. The Church (and sometimes the world) has come to honor those Christians who opposed Hitler in the face of threats, concentration camps, and death.

Communist states have followed a somewhat different pattern, because Marxist doctrine is formally opposed to religion. Nevertheless, despite official atheism and sporadic propaganda against religion, the governments have not gone to the trouble of persecuting all religion. Even the Soviet government has sought the support of the Church, as when Stalin publicly hailed the patriach of Moscow during the Nazi invasion. More characteristically the Communist powers have ostensibly allowed complete freedom of religion and offered the churches a few crumbs of support, provided the religious groups kept to the business of liturgy and spiritual counsel, avoiding any interference in political and economic issues.

Similar pressures are powerful in the United States of America. Those most frequently exerting such pressures treasure religion as a support in the ideological struggle against communism. But as soon as the social ethic of the churches undermines

satisfaction in the American way of life, they complain that
religion is getting out of its proper sphere. That sphere presum-
ably includes cultic activities for marriage and death, worship
on Sunday, the study of those parts of the Bible and those
doctrines regarded as socially harmless—but not ethical judgments on international relations, racial justice, civil rights, or
the working of the economy.

BOLDNESS AND RESTRAINT

It may appear strange that a culture tracing its spiritual
ancestry to the Pilgrim Fathers should ever seriously wonder
whether its faith ought to have social consequences. The rugged
Pilgrim spirit sought to subdue the whole world to God. The
New England theocracy brought every human activity into the
orbit of Christian behavior. No Puritan argued that religion
should stay out of business and politics. The role of faith was
to dominate and discipline the lives of men who in their sin
were all too ready to rebel against the divine law.

But two major types of changes followed quickly in American
life. First, as the economy developed, a distorted Puritanism
sometimes misunderstood its own Calvinistic origins and blessed
predatory individualism and economic greed. Whether the issue
was slavery, the right to build a fortune by paying low wages,
or national expansion, someone was always ready to justify
privilege as a divinely given reward and responsibility.

Then, second, a set of counterforces sought to detach religion
from any social concern. Puritanism itself, by claiming divine
approval for fallible human judgments and intolerance, provoked a legitimate impulse to free society from ecclesiastical
domination. The separation of church and state was sometimes
taken to mean that religion should ignore problems of public
morality. The waves of revivalism, so influential in the developing West, evoked intense individual experiences but had less

to do with the shape of society.[1] Pietism, coming from Europe, cultivated the devotional life at the cost of neglecting social responsibility.

From these two kinds of tendencies came the distinctively American form of the universal social impulse to use religion or to trivialize it. Thus the public discussions of social ethics in America have often appealed to two mutually inconsistent premises. The first premise is that Christianity supports the American way of life, whether the issue concerns national interests in a world society or the interests of established classes in the domestic society. The second premise is that religion should mind its proper business and not intrude into economics and politics. Our society, by and large, is able to call on either premise, depending on the convenience of the situation.

The classic American struggle of conscience centered on the issue of slavery. To review the Christian discussions of slavery, many of them barely a century old, is to find three broad types of argument frequently repeated:

- The Bible and Christian belief support slavery.
- Slavery is not a religious issue. The church should preach the gospel but should not enter into the political controversy.
- The church has a Christian responsibility to oppose slavery.

In retrospect it is easy to see that the first two arguments usually flowed from self-interest or from captivity to a culture that prevented clear thinking about Christian faith and ethics. The remarkable thing about the third argument is that men sometimes were persuaded by it despite their self-interest and the pressure of culture.

[1] Timothy L. Smith, in *Revivalism and Social Reform* (Nashville, Tenn.: Abingdon Press, 1957), has shown that the frontier revivals had very real consequences in social behavior. But his own evidence touches only a limited number of social problems, such as drunkenness, crime and disorder, personal dealings with neighbors, and, in some cases, slavery. The revivalists had little to say about many of the great forces molding American society.

The same three forms of argument have recurred among churchmen as various specific issues have emerged, for example, the ten-hour day, rising wages,[2] immigration, foreign policies, and desegregation. When the issue is sufficiently far past, we may often wonder how Christians could have been so unconcerned for justice, so insensitive to human need, so agile in warping Christian ethics to their own interest. When the issue is closer at hand, we find it more perplexing. How can we be sure what a Christian ethic has to say about the United States and the Soviet Union or Latin America, about domestic problems of health, education, and automation?

The obvious mistakes of our forefathers and our own bewilderment remind us of the *genuine difficulties* in working out a Christian social ethic. Seldom has the church the right to prescribe social policies confidently with a "Thus saith the Lord." Christian minds, like all other human minds, are fallible. The Christian approaches social problems with a biblical understanding of his responsibility to God and neighbor, but he does not find a modern political and economic program in the Bible. A wise social ethic requires an understanding of society and its processes. We misunderstand our world both because of error and because of sin. That is, we often do not know as much as we need to know for wise thinking, and we appropriate what we do know through our prejudices. Hence social ethics requires continually both the enlarging of our minds and the purging of our spirits.

The layman—the industrialist, the laborer, the politician, the farmer, the social worker, the policeman—rightly resents the minister who, with no knowledge of social and economic processes, prescribes answers for our social ills. Almost every Christian has suffered under dogmatic ethical preaching, when he suspected that the minister was speaking from ignorance or

[2] The often dismal story of American Christianity on economic issues is recorded in Henry F. May, *Protestant Churches and Industrial America* (New York: Harper & Brothers, 1949).

prejudice rather than from the gospel. Depending on which church he attended at a particular time, the Christian might hear that pacifism was his Christian duty or was ethically irresponsible. He might hear capitalism blessed or condemned, might hear a plea for harsher treatment or for more mercy toward juvenile deliquents.

The answer for such problems is not for the church to avoid controversial issues. That would be renunciation of the faith of prophets, of Jesus Christ, of apostles and martyrs. The answer is to undertake the discipline of understanding the gospel and the world, then to act with both the boldness of Christian disciples and the restraint of men who know they can err.

Each age presents a peculiar set of social problems to mankind and a peculiar call to Christian fidelity. Out of the perplexities of our time is emerging a Christian social ethic for responsible living in this day.

THE HERITAGE OF RAUSCHENBUSCH AND KIERKEGAARD

Christian social ethics today directs men's attention both to Scripture and to the latest television. Those who expect comments on modern society are often startled by its use of the Bible and classical doctrine. Those who want traditional Christianity are frequently offended by its interest in economic facts, international developments, studies of the influence of mass communication.

This social ethic rejects the old clichés that separate biblical religion from modern social concern. To those who advise the church to pay more attention to religion and less to things of the world, Christian ethics answers in terms of Scripture:

> When it describes the mighty deeds of God, the New Testament uses political, juridical, sociological, and other secular terms. Kingdom of God, Son of David, King of the

Jews, Redemption, Faith, Forgiveness, Healing, Freedom,
Service—all such words by which the person and work of
Jesus Christ are described are secular words. This secular
terminology of the New Testament is not only a form of
speech. For the coming of Jesus Christ in the flesh and in
the power of the Spirit is a "secular" event. It is an event
in the world and for the world.[3]

The latest Christian social ethic thus has its roots and source
in the biblical faith. It also has a more recent ancestry in Christian thought. Although its family tree is as complex as any other,
two persons loom large in it. The two were so different that, if
they could have met, they would surely have argued and misunderstood each other. But contemporary Christian ethics has
learned profoundly from both.

Walter Rauschenbusch (1861-1918) was the most prominent
spokesman for the social gospel. This movement, in spite of
the fashion that calls it "typically American," was part of a
world-wide awakening of Christians to their social responsibilities. Europeans and Americans, Roman Catholics and Protestants made their contributions. Rauschenbusch is both a
representative and a symbol of that new Christian social ethic.

Rauschenbusch and the social gospel were not original in
addressing the Christian ethic to the social order. Roman
Catholicism had for centuries developed the idea of Christendom in which the whole society (despite the obvious presence
of sin) was responsible to moral law. Protestantism, especially
as we have noticed in Calvinism, upheld and often enforced a
rigorous social ethic. Many of the basic themes of the social
gospel were centuries-old.

Yet many elements in the social gospel were new. It faced
for the first time ethical issues of an industrial society. Organized capital and labor, production in great factories, financial

---

[3] *A Theological Reflection of the Work of Evangelism*, World Council
of Churches, Division of Studies Bulletin, Vol. V, Nos. 1-2, Nov., 1959,
p. 13.

and credit structures, new kinds of exploitation, and slums called for ethical decisions with few helpful precedents. So it turned from scholastic processes of ethics and authoritative codes to a broad concern for human well-being in modern society. It had a historical awareness that the structures of society are not immutable, that the answers of the Middle Ages or the seventeenth century were not adequate to new situations. It approached social problems with democratic rather than hierarchical conceptions of society. Alert to the developing social sciences, it saw new possibilities for political and social institutions. It recognized that personal works of mercy, though always demanded by faith, might do far less to relieve suffering than a change in public policy, that personal generosity might, in fact, be an escape from the real ethical responsibility of men of power. All these ideas remain important for contemporary Christian ethics.

Critics of the social gospel can easily point to its errors. Though it recovered much of the biblical ethic that had been conveniently lost, it in turn missed aspects of the gospel message. Although it was urgently aware of sin, especially the sin of greed, the social gospel often did not see the subtler aspects and the stubborn staying powers of sin. Under the influence of the widespread faith in progress, it saw the kingdom of God as a goal for society, missing its eschatological quality. It did not do justice to the tragic character of history that has become so obvious in more recent years. Lacking the refinements that were to come in social sciences, it saw only partially the ways in which power, operating through impersonal mechanisms, determines the fate of persons.

Criticism of the social gospel has by this time become the vogue. But the greatest critics of the social gospel—for example, Reinhold Niebuhr—have been the most indebted to it. They modify its theological and social doctrines radically, yet accept its assumptions about the social responsibility of Christian faith.

To turn from Walter Rauschenbusch to Søren Kierkegaard is

to enter a different world of thought. Kierkegaard (1813-1855) died before Rauschenbusch was born, but his major impact came after the death of Rauschenbusch. The faith of Kierkegaard was so intensely personal and his opposition to the contemporary equivalent of a social gospel was so great that he might seem to have no contribution at all to a social ethic. Yet with peculiar force he has helped Christians to understand the relation between the gospel and culture.

Kierkegaard showed more powerfully than any other writer before or since that the church has been captured by culture. The original daring faith in a Christ who calls men to follow and suffer with him has become transmuted into the stodgy cult of respectability. Men, he said, have cunningly transformed Christianity into the opposite of discipleship. Instead of disturbing and transforming persons, the church makes them comfortable in their settled ways. At about the same time that Marx was describing religion as "the opiate of the people," Kierkegaard with equal passion and far greater psychological penetration was exposing the self-deception that goes on in the church. The influence of Kierkegaard would not, by itself, convince a Christian today to work for public school desegregation or for a more enlightened foreign policy. But Kierkegaard unmasks the intricate devices by which churchmen blend their racial prejudices and their nationalism with Christianity in an idolatrous religion.

Kierkegaard's second contribution to a social ethic was his acute recognition of the forces in modern society that were beginning to depersonalize human beings. He saw that culture can harm men with its beneficence as truly as with its cruelty. A century after his death, hundreds of social critics were pointing to the ways in which persuasive manipulation lures men to give up their freedom, pressures them into conformity, and treats them as consumers rather than selves. Kierkegaard was completely ignorant of the clinical and statistical techniques by which psychologists, sociologists, and cultural anthropologists come to their conclusions. But his penetrating imagination sketched out most of the lines of contemporary social criticism.

The emerging Christian social ethic, alert to biblical faith and the latest news, tutored by Rauschenbusch and Kierkegaard, faces the ethical issues peculiar to this age. Rauschenbusch alerts it to the injustices of a society that crushes opportunity for migrant workers, slum dwellers, and racial minorities. Kierkegaard alerts it to the blandishments of the same society as it surrounds men with comforts and muffles the unsettling demands of a transcendent God.

THE BURDEN OF THE AMERICAN CHURCH

Whether the Church can rise to the urgent demands of the day is an open question. The peculiar social problems of our time require of mankind exceptional wisdom, courage, and tenacity—or a more indulgent providence than we have a right to count on. Even an utterly faithful church might hesitate before the scope of human dilemmas today. The existing church may be overwhelmed by the challenge.

Men of good will are bewildered by the needs of our time. In the face of many a question they must honestly wonder, What is the right way?

The overwhelming contemporary problem is nuclear war. Anyone who looks squarely at the threat to mankind, to the germ plasm from which future generations will come, and to the planet itself must feel horror before the monstrous destruction now possible. Certainly Christian ethics must seek peace, must subordinate strictly national interests to world interests, must ask that foreign policy never lead us to initiate the ultimate disaster.

The difficulty is to devise the statecraft that will assure peace. If America were to renounce nuclear weapons, would this action (as some say) contribute a favorable climate for peace through-

out the world? Or would it remove the anxious balance of terror
that has thus far held off thermonuclear destruction? Since
America is, in fact, not going to disarm unilaterally, can the
Church influence international policies that have some actual
chance of changing the perilous situation?

To turn to another question, how shall America use its vast
wealth in a needy world? The United States, with six per cent
of the world's population, has approximately half the world's
wealth. Obviously Christian ethics calls for generosity. But how
generous can a nation be persuaded to be? What kinds of
generosity will help poverty, and what kinds will only alleviate
and prolong it?

The meaning of Christian love seems so clear and direct in
the New Testament that the present-day Christian feels (and
probably ought to feel) some impatience with questions like
these. Churchmen often complain that *ambiguity* has become
the most prominent word in Christian ethics, as men discover
repeatedly that contemporary problems have no clear and simple
answers. Yet there is something irresponsible in bursting through
ambiguities for the emotional satisfaction of a direct answer
that really does not meet the questions of our time.

If the Christian is often puzzled by the question, What is
right, he may find equal difficulty in a second question, What
can I do? In our complex, technological society the diffusion
of responsibility is such that we scarcely know who makes major
decisions. The citizens of a democracy all share a responsibility
for the acts of the nation. But not many citizens participate
in decisions of weapon making or diplomacy. Often the specific
decisions require such technical knowledge that the average
person cannot make wise judgments.

A comparable problem arises in the economy. The owners of
a business have responsibility for the ethics of their operation.
But the owners are no longer a few identifiable people. The
typical college teacher is an owner in about seventy-five corporations—not because teachers are a financially powerful group but

because the major teachers' pension fund invests participants' money in common stocks. When newspapers report bad ethical practices of corporations, the teacher rarely knows whether or not he is part-owner of the companies involved. If he feels a conscientious concern, he also knows that he cannot investigate the activities of seventy-five corporations and still find time to teach. He has an ethical responsibility, but he does not always know how to exercise it.

These questions—What is right? and What can one do about it?—make difficulties for the most conscientious churchmen. But they are vastly compounded by the captivity of the church to culture. The American church has for the most part dealt ineffectually with racial issues because its own conscience is largely the divided conscience of American society. The institutions of the church have fostered segregation more often than they have overcome it. The economic views of churchmen by and large owe far more to middle-class culture than to the upsetting teachings of the Bible. Most American Christians, when they are thinking about other areas of the world, can scarcely shake themselves loose from nationalistic and economic feelings that obscure factual realities and ethics.

Powerful forces in American society work to enforce the captivity of the church. When prominent Christian leaders and church agencies criticize the dominant cultural ideology, they meet bitter attacks. The succession of accusations has come from such sources as the McCarthy Committee, the notorious Air Force training manual, the broadcasts of Fulton Lewis, Jr. on hundreds of radio stations, and spokesmen of the John Birch Society. The targets of fire include the major denominations and the National Council of Churches. Usually the accusers claim Communist influence in the churches—often because the churches support the social policies long a part of American life. The charges are remarkably undocumented and easily refuted. But the financial power behind the attacks is impressive, both in money to support critics and in withdrawal of contributions from churches.

The polemics frequently rest on the two incompatible premises we have already noted—that the church should be a bulwark of the *status quo* (often the *status quo* of several decades ago) and that the church should confine itself to spiritual affairs and stay out of social issues. When churches take stands against communism (as they frequently do), they are applauded. If they are critical of American institutions, they are accused of becoming political.

Thus Eugene Carson Blake, the chief executive official of the United Presbyterian Church in the U.S.A., has commented:

> In all my ministry I have never been criticized for "meddling" in political affairs by any church member who agreed with the views expressed.
>
> The stake that the Protestant churches have in this whole business is to keep themselves free to teach and preach the gospel. Those who are pressing the church to keep out of economic and political areas, whether they know it or not, are attempting to make in this country a tame, kept church such as all totalitarian states attempt.[4]

Christians may draw one comfort from the violent contemporary attacks upon the churches. They are evidence that American Christianity has not succumbed completely to captivity. It still has the vitality and fidelity to distinguish itself from the synthetic religion of home and country. Its biblical and theological consciousness give it some leverage against the weight of culture, which works to subdue every religion.

Apparently, however, the normal churchman does not take very seriously the social ethic that comes from Christian faith. At least one survey of opinion so indicates:

[4] Reported by John Wicklein in the *New York Times*, March 28, 1960, p. 25.

Although over ninety per cent of American adults identify themselves with one of the major religious groups, a
majority believe that their religion does not affect their
ideas of politics and business. Interviewers for the American Institute of Public Opinion asked those who considered religion to be something "very important" in their
lives, "Would you say your religious beliefs have any effect
on your ideas of politics and business?" Fifty-four per cent
said no.[5]

Evidently most churchmen expect their religion either to
endorse their behavior or to keep out of the way when something serious is at stake. The church is called to preach the
daring biblical faith to a society that wants to take its religion
with its tranquilizers. The culture is hardly able to understand
Thomas Jefferson's saying, "I tremble for my country when I
reflect that God is just." It is even less ready to hear the call
to faithfulness that comes from a crucified Lord.

SIGNS OF HOPE

In the face of such difficulties Christian social ethics has had
some effect in helping the church and culture to understand
the gospel. Its accomplishments are grounds not for pride but
for thankfulness and hope.

On the broad scale the churches have achieved a notable
consensus on many of the social implications of Christianity
for our time. The breadth and depth of consensus became
obvious with the publication on July 21, 1961, of the Encyclical,
Mater et Magistra, of Pope John XXIII. The agreement between this document and recent declarations of the World
Council of Churches, the National Council of the Churches

[5] J. Milton Yinger, *Religion, Society and the Individual* (New York:
The Macmillan Company, 1957), Vol. 1, pp. 25-26. By permission of The
Macmillan Company.

of Christ in the U.S.A., and the major Protestant denominations was remarkable. The papal letter disagreed with Protestant teaching on birth control, and it sometimes used a doctrinal and scholastic language unfamiliar to Protestants. Otherwise the agreements were overwhelmingly impressive.

The consensus was not new. Scholars had seen it for many years. But now it has become evident to anyone who is willing to observe. No longer can it be said that the range of weighty Christian thought is indistinguishable from the spectrum in society at large. Granted the right of Christians to dissent (on grounds of conscience, doctrine, and reason, not on grounds of personal or group advantage), the main streams of Protestant and Roman Catholic social thought concur on many major issues: on the responsibility of wealthy nations in our world, on rejection of communism and economic individualism, on the necessity of the increasing socialization of life with due care for the dangers involved, on many aspects of the world ideological struggle, on the role of technology in modern society, on taxation, and so on.

Like the long succession of Protestant stands, the Pope's letter was derided from both left and right in the ideological spectrum. Part of the persuasiveness of the main stream of Christian social ethics in our time has been the nature of the attacks upon it. Its main claim to authenticity, however, is not its moderate position but its fidelity to the biblical heritage.

This emerging Christian consensus is one major fact in the Christian social record of our time. The other major fact is the courageous witness of individuals and small groups in the face of cruel persecution of dictators and the kindlier pressure of culture. We have lived and are living through another age of the martyrs. The story of Christians who defied Hitler has been written into modern history. Behind the iron curtain other Christians have maintained the faith, neither capitulating to nor hating their rulers but engaging in their ministry of reconciliation. In South Africa and the United States, where the church at large has often supported racial injustice, creative minorities of black men and white have shown the power of faith. From such persons and activities comes the encouraging news that although religious institutions often capitulate to cultural pressures, the gospel still awakens living faithfulness.

In the variety of Christian vocations there is a social ethic of the catacombs and of the legislative halls of nations. Our generation has seen both. Despite fanaticism and weakness, apostasy and torpor, prejudice and complacency among churchmen, there is room for gratitude to God for the social concern of some of his people.

The time has come when the Church must face new social problems on unwalked paths. To ease the threat of nuclear war will require bold imagination, hard thinking, and willingness to face uncomfortable facts. Economic ethics has taken on new dimensions. Beside the old problem of injustice and poverty, which persists for some in the United States and many in the world, we have the new problem of prosperity in a society where production requires extravagant consumption, while machines do most of the work. The issue of freedom is no longer that of emancipation from chattel slavery and tyranny alone, but also that of maintaining personal integrity in a world where we must live closer to our fellow men and somehow handle the pressure to conform. The old problem of work—of long hours under cruel conditions—is giving way to the new problem of meaningless work and meaningless leisure. The ethics of sex has new implications in a world where the population explosion threatens safety and where mass media turn sex from sacred mystery to an advertising gimmick.

To meet the unexplored issues of the future will require no mere reiteration of ancient precepts. The Church must listen to the findings of social scientists, must learn from every available source, must consider proposals never imagined before. But it must do so in fidelity to its Lord and in the perspective of biblical faith. As to facts about society, the world must be the teacher of the Church. But facts never constitute a goal or a policy. Information is not sensitivity to human need. Christian ethics appropriates facts within the context of a covenant that binds each person to God and to the community of mankind.

Thus the method of Christian social ethics requires the continuous interpenetration of biblical faith and the most modern scientific understanding. A generation of Christian scholars, of whom Reinhold Niebuhr is the foremost ground breaker, has been working out the method, and their work continues.

Beyond wise methods Christian ethics requires fidelity and courage. Arnold Toynbee argues that the great religion of modern man is "unavowed worship" of the state.[6] Richard Niebuhr describes the dominant faith as trust and devotion directed toward social unity—family, tribe, class, nation, or, in rare cases, humanity.[7] Against these mighty faiths Christian social ethics seeks to live by faith in the God and father of our Lord Jesus Christ, trusting that in worship of him we shall serve mankind better than in worship of society.

[6] Arnold J. Toynbee, *An Historian's Approach to Religion* (New York: Oxford University Press, 1956), p. 213.

[7] H. Richard Niebuhr, *Radical Monotheism and Western Culture* (New York: Harper & Brothers, 1960).

PAUL H. ELMEN

The Arts

WHEN the goal of every man is seen to be the achievement of a rich personal experience set in the matrix of a comprehensive and unshakable order, the relevance of the arts to the work of the Church seems clear. For both are concerned with freedom within a structure which has enough authority to arrest endless process and confront chaos with a significant form. And both are threatened by massive and formless events which caricature their freedom, and which in some moods seem strong enough to destroy their cherished symmetries.

The painter, the sculptor, the musician, the dancer may be described as men who search endlessly for an absolute form which is their own discovery, and yet which also has the character of being inevitable. So the artist creates within his own tradition; and so the Church tries to maintain a primitive freshness within its ancestral forms. But the very great difficulty of achieving this newness-within-oldness is made exquisitely complex if it must proceed within a chaotic and spreading secularity. In a land where Whirl is king, the artist's ordering lacks permanence; and in a world where all coherence is lost, the authority of the Church, which derives from its compelling sense of direction, seems arbitrary and uncertain.

Probably there have always been men who have failed to find a controlling purpose in life, and who have sought to avoid an unflattering singularity by elevating this lack of meaning into a universal norm. But surely no time before our own has heard so many voices describing the fragmentary character of existence, and seeming partly to enjoy the *frisson* of knowing

81

that no archetypal plan guides our headlong journey through space and time. Up to now such speculation has had a personal and whimsical tone, like the claim of Tweedledum that Alice and Tweedledee and he himself were all figures in the Red King's dream. But today a large and influential number of artists are agreed that life is a kind of vast *commedia dell' arte*, with each of us getting along without a script by improvising dialogue and peering out from behind a series of masks.

The challenge of absurdity to all traditional purposes has confronted the Church with its newest apologetic task. The problem could be approached philosophically, since it is really the question of contingent status in new dress, but it would seem most promising to limit the inquiry to its treatment in the arts. Examples could be chosen from a wide area. In modern sculpture, for instance, the artist has shaken off the long domination of Greek rationality and with a refreshing impudence has asked us to consider rusting iron, unrecognizable shapes, and satires on the sturdy common sense of machines; the most exciting modern painting has abandoned representation in favor of a nonobjective art which illustrates our brokenness and confusion, and which in its accidental techniques seems perfectly to mirror our lack of ultimate purpose; and "the new music" delivers its atonalities with great clarity through stereophonic speakers, confirming our impression that we are alone and afraid, in a world we never made. But the literary arts as well illustrate this growing sense of absurdity, and they have the advantage that the writer has often been explicit about his purpose, and in any case has given us a printed page which can be discussed with greater confidence that we have been fair to his intention. In the novels and plays which are being discussed on every hand the Church can profitably confront the new notions of Being which are said to be independent of the logical sequences in conceptual thought, and independent as well of God.

THE ABSURD

In ordinary usage, *absurd* means "ridiculous," or "silly," and there is a strong suggestion that the matter is funny or too trivial to bother about; in the usage that has become common since World War II the word is also used for that which is contrary to reason and so is devoid of rational purpose. Since the whole of life seems to many writers to be cut off from religious, metaphysical, and transcendental roots, and so to lack ultimate meaning, the word is losing its trivial connotation and carries now the solemn burden of describing the lostness of modern man. When values were more firmly established, the absurd seemed comic; but now it seems the terrifying nexus where a great human need encounters the unreasonable silence of the world.

Some will of course protest that the world makes sense most of the time. Immediate purposes seem clear enough, and ordinary people seem content to work and to play and to rest without worrying about such baffling problems as the origin and destiny of man. The butcher pounds his block, the masseur kneads his muscles, and the salesman calls on his customers with a sense of urgency, even though the place of all these deeds in a great drama is never identified. But according to Albert Camus, whom Sartre called "the Descartes of the Absurd," [1] routine activity is no protection against a sudden discovery of nonsense. Routine might in fact bring it on:

> It happens that the stage sets collapse. Rising, streetcar, four hours in the office or factory, meal, streetcar, four hours of work, meal, sleep, and Monday Tuesday Wednesday Thursday Friday and Saturday according to the same rhythm—this path is easily followed most of the time. But one day the "why" arises and everything begins in that weariness tinged with amazement. [2]

[1] In "Tribute to Albert Camus," *The Reporter*, Feb. 4, 1960, p. 34.
[2] *The Myth of Sisyphus*, Justin O'Brien, tr. (New York: Alfred A. Knopf, Inc., 1955), pp. 12-13.

We are amazed because the obvious question of why we do these things cannot be more easily answered; and we are weary because we suspect that the question cannot be answered at all. If existence has no meaning, we are lunatics. Yet to what other conclusion can we come? If anyone pauses in his routine and asks himself what plausible reason could be advanced for the fact that one is flung into life like a stone, given a few ambiguous years of existence, and then plucked out of life, to be mourned briefly by one's family and friends before being utterly forgotten, the farcical quality of existence becomes apparent. Why this life, at this time? Why any life at all? What can break the tedium of the grave? Such are the questions that lead to the conclusion that all logical sequence is illusory. Man is a stranger in a universe which not only fails to welcome him, but seems unaware that he is there. "What I fail to understand," said Camus, "is nonsense." [3] The perfect symbol for the human adventure is Sisyphus, condemned forever to push a heavy stone up a hill though the stone keeps rolling down and can never be pushed to the top.[4]

If the routine of our daily life dulls our sensitivity and makes us unable to recognize the futility of such repetition, it may be that on some ordinary day we discover the absurd insolence of things. It was Jean-Paul Sartre in his novel La Nausée (1938) who pointed out that the world was oddly filled with things, and that these objects had no rational explanation, but were simply and even obscenely there. The protagonist Roquentin stands horrified before a tree root in the public garden at Bouville. While Juliana of Norwich found in the contemplation of a hazelnut the assurance that all things would be well, Roquentin found in the dark otherness of the root the proof that all

3 *Ibid.*, p. 27.
4 See Victor Brombert, "Camus and the Novel of the 'Absurd,'" *Yale French Studies*, I (Spring-Summer, 1948), 119-123; and Germaine Brée, *Camus* (New Brunswick, N.J.: Rutgers University Press, 1961), pp. 198-211.

was lost. Roots hold trees up and supply them with food; but function cannot explain why this root should hold this tree, or why there should be a tree at all in this place. Abstraction, which is the lifeblood of rationality, was powerless before concretion. One could not even say that the root was black: it was something more than black and something less than black. One could only say with confidence that the root was there, absurd, menacing, *de trop.* The world seemed vicious, flowing with inexplicable objects like a sea of lava, and since no one could take in so many discrete things, Roquentin felt sick to his stomach. "This park," he said to his astonished companion, "smells of vomit."

Even those who do not feel particularly menaced by the unexplained givenness of things must sooner or later deal with the mystery of innocent suffering. The impossibility of justifying the tears of a child caused Ivan to hand back his ticket to the world in *The Brothers Karamazov.* In Camus' novel *The Plague,* the humanist doctor, Rieux, and the priest, Father Paneloux, wait anxiously at the bedside of a child dying from the epidemic disease. Father Paneloux had preached a sermon to his flock in which he had spoken of the plague as God's flail, punishing the people for their sins. When the child dies, Dr. Rieux turns on Father Paneloux and says fiercely, "Ah! That child, anyhow, was innocent, and you know it as well as I do!" The priest followed him out into the playground:

> "Why was there anger in your voice just now? What we've been seeing was as unbearable to me as it was to you."
> Rieux turned toward Paneloux.
> "I know. I'm sorry. But weariness is a kind of madness. And there are times when the only feeling I have is one of mad revolt."
> "I understand," Paneloux said in a low voice. "That sort of thing is revolting because it passes our human understanding. But perhaps we should love what we cannot understand."
> Rieux straightened up slowly. He gazed at Paneloux,

summoning to his gaze all the strength and fervor he could
muster against his weariness. Then he shook his head.

"No, Father. I've a very different idea of love. And until
my dying day I shall refuse to love a scheme of things in
which children are put to torture." [5]

Suffering where there is clearly no guilt is preposterous; and
so is death itself. Whatever appearance of pattern may lend
dignity to our days, the inevitable death which lies in wait for
us makes a mockery of our life. Death is the final outrage which
obliterates meaning so completely that one cannot speak rationally about it, but can only experience its annihilation. Yet
it is not the prospect of our own death which we experience
most vividly, but rather the death of someone we love. Lear had
known real and feigned madness on the heath, but he was not
to experience the full horror of irrationality until he held the
dead Cordelia in his arms:

> "Why should a dog, a horse, a rat, have life,
> And thou no breath at all? Thou'lt come no more,
> Never, never, never, never, never!"

That anyone could live so completely in our love and then pass
out of existence seems a spoliation beyond the barbarism of
Father Time, the god who eats his children. When Matthew
records the slaughter of the innocent Israelite boys, who did not
even know that they died in the place of Jesus, he remembers
Jeremiah's account of a heartbroken mother: "In Rama was
there a voice heard ... Rachel weeping for her children, and
would not be comforted, because they are not."

It would be a mistake to think of this attitude toward death
as a literary convention, or as a philosophical point of view. As
the creators of the *danse macabre* took their inspiration from
the wasted figures who writhed on their pallets in plague-stricken
towns, so the French *absurdistes* take their cue from the expe-

[5] Stuart Gilbert, tr. (New York: Alfred A. Knopf, Inc., 1960), pp.
196-197.

rience of life itself. It seemed to them monstrous that Antoine de Saint-Exupéry should be missing in action in 1944; that Shestov's brilliant pupil Fondane should be one of the victims of Dachau; and that Camus' Facel-Vega should carry him to his death against a tree early in 1960. Sartre in particular had reason to hope that since no one had understood the limitation of our labyrinth so clearly as Camus, he of all men might find his way out. But on the day that Camus died, the impotence of the shaping mind was confirmed. The mind might be capable of a gallant protest, but in the end the inhuman would assert its mad dominion over the human. *"Il était une de nos fiertés,"* wrote André Rousseaux in *La Journée* on the day of the crash. *"Notre confiance en une certaine noblesse de la nature humaine reçoit ce soir une atteinte."*

When the imagination clings to a vision of collapsing authority, the whole outer world seems to crumble. God loses his magisterial and merciful power, and becomes a projection of man's need—Husserl's most flamboyant intentionality. Nietzsche's Zarathustra had already pronounced the demise of God. Coming down from the mountain, he sees an old man making up hymns, singing them, laughing, weeping, and mumbling, "Thus do I praise God." When Zarathustra is alone he says to himself, "Could it be possible! The old saint in the forest hath not heard that *God is dead!*" [6] What he means is that regardless of their ceremonial habit or traditions of belief, the people in the village called the Pied Cow arranged their affairs without reference to a transcendental yea or nay, being born, growing up, tending to their work, and dying as though there were no God.

Not only does religion crumble, but all systems of value which structure our days turn out to be our enemy. The cult of absurdity results in much more than the ability to stay home from church without compunction; all "those large dreams by which

[6] *Thus Spake Zarathustra*, I, 2, in *The Philosophy of Nietzsche* (New York: Modern Library, 1959), p. 27.

men long live well" lose their organizing power. In a world without purpose there can be no coherent myths, no symbolic depth, no natural law, no metaphysical order, no rational universals for science to discover. Not only can there be no valid Church, but there can be no political party, no state, and no family. The world robbed of its origin and destiny, has been robbed of its truth as well. Instead of a truly human history comes Nietzsche's nightmare—the eternally recurrent.

The outer world crumbles, and the inner world does not long survive. If everything is absurd, there can be no Self, in the sense of an enduring entity which gives coherence to our acts. This inevitable consequent, deeply offensive to every creative artist, led Baudelaire and Gide to incessant questions concerning their own identity, and led Proust to write *À la Recherche du Temps Perdu*: was Marcel the adult linked in any essential way to the Marcel who as a boy tasted the madeleine and the tisane at Combray? Proust thinks so, but Samuel Beckett thinks otherwise in his recent play *Krapp's Last Tape*. The old man Krapp wonders who he is, and how he is related to the Krapp of thirty years earlier. By means of a tape recorder he has been able to make annual recordings of his insights, and as an old man he can look back upon his observations in any previous year, which are in turn observations upon the past. Krapp perceives no continuity, and the curtain falls as he sits staring at the silent but running recorder, much as Vladimir and Estragon wait futilely for a Godot who never comes.

Those who have embraced the philosophy of absurdity seem to alternate between a sense of delicious freedom, like a boy playing hooky from school, and a sense of heavy depression when it becomes clear that they themselves and the world around them are careening through space on no errand at all. What the doctrine of absurdity promises is a sadness and loneliness deeper than words, and the return of the ancient fear of Eunapius, the fourth-century Roman philosopher, who dreaded most of all a "fabulous and formless darkness mastering the loveliness of the world."

THE CHRISTIAN AND THE ABSURD

Christian apologetics finds a surprising ground of agreement with the analyses which we have been observing. Once the problem is stated in a certain way, everything follows in the order which contemporary nihilism has pointed out. If it is true that there is no God, or only a God who has died, there can be of course no clue in existence to the divine purpose; and it is then no doubt the part of bravery to face this emptiness in its full and terrifying vacuity. Christianity finds no quarrel here. In fact, the assertion that life lacks meaning apart from God is precisely what religious men have been saying for centuries, but without quite knowing what they said, and so being unable to find a dramatic expression. "The children of this world," said our Lord, "are in their generation wiser than the children of light."

The inability of men to save themselves has always been a theological commonplace. It has often been pointed out that in the biblical world view there is no independent anthropology, or sociology, or political theory, apart from the divine plan. The world is absurd, apart from God. Nor does the Bible flinch before the belief that from the human standpoint God is absurd: his wisdom is inscrutable and his ways past finding out. The Creation, for example, is not the imposition of form on matter that is the grounds of its rationality in the *Timaeus*; in Genesis, God creates *ex nihil*, exercising an absolute authority which must be forever a mystery. The point is that in the Bible, the order of life is seen only against the will and purpose of God, and there is no provision whatever for any human initiative which might bring cosmos out of chaos. Such is God's transcendence, even when it is manifest in history; and before that awesome unity any human effort to create its own center of meaning is absurd. As Camus observed, "The absurd is sin without God." [7]

God's communication with man is in the form of revelation. The limitation of human speech forces us to describe God's plan for our salvation as a Covenant, suggesting that our collusion was necessary for the pact; but human comprehension falters before a contract in which the chief bargainer is the Absolute. The doctrine of grace is that a transcendent initiative operates at the edge of all human enterprise. There is no feature of the long biblical account which does not imply the same opaqueness to human understanding. We read, for example, of the Elect, who are a people chosen to be bearers of the blessing; but the Elect are not chosen by any logical necessity. The worship of this God is also beyond reason and common sense. Shall we bring him an offering? But all things are his, every beast of the forest, and the cattle upon a thousand hills. The presumption in reducing God to rational categories is rebuked in his terrifying utterance, "If I were hungry I would not tell thee."

The Book of Job is the classical account in the Old Testament of the perennial vanity which attempts to bring the dark mystery of concrete existence into some kind of conceptual scheme. Why does Job suffer? Is it for some reason that could be spelled out for an unbeliever? Is Job being punished for his sins? Is he being tested, or perhaps instructed? From the beginning Job understands that no such categories are adequate for the action of an absolute power, but he does not really understand his own view until God speaks to him out of the whirlwind: "Where wast thou when I laid the foundations of the earth?" What human imagination invented the forms of the given? What human creativity fathered the rain? Now Job feels the full force of the argument: he can not bind the unicorn with his band in the furrow, nor can he clothe the horse's neck with its strange power.

Job's epiphany comes when he understands that suffering is

7 *The Myth of Sisyphus, op. cit.,* p. 40.

indeed a mystery, but no more a mystery than the most commonplace events you can imagine: the ostrich clumsy in flight,
the wild ass patient in his stall, the moon walking in brightness.
Job's redemption draws near when he not only perceives the
absurdity of every conceivable thing to the human mind, but
refuses to draw the conclusion that there is no center of meaning beyond our knowing: "I know that thou canst do every
thing, and that no thought can be withholden from thee." God,
he discovers, is not an abstract principle to be seized and ordered by the mind like an idea; God is a Presence, to be encountered with fear and trembling: "I have heard of thee by the
hearing of the ear: but now mine eye seeth thee."

Similarly, the Book of Ecclesiastes ceases to be a puzzling
document in the canon when it is seen to be a realistic appraisal
of what is possible by human effort unaided by divine mercy:
"I returned, and saw under the sun that the race is not to the
swift, nor the battle to the strong, neither yet bread to the wise,
nor yet riches to men of understanding, nor yet favour to men
of skill; but time and chance happeneth to them all." The very
form of the book supports the content: there is no development
of theological argument, and no story. Instead there are isolated
gnomic passages, conveying to the reader a complex impression
of an absurd universe, which rewards and punishes according to
no known formula. The book concludes with Candide's decision: since the universe is opaque to our understanding, the wise
man turns to an immediate purpose, the cultivation of his garden. Sow your seed, says the Preacher, in the morning (when
you can see what you are doing), but sow your seed while dusk
is coming on as well, for the future is not so much in man's
grasp as ordinary sowers believe. You do not really know which
seed shall prosper, "either this or that, or whether they both
shall be alike good."

But it is perhaps not necessary to produce more instances of
what can be found on every page of the Bible. No human mind
operating without grace can believe that God could become

man. When man is informed that God's son was born in a manger, that his mother was a virgin, and that like the boy next door he grew in wisdom and stature, the best he can do in reply is Mary's whisper, "Be it unto me according to thy word." The miracles Christ performed are surds as obviously as the square root of three. At the crucifixion, where God is put to death between two thieves, the limit is reached for all human possibility, including the rational. You can believe in a God who suffers, who dies, and who is raised up in three days; but you cannot make him seem plausible to an unbeliever. It was part of Paul's achievement that he faced up to the patent absurdity and found the audacious language which would gather it all into the divine plan. "God hath chosen the foolish things of this world," he told the church in Corinth, "that he may put to shame the things that are wise." Man sees through a glass darkly, he said, anticipating with his bold metaphor the controlling image of the mirror in the absurdist Jean Genet. Though the *kerygma* is enveloped in *non sequiturs*, the Christian must accept the fact and must be equal to our Lord's plea that we should not be ashamed.

Two dissimilar themes have been explored by theologians: the reasonableness of God (visible in a reasonable universe), and the dark willfulness of God (visible in his mysterious universe). In the former tradition could be listed the Pharisees, early Greek Christianity, Origen, Pelagius, the Franciscans, the nominalists, humanists, Arminians, Socinians, and others. These have found comfort in the abstract virtues which can rightly be ascribed to God, and have held that the infidel has no excuse, since the Creator is visible in his creation. But even these theologians have not understood reason as a purely human instrument; they have understood it to be the vestige of God's likeness. Another long line of theologians has spelled out the weakness of even the most brilliant speculation concerning the meaning of life apart from the revelation of God: Paul, Tertullian, Augustine, Luther, Calvin, St. John of the Cross, Dionysius the

Pseudo-Areopagite, Boehme, and Barth. There is opportunity here to call in the witness of only two of these.

Tertullian early in the third century was making the claim that the scandal of the *kerygma* was the best proof of its truth. He was furious at Marcion, who seemed to him to be dissipating the mystery and power of the divine visitation by trying to subsume it under logical process. Some allowance must be made for Tertullian's passion (he sneers at Marcion, *"sceletissime hominum"*); but he sees with utter lucidity that if God came to earth, his arrival could not possibly have been ordinary and unexceptionable. In a famous passage he cries, "The Son of God died: it is immediately credible—because it is silly [*quia pudendum est*]. He was buried, and rose again: it is certain—because it is impossible." [8]

But contemporary apostles of the absurd, who are more interested in the irrationality of life, find their patron in the nineteenth-century Dane, Søren Kierkegaard. The problem which engaged him above all others was what he called the Paradox, namely that Eternal Truth is in some way brought into relation with the existing individual. Perhaps his most influential treatment of the subject is in his account of Abraham's sacrifice in *Fear and Trembling*. Abraham is not simply tried to test his obedience, says Kierkegaard; his trial is not so easily explained. Nor is the test ethical, since we have here a "teleological suspension of the ethical." Abraham is tested by confronting him with the absurd. What proves him a true Knight of Faith is that he finds his way past absurdity to belief. So what we can learn from Abraham is simply astonishment. "To be able to lose one's reason, and therefore the whole of finiteness of which reason is the broker, and then by virtue of the absurd to gain precisely the same finitude—that appalls my soul." [9] He urges

---

[8] *De Carne Christi:* 5, in Tertullian's *Treatise on the Incarnation*, Ernest Evans, ed. (London: The Macmillan Company, 1957), p. 99.

[9] *Fear and Trembling*, Walter Lowrie, tr. (New York: Doubleday & Co., Inc., 1954), p. 47, Anchor Book.

Christians not to lose heart before the preposterous, but on the contrary to make "the absurd, the paradox, the possibility of offense" the decisive criterion of Christianity. "And that this should be indicated in every definition of Christianity is of the utmost importance, for the offense is Christianity's defense against all speculation." [10]

The way in which Eternal Truth is present in the existing individual cannot be mediated, because mediation depends upon universals, and this relationship in its particularity is by definition paradoxical and inaccessible to thought. The diagnosis of contemporary nihilists is enthusiastically supported by Christian teaching: it is true, as they have said, that nothing in secular history is necessary, in the sense that it could not have been otherwise. It remains now to consider at what point Christianity must demur from these contemporary analyses, maintaining stubbornly that the realm of individual life must not be considered lost, despite its problematic and even tragic character to speculative abstraction.

TO DEFY THE CHAOTIC

When the question is raised as to what response is possible to a universe which has been found to be absurd, the answer may be formulated in terms of the three categories first established by Kierkegaard: the aesthetic, the ethical, and the religious. The aesthete is the detached man, the connoisseur, who avoids at all costs the seriousness of existential participation. But all men can sympathize with the impulse to defy the chaotic by creating a work of art which in itself will have unity and harmony and even radiance despite the surrounding confusion. André Gide, one of the priests of the absurd, wrote in his Journal on April 25, 1918, "The aesthetic point of view is the only

10 *The Sickness unto Death*, Walter Lowrie, tr. (New York: Doubleday & Co., Inc., 1954), p. 214, Anchor Book.

one from which to speak of my work soundly." [11] He felt passionately that the particular has its own enchantment, which can be enjoyed in a detached way despite the absence of any perceptible organization in the universe. In *Les Nourritures Terrestres* he recognizes the uniqueness of everything, and an absence of ultimate purpose; but he argues that the fruits of the earth are good for all that, having the kind of immediate intelligibility which Husserl described, and are in any case the only nourishment that life has to offer.[12]

When all systems of value have been proved to be fictitious, the way is prepared for what Gide calls "the gratuitous act," the one distinctly human response. Such a deed is not dictated by self-interest, nor does it often please the community; but it has the merit of having been freely chosen, with no compelling motive turning men into puppets. Such an act was the impulsive killing of the old man in *Les Caves du Vatican*. Man's glory is his ability to maintain aesthetic distance, moving in bemused and unpredictable ways, like Kierkegaard's Don Juan the Seducer, or like Camus' Caligula, or like Nietzsche's Superman. Such a man is strong enough to live in a world where nothing is explained, and even to derive some pleasure from the strange and hopeless heroism demanded of him.

Artists have always found in the beauty of their forms the most gratifying kind of order, but they have not always elevated their source of peace into a universal remedy, as did Flaubert, the Goncourts, Rimbaud, Valéry, the writers of the *fin de siècle*, and so many of our contemporaries. Poetry has seemed to many to be an admirable icon, or image of the real world, structuring in miniature the random discords of experience. "We turn to poetry," said Matthew Arnold, "to interpret life for us, to con-

[11] *The Journals of André Gide*, Justin O'Brien, tr. (New York: Alfred A. Knopf, Inc., 1948), II, 229.
[12] See Everett W. Knight, *Literature Considered as Philosophy* (London: The Macmillan Company, 1957), p. 99.

sole us, to sustain us." [13] The early I. A. Richards thought that poetry is "capable of saving us." [14] And Wallace Stevens has often asserted that since religion has lost its power, only the order and effulgence of art can overcome the world's barrenness.[15]

Of dubious artistic merit but of unquestionable theological interest is "the theater of the absurd." [16] Such playwrights as Samuel Beckett, Arthur Adamov, Eugene Ionesco, and Jean Genet have written works which succeed with agonizing power in exposing the radical disorder of our age. Such plays as Jack Gelber's "The Apple" and Edward Albee's "The American Dream" are typical of this genre, in which there are no events in sequence, but only isolated situations; no valid characters, since each actor is called upon to establish his being from moment to moment; no moral imperatives, since absolute freedom reigns. The language wanders vaguely from trivialities to profundity, as in "Waiting for Godot," and the time sequence is circular, the curtain frequently falling just as the whole play begins again. Audiences flinch as they witness these hypnotic presentations of their own aimlessness, but here and there are said to be spectators who are filled with exhilaration at this fearless confrontation of the suffering implicit in all being. They leave the theater with the kind of purgation which Zen is said to bring to those of its devotees who dare to approach reality without the protection of a conceptual screen.

One must ask certain questions about the purgation possible from artistic form, or from the parody of that form in the theater of the absurd and in the anti-novel (both of which have rapidly acquired a form of their own). At best the artist knows that his achievement is full of irony, for if there are no established values, his own impromptu creation cannot hope to sur-

---

[13] "The Study of Poetry," in *Essays in Criticism, Second Series,* S. R. Littlewood, ed. (New York: St. Martin's Press, 1930), p. 2.
[14] *Science and Poetry* (New York, 1926), p. 95.
[15] See Joseph N. Riddel, "The Metaphysical Changes of Stevens' 'Esthétique du Mal,'" *Twentieth Century Literature,* VII (July, 1961), 64-79.
[16] See Martin Esslin, *The Theatre of the Absurd* (New York, 1961).

vive. It is perhaps for some such reason that the artist normally shows little interest in his past work, and turns hopefully to his next project. However absorbing his work may be while it is in process of creation, when it is finished it is no more secure a refuge than Coleridge's Xanadu; Kubla Khan's great wall could not protect him from the deep, sinister streams which welled up inside the garden and brought "ancestral voices prophesying war." Or one thinks of Kafka's early story, "The Great Wall of China." The building of the wall has gone on expertly for decades, but it is disclosed that there is a limitation: there are great gaps in the wall! "How can a wall protect," asks the narrator solemnly, "if it is not a continuous structure?" How can beauty, he might have asked, protect us from a demonic invasion which finds its way easily through the gaps in the intermittent wall which is the whole aesthetic enterprise?

The great works of art have themselves to be included in a comprehensive frame of reference if they are not themselves to be anarchic elements in an already chaotic structure. The thesis of Malraux's *Les Voix du Silence* is that although art between the Renaissance and the late nineteenth century was representational, and so dependent upon a community of meaning outside itself, since Goya it has been nonrepresentational, as it was before the Renaissance. The whole history of art points to the creation of unique objects which have their own integrity. Art therefore is able to transform destiny into freedom, and so is "man's eternal revenge." [17] Like the revolutionary, the artist helps man to achieve a godlike status which does not depend upon anything outside itself.

The irony is, however, that the freedom of the artist is never so complete as the Left Bank would like it to be. Something greater than man controls the dynamics of his freedom and gives it the form which creative spirits love more deeply than other men. The epigraph in Malraux's latest book, *The Metamorphosis of the Gods* (1961) is taken from Van Gogh: "In life and

[17] *Les Voix du Silence* (1952), p. 635.

painting I can quite well dispense with God. But, suffering as I am, I cannot dispense with something *greater than myself*, something that is my whole life: *the power of creating*." The movement in the genre of absurdity has been away from the presentation of discrete particularity toward some kind of abstract principle, such as creation, or rebellion, or fraternity. The detached aesthete soon tires of studying his fingernails, like Joyce's artist, and takes the path of Berthold Brecht, who abandoned the theater of the absurd for the theater of social protest. The aesthetic position, in other words, is not tenable for long except by deeply degenerate spirits.

Most commonly what strays into an aesthetic position is an ethic of rebellion. In Camus' novel *The Stranger*, Meursault is an archetypal example of the outsider who will not recognize the authority of convention and finally strikes out blindly against the pressures of society. He reacts violently against the ordinary prison chaplain who has come to hear his confession. With nothing but scorn for the simple-minded timidity which accepts the usual norms, Meursault chooses instead himself, even if that self is soon to die. The principle of rebellion has freed him and made him understand the simple innocence of the world process. Camus' *The Rebel* is the proper commentary for such novels as *The Stranger* and *The Plague*.[18] It also establishes the grounds for the positive elements in the metaphysic of revolt which might not be noticed in the novels of Malraux, T. E. Lawrence, Saint-Exupéry, and Sartre. Almost imperceptibly, as in the novels by the late Camus, the ethics of rebellion slide into an ethic of compassion or comradeship. In Malraux's *The Walnut Trees of Altenburg*, for instance, the threat of meaningless death is seen to be averted by a principle of human companionship, "*la fraternité virile*." A great many contemporary novelists, from

[18] See Louis R. Rossi, "Albert Camus: the Plague of Absurdity," *Kenyon Review*, XX (Summer, 1958), 399-422; Philip Hallie, "Camus and the Literature of Revolt," *College English*, XVI (1954), 25-32, 83; and Thomas J. Hanna, "Albert Camus and the Christian Faith," *Journal of Religion*, XXXVI (Oct. 1956), 224-233.

Silone to Hemingway, have observed that the *revolté* may feel a warm sympathy and affection for the rest of the human family, which shares his predicament.[19] There seems to be a rhythm of rebellion, abstraction *("bon sentiment")*, and sentimentality.

The drift of absurd theory into some form of Sartrean engagement indicates a basic flaw in the position. There is no great difficulty in maintaining, with a kind of aesthetic detachment, that life is senseless; if life is farcical, one can be forgiven for laughing. But even here there is a problem in consistency, because the word *absurd* is a word which can exist only in relation. There must be a position from which everything else can be adjudged absurd, and this position must certainly be rational. The confusion becomes clear when the appeal is made to rebellion, or to compassion, or to some other abstraction. If the universe is absurd, nothing at all can be salvaged from its absurdity, not even the assertion that life is absurd. The problem is not a quibble, in its aesthetic or ethical form, and it is not answered by Beckett's reply when Gessner charged him with inconsistency in writing words about absurdity: *"Que voulez-vous, Monsieur? C'est les mots; on n'a rien d'autre."* [20] *Absurd* bears within itself a saving power which drives toward its own contradiction; when you say the word you protest in the name of the rational; if everything were absurd, no one would ever know it.[21]

The positive element which is present in the most sullen negativity is the point at which a most fruitful conversation could begin between the Church and the writers we have been

[19] "Before the appearance of Malraux's novels 'masculine brotherhood' ...had been absent from French literature for fifty years," Everett W. Knight, *Literature Considered as Philosophy* (New York: The Macmillan Company), p. 130.

[20] Esslin, *The Theatre of the Absurd*, p. 44.

[21] According to Waldo Frank, "One can call life absurd only by a positive axiom or measure making it absurd" ("Life in the Face of Absurdity," *New Republic*, 133 [Sept. 19, 1955], 19). For this reason Simone de Beauvoir prefers to use the word "ambiguity" in *The Ethics of Ambiguity*, Bernard Frechtman, tr. (New York, 1948), p. 129.

considering. They would perhaps not be prepared for Kierkegaard's dramatic leap from the absurdity of life to the foolishness of the gospel. Sartre identifies such transilience as "bad
faith," and Camus sneered at Chestov and at Jaspers, who
trusted in a leap that "suddenly and through a blind act of
human confidence, explains everything." [22] But when the early
Camus rejects suicide, as the later Camus rejects murder, and
when Sartre supports political projects, they also have performed
a leap and have affirmed value and are full of hope. Love can
enter so long as there is hope, according to Dante's Manfred in
the *Purgatorio:* "Not by curse of theirs is man so lost, but Love
eternal can return, so long as hope abideth green of leaf." [23]

The Church should be grateful to the literary artists and to
all other artists who have provided this unexpected demonstration that the Renaissance impulse to fulfill life within human
history has proved abortive. It is true and it is worth saying that
within the world process there is no *arché* visible, in the sense
of a fixed and stable figure on which all change depends. But
the church prefers to call this sense of impoverishment by the
more familiar name of Purgation, the first step on the mystic
way, "Qwhat is poverte of spirit bot mekenes of mynde," asked
Richard Rolle, "be the qwhilk a mane knawes his awen infir-
mite? Seand that he to parfyte stabilnes maye not cum bot be
the grace of God." [24] Loyola might well be right that the third
sacrifice, the sacrifice of the intellect, might be the offering in
which God takes the greatest delight.

It is not possible to receive salvation from God until the
human predicament is seen to be as desperate as the nihilists
have said it is. But the Christian does not believe that salvation
is possible from the mere recognition that man has need of it.
Evil spirits, as our Lord warned, are likely to fill a house swept

[22] *Myth of Sisyphus*, p. 33.
[23] *Purgatorio*, III, 11. 133-135.
[24] *The Mending of Life*, Richard Misyn, ed. (EETS, 106, London,
1896), p. 110.

clean. Surely there is a kind of purgation in the discovery of the world's incoherence: Meursault, for example, feels "purged of evil" after he has driven out the chaplain in *The Stranger*. But if what is purged away is the only remaining possibility of coherence, the process is very like the act of blood-letting which brought some of our mildly ill ancestors to death's door.

The nihilist purgation does not lead to health and wholeness because it does not lead to an illumination where the distant goal is visible. There are strident claims that what is achieved is lucidity; but lucidity is a quality which perhaps only should be ascribed to others. Lucidity in any case is a quality which may be achieved by ignoring some of the possibilities. Even Descartes felt that the first of the "clear and distinct ideas" was the existence of God. The nihilist illumination by lucidity cannot lead to the Spirit who can be found after unutterable groanings. Nor is there even a promise of union in this version of the mystic way, but rather the certainty of separation, estrangement, and loneliness, one of the archetypal experiences of our time. At the end of *The Stranger*, Meursault lays his heart open to "the benign indifference of the universe." He then claims to be happy in a way the most credulous Christian finds it difficult to believe: "For all to be accomplished, for me to feel less lonely, all that remained to hope was that on the day of my execution there should be a huge crowd of spectators and that they should greet me with howls of execration." [25]

This is the philosophy of a stag at bay. In the face of such perversion, the Christian apologist can only sigh and present once again the grounds of his faith. The meaning of creation is indeed a mystery beyond intelligence; faith begins at the edge of comprehension. If the universe were comprehensible it would have a finished structure in which human freedom would certainly be illusory. But faith has its reasons. They depend upon revelation, which comes from beyond intelligence. The Chris-

[25] Albert Camus, *The Stranger*, Stuart Gilbert, tr. (New York: Alfred A. Knopf, Inc., 1957), p. 154.

tain has no novel insight into the radical facticity of things—
Sartre's tree root, my single nose and my twin ears—except to
say, "It pleased God that it be so." Such sense as life makes
for us is not the achievement of our intelligence, but is a gift
from the Creator. And this is why Camus has Father Paneloux
turn to the humanist Dr. Rieux and say sadly, "Ah, doctor, I've
just realized what is meant by 'grace.'" [26]

The Christian affirms that God has a freedom beyond the
structures of existence, and so appears in history as Creator,
Judge, and Redeemer. The chaos which the *absurdistes* have
discovered is the same chaos which God ordered in biblical
myth. "For the word of the cross is folly to those who are perish-
ing," wrote Paul to the Corinthian church, "but to us who are
being saved it is the power of God." There is nothing to fear,
because "the foolishness of God is wiser than men, and the
weakness of God is stronger than men." His folly is wise past
telling, and his weakness is strong past knowing. As the angel
asked Sarah, who was laughing at the absurd possibility that
she bear a child at ninety, "Is any thing too hard for the Lord?"
Since with God all things are possible, the Christian is able to
affirm that life has meaning, even after making the admission
that the center and source of that meaning lies beyond history.

We need not perhaps insist that we do not know everything,
but neither should it be necessary to insist that we know something. We have the kindly light that showed Newman his next
step. We know that values are real. "Thus saith God the Lord,
he that created the heavens, and stretched them out; he that
spread forth the earth, and that which cometh out of it; he that
giveth breath unto the people upon it, and spirit to them that
walk therein: I the Lord have called thee in righteousness, and
will hold thine hand, and will keep thee" (Isaiah 42:5-6). We
can sympathize with Sartre's predicament: "I cannot judge the
world, since my judgments are a part of it." [27] So said Paul, but

26 *The Plague, op. cit.,* p. 197.
27 *Situations* I (Paris, 1947), p. 136.

he added, "he that judgeth me is the Lord." No one under that awful gaze would write Sartre's foolish conclusion that "it amounts to the same thing whether one gets drunk alone or is a leader of nations." [28]

As T. S. Eliot has observed, we are engaged in the experiment of creating a purely secular culture. So much contemporary writing seems to the believer to be composed of odd bits taken without discrimination from orthodoxy, and unrelated to the history of salvation. It is as though one took everything from Pascal, except his Christ; and everything from Kierkegaard, except his saving leap; and everything from Cape Canaveral, except its rockets. The result is disastrous, without the impressive quality of a firm and comprehensive atheism; a little piety, like a little learning, is a dangerous thing. The Christian will continue to believe, as he has for 2,000 years, that despite the distraction of our days and the mystery of time, each of us fulfills in some inscrutable way a divine purpose. The sovereign God, from somewhere beyond our lucidity and our perplexity, is the lifter-up of our countenance. It makes a difference. As Chesterton wrote in "The Ballad of the White Horse,"

> the men signed of the cross of Christ
> Go gaily in the dark.[29]

[28] *Being and Nothingness*, Hazel E. Barnes, tr. (New York: 1956), p. 627.
[29] *Collected Poems* (New York: Dodd, Mead & Co., 1911).

J. EDWARD DIRKS

Education

EVERY discussion of the relationship of Christianity and education—a relationship recalling numerous historical movements and diversified themes or emphases—leads not only to a consideration of the training of Christians in the life of the church but also to a consideration of the secular. This has been apparent from the early centuries when educational responsibilities were broadened to include the liberal arts and the pursuit of truth by reason as well as by faith. The Reformation gave impetus to new emphases upon the so-called secular vocations and helped to give birth to modern curricula and teaching methods. Nevertheless, the traditional consideration of secularized education among Christians has often been confined to a variety of forms of deprecating such secularization of education.

Now—in this as in everything else connected with the role of the church in modern culture and in education—some basic changes can be perceived. The most important is a realignment of ideas, rooted in recent theological developments, with the secular coming to be understood as a positive movement which is both a complement and a true ally of the Christian. Contemporary secular education demands a kind of freedom which challenges Christianity to consider anew the basis of "the freedom for which Christ has set us free." It is also only in the exercise of this freedom within education that Protestantism, when it is true to its Reformation tradition, can hope to be effective.

Before it is possible to outline and discuss some of the more important problems and opportunities that lie ahead for Christianity's educational frontiers, we must examine several of the more significant factors which, present in both contemporary Christianity and education, suggest the major contextual conditions. We shall be reminded, therefore, of what each of these movements brings to their meeting on the frontier and what they both find as already there, "given" in the present situation. Although any effort to be comprehensive and complete must be set aside in this brief section, a description of the frontier itself must be attempted under several headings.

THE THEOLOGICAL RENAISSANCE

During the past several decades professional leaders in the churches and increasing numbers of the laity have become aware of a reawakened theological interest. Signs have been accumulating to indicate that the theological depression of the modern period has been drawing to its close and that new directions in biblical scholarship, theological formulation, and interconnections between faith and culture have been under way. Christian thought has been advancing in different ways; horizons have been broadened while analyses have been deepened; and major developments in Christian theology have had their bearing upon Christianity's own educational endeavors as well as upon the areas of scholarly inquiry in the arts and sciences where the search for basic foundations has been proceeding. The renewed interest in theology itself has led toward many different efforts of interpreting the faith of the Christian church in relation to other knowledge and with special concern for the tests of truth.

Three basic concerns shape this theological movement today in Protestantism and also increasingly in Catholicism. The first of these is the concern for the uniqueness and integrity of the Christian faith as it is rooted in the biblical witness to God's revelation in Jesus Christ. The beginnings of the theological renaissance may well prove to reside in the readiness of theologians to leave some of the narrow preoccupations of the past or even their dialogue with other scholarly pursuits in order to come to the rescue of the Church in urgent need of recovering its distinctive message—its "Word" from beyond the world. In continental Europe, for example, the recovery of theological concern for the uniqueness of the gospel was directly part of the same historical situation in which the churches were threatened by totalitarianism. In this situation, as in the Protestant Reformation, there was the need to return to the sources, to the Scriptures, to the essential Christian doctrines, and to an emphasis upon Christian faith as proclamation. This renaissance has therefore involved academic scholarship and it has instilled a new vitality and vigor in a whole generation of younger thoughtful Christian leaders and educators.

The second concern which is noteworthy in contemporary theological developments is the establishment of the Christian view of the uniqueness and value of persons and their relationships within a meaningful community. This brings to mind the importance assigned to such areas as psychology and sociology in contemporary theology. Whereas the history of Christian thought shows early efforts to establish the central importance of nature and later of history as authentic means of God's self-revelation, recent theological endeavors assign similar importance to personal and corporate human emphases as Christian faith is seen in the context of personal encounter and man's existence in community. The I-Thou relationship of faith has been stressed primarily as a possible basis for meaningful personal existence within technical modern civilization. The educator for whom this represents a matter of concern is in a position to explore the issues in depth and to appraise the tensions they create.

The third concern which must be mentioned is the concern for the relevance of the Christian message to the radical questions, anxieties, and struggles of contemporary man. The root-metaphor for the periods which gave chief stress to "justification by faith" was primarily one which saw the world in legal terms, emphasizing lawful order, punishment, and justification. In contemporary thought, the basic metaphor is more likely to be a "field of forces" theory, changing the emphases in the direction of tensions, dialogue, and wholeness. Moreover, a theologian such as Paul Tillich interprets man primarily from the standpoint of the universal question concerning the meaning of his existence. What does it mean to be? What threatens our being? Reflection on these questions prompts a person to acknowledge his anxiety. To such a process the Christian faith offers its message; it is an answer to man's ultimate questions. This type of approach has its immediate educational implications, for it suggests that Christianity is communicated in a two-sided way, with respect to questions and answers; and it opens up for the educator a new possibility of interpreting religious symbols, language, and doctrine.

Beyond the general importance of a theological renewal around such concerns as these for the life and work of the Church, there are particular educational implications which should be noted. The educator is engaged directly, as well as indirectly, with the concrete problems of persons and their existential questions; though no theological formulation can exhaust the depth of man's spiritual need, the educator can point to the need and often refer to various types of responses or answers to it. The educator is, furthermore, involved with all the points of growth in human life, including the crises with respect to personal goals of human living. To bring these points into a framework of theological perspective can be educationally enriching whatever may be its results for Christian faith itself. Finally, the educator is in a position where he can contribute to the understanding of the nature of Christian faith and the Christian community. The faith is dynamic, and the community is a living organism. Their forms and directions are fruitful in educational ways, and, in addition, since theology is the ongoing interpretation of the Christian way of believing and living, those who contribute through education to this process become part of the contemporary theological movement itself. Educators, therefore, not only draw upon insight from theology, but also help to create the material and the criticism which makes a living theology possible.

THE RECOVERY OF THE LAITY

The new emphasis upon the laity and upon the church as a people is one of the prominent features or conditions of Christianity on the educational frontier. Whereas, for example, the first half of the twentieth century gave evidence of the church's educational devotion to the study of children and the development of programs for youth, the second half promises to center on the study of adults and the development of programs for the Christian education of adults. The recovery of the laity is not only parallel with a theological renaissance; an underlying connection between the two is to be found. Biblical and theological illiteracy of the large majority of church members was long decried as one of the areas of greatest educational needs in the church. Today the large number of training programs, centers for lay theology, and publications for adults is indicative of the attempts which are being made to correct this situation. Increasing recognition is evident of the problems which the church faces unless it has an informed and articulate laity; when it lacks a theologically sophisticated laity, it has only clerical, and therefore "outside," voices in the work-a-day world of business, industry, education, politics, labor, and the like; further, it has no resources within itself for carrying out an educational program without the necessary lay teachers.

The role of the adult and the place of the laity have been given renewed attention for many reasons. New interest in adult education, the understanding of education not as preparation

for but coextensive with human life, and the lengthening dura-
tion of life are all part of the new situation. Clarification of
the Church as a covenant community with a mission to perform,
the rediscovery of the doctrine of the priesthood of all believers,
and the growing recognition of the Christian's vocation where
he serves in the world, all point to the need for a theological
re-education of the laity. And the ingredients in the theological
renewal already discussed are directly relevant for this re-education. Instead of having the church viewed as the responsibility
of a professional minister, assisted by those laymen who have
the time and interest, the contemporary emphasis is reversed
so that the church is first and primarily a congregation whom
the minister is called upon to train and assist in being God's
people in the world.

Many different organizational approaches and methods have
been used in the theological re-education of the laity. The
sermon is often used for teaching, and the adult Bible class
continues to be an important standard agency. Closely allied
with the small-group Bible study movement is the increasing
number of Christian nurture groups, with some churches organizing their entire adult constituencies into small Christian-
growth groups. Parish life conferences, congregational retreats,
and interdenominational institutes for adult education are increasingly part of the newer patterns. More radical efforts are
evident in such approaches as the emerging interest in the use
of the fine arts in the church, the establishment under a congregation's auspices of a coffee-house which becomes an avenue
for adult lay evangelism among non-Christians and especially
among intellectuals, and the development of lay centers for
conferences devoted to study and Christian nurture. Recognizing itself as set amid a secularized world and moral ambiguities, many of which penetrated its own life during an era
of nontheological interest, the Church has made efforts to
correct its work in evangelism and self-understanding among
the laity. When the traditional patterns have seemed to be

threatened by lack of intensive dealing with subjects and by educational programs that are too sporadic, then efforts have been made to create new designs for more effective recruitment and training of lay leaders. Few of these have gone as far as the "Church-and-World Centers" or the Evangelical Academies on the European continent in the postwar period. But what has been taking place already brings the churches to their educational frontier with a greater clarity about the role of laity (even in the minds of the clergy) than was true several decades ago. Even the theology of the laity, about which we shall speak later, is a phrase more often heard and understood in wider circles of the life of the church.

THE ROLE OF COLLEGES AND UNIVERSITIES

The past several decades have given clear evidence for the assertion that our era is marked by revolution, that it is sweeping the earth in far more radical ways than most of us can admit, and that it is affecting the lives of millions of people who have been finding their way toward a new dignity, freedom, and equality because of this revolution. In the same critical hour higher education has been moving toward the center of the stage as a key means of advancing these far-reaching changes, disciplining the possible excesses inherent in its forward sweeps, and training the leadership needed for constructive development into the future. Because of this revolution, or as the sign of it, an old order has been passing from the scene and the more profound and convulsive character of a new era is beginning to take shape. Its contours are still difficult to describe, but one feature is becoming apparent—the importance of higher learning, the premium it places on scientific training, the hope that it may find ways of meeting technological needs with an education informed by the heritage of a humane culture, and the promise that it may give to the future leaders whose critical intelligence has been sharpened and whose range of understanding has been broadened.

Only during the past two or three decades has there been an increased and new awareness of the central importance of higher education for Christianity. But during those same decades much of the critical thought which has been converging on the purposes and problems of colleges and universities has been a preoccupation of Christians. In England, the earliest signs of difficulty for the liberal modern university appeared when these institutions on the Continent, long revered for their academic and scholarly transcendence of the ordinary levels of society, knuckled under to fascism. Criticisms began to be heard to the effect that studies in the modern universities were irrelevant to the urgent needs of the contemporary world. A different approach to relevance was outlined in such books as Arnold S. Nash's *The University and the Modern World,* and Sir Walter Moberly's *The Crisis in the University.*[1] Their arguments and perspectives have been restated in many ways since they first appeared during and shortly following the Second World War.

According to this line of thought, a university exists primarily to give a country's youth, especially its ablest, a pause to think, to learn, and to reflect; to acquire intellectual (and perhaps social and aesthetic) standards which will enable them to see through bogus arguments quickly and to develop valid ones with conviction; and to realize that as the mind moves with curiosity to the edges of knowledge it finds not static formulae but dynamic truth, the truth which is not a terminus to searching but a path in which to walk. The core of this process is the mastery of the disciplines of scholarly endeavor, intensive study in several areas and the development of an acquaintance with other subjects, and training in the arts and skills of communicating truth to others. The objection that education in this direction is socially unjustifiable is met by the claim that

[1] The Macmillan Company, 1959.

it is in fact closely relevant to the needs of an increasingly specialized and intricate society, for no other method simultaneously concentrates and expands the powers of the mind, thus
enabling the person to grasp and criticize a whole range of
practical subjects and to bring an independent judgment to
bear upon them. Studies perfect nature and are perfected by
experience. Conversely, experience without studies can lead to
narrow and uncreative views and the retention of traditional
methods at the expense of clarity and efficiency.

This view of what a university education should do recalls
the essential heritage of higher learning, because it assumes
that the mind's development and growth, within the context
of broad understanding, avoids the danger that in doing only
what is believed to be "relevant" to today's needs, it may prove
to be painfully irrelevant to tomorrow's. Beyond this, the search
for a responsible understanding of university education gives
renewed importance to studies which send students' roots
deeper into their cultural heritage. Today there is increasing
recognition that cultural educational dimensions call for a more
universal curriculum than we have known. Such studies require
time and, when they are accepted as being fundamentally important, then difficulties are posed for education along technological lines, toward narrow nationalistic political ends or
for the achievement of cultural parochialism and isolation. To
insist that colleges and universities must exercise a critical function in our culture, that time must be allowed for creative
thought, and that incentives must be provided for an historical
approach to human issues in the contemporary world, all call
for, and are in part prompted by, a profound Christian concern
about learning and society. If there is to be more than shallow
thought and vulgarized culture, then there must be not only
a new dedication to the cultivation of the mind, but also a
growth in world-mindedness that will assure the future of
educated persons who will find all historical epochs, all persons
throughout the earth, and all significant streams of thought and

culture ethically relevant. Without the perspective that such a sophistication would afford, Christianity's work on the higher educational frontier is doomed as marginal and something extra. Insofar as Christianity's efforts include the concern for such a sophistication, its mission in higher education is comprehensive of the university's own best future.

REAPPRAISAL OF SECULARIZATION

Education is, by and large, stubbornly secular in its motivations. By accentuating a questioning and critical attitude, in requiring freedom to pursue the truth to the very brink of perception, and in a deep historical legacy of autonomy and independence among communities of teachers and scholars, there has been a long tradition of secularity in many levels of education. To be sure, the church has established educational institutions and given priority to certain religious purposes inherent in learning, but the pressures toward secularization in education have continued wherever the search for human self-realization, the fulfillment of man's life in the world, through knowledge and culture, has been encouraged. The mood, ethos, and explicit aims of education are, therefore, set in a position of contrast and tension with much that is essential to Christianity. For this reason the Church has long found itself uneasy, ambivalent, or hostile toward human culture; H. Richard Niebuhr in *Christ and Culture* [2] suggests at least five different theological approaches to culture in historic Christianity. And every discussion concerning the contemporary interconnections between Christianity and education sooner or later finds itself involved in the meaning of the secular.

Until a decade or two ago any consideration of secularization in a Christian framework, if it took place at all, became an

[2] Harper & Brothers, 1951.

occasion for refutation, criticism, and regret. Secularization in modern history appeared as a process with many unfortunate consequences; it represented a denial of all spiritual realities and needs; it suggested a philosophy of life drained of religious meanings, insisting that man now knew his self-sufficiency in a self-explanantory world. Such secularity avoids conviction and commitment, and it may be tempted by both complacent optimism and existentialist despair; in its radical relativism goals are narrowed, human concerns of any depth are neutralized, and any consideration of world views is dismissed as unimportant. But, within the recovery of a vigorous prophetic type of Christianity, which has occurred with the theological renaissance already described, secularization has come to be understood in a different sense as a positive movement and perhaps as a true ally of Christianity itself. Christianity is, after all, the most secular of all religions; faith issues in an obedience demanded in this world; and true secularity for man may demand the kind of freedom which is offered the Christian in the gospel itself.

Within this positive framework the historical process of secularization is viewed not as the gradual withdrawal of the various orders of life from ecclesiastical and religious control, but as the search for human meaning and action in "a world come of age," where men are expected to be mature and responsible, not made and kept dependent. Moreover, instead of his having to assent to metaphysical explanations and comprehensive systems of thought which resemble ideologies, secularized men may live by faith, as trust, and with this freedom entertain skepticism and agnosticism about the final details of ultimate reality. Curiosity and disbelief, intellectual skepticism and existential confidence, the openness of science and the security of faith, all have their place and need not be interpreted as opposites excluding one another. Such a reappraisal of secularization, expressed in the writings of theologians such as Dietrich Bonhoeffer, Rudolf Bultmann, and Karl Barth, to name only a few, not only tends to reconstruct cultural history but also assigns a new importance to the secular attitude. The historical drama is not solely from a sacral society toward a secularized one, but it is a drama that opens with a natural state which is conceived in sacred terms and proceeds toward a breaking of this bondage for the end of properly sanctifying the world. And the secular attitude is made possible, in part, by faith as a restoration of freedom and responsibility in and for the world; faith breaks the powers of idolatry and offers the world to men for their appreciation, understanding, and even dominion.

It can readily be seen that such a line of thought concerning secularization makes possible an openness toward the secular realm designated as education. It opens the way toward a life of dialogue between the Christian and the non-Christian in which a basic co-humanity is assumed. It makes possible the objective study of any reality and the raising of all fundamental questions for inquiry. To seek knowledge in a secular way is to recognize knowledge as something dynamic and open, a force that can help to meet the needs of the human community. Education, then, is for the relative and provisional solution of human problems; it is a process that has pragmatic ends. Upon this basis, Christianity can move with vigor toward the educational frontier and assist it to do its own proper work; yet it can avoid the danger of the kind of idolatry that is implicit in the notion that men can be saved by education.

PROBLEMS AND OPPORTUNITIES AHEAD

We have reviewed the more significant signs of progress in recent educational ventures associated with Christianity—a reawakened theological awareness and interest, a new understanding of the Church as a covenant community of the laity, an awareness of the central importance of higher education in the world-wide cultural revolution, and the beginnings of a different theological appraisal of secularization to prepare for an engagement with the realm of education in its primary secular aspects. We must now suggest the more important problems and opportunities that lie ahead for Christianity's future work on the educational frontier. This calls for a clear recognition of the values inherent in previous contributions and patterns on this frontier. Much that has already taken place in the past, and much that is now under way along the lines suggested above, must still be carried forward and completed. But undertaking only yesterday's responsibilities is not enough; the dynamics of our time take us beyond yesterday's solutions. Some of the things yet to be done and some of the ways in which they might be done have yet to be given attention. Among these there are the following challenges:

To Develop a Theology of Education

Several books and a large number of journal articles have begun to suggest the possibilities of a theology of education. A study toward this same end has been under way for several years under the auspices of the Commission on Higher Education of the National Council of Churches; it has involved philosophers of education, educational leaders, and theologians. The efforts that are being made suggest the need for bringing within reach something which is believed potentially to exist but which does not now exist, namely, a distinctive Christian philosophy of education, informed by Protestant themes, history, and experience. Educational philosophers insist that what is being sought must fill a tragic gap in their disciplines; although there is a Roman Catholic philosophy of education and it is available for study, nothing exists to bring students into touch with a comprehensive Protestant approach to education. Educational leaders, teachers in many different fields, and those who serve as ministers in educational institutions all confess to the same need.

What should be advanced in this regard has a number of dimensions. One of these is historical, partly biblical and partly the experience and insight of Christians, particularly those of the Reformation and its heritage. The collecting of readings from the reformers and educators in Protestantism's history is not an impossible task; the fact that much of this is not readily available to the contemporary student of education deprives him of one important line of development and thought within his field. A second dimension is philosophical, however beset with problems this may be. Here the purposes and the methods of education would be given most central attention and, if it were informed by the historical material, the effort to work out some of the philosophical materials would suggest the most fruitful insights of the Christian tradition for an understanding of education. The third dimension is theological. Whether or not any theological system can be considered as giving explicit directions to education is a question which will be viewed differently by interpreters in both theology and education. Theology offers perspectives on the nature of Christian faith and guidance to the sources of its insight and values. Insofar as Christianity has to do with the universal problems and ultimate questions of human existence, such perspectives and guidance also speak to the area of education. But theology would not come to education as a completely independent discipline; it would reflect upon the activities which involve Christian nurture, and it would be illuminated by educational theory in its definition of the goals and activities of learning. Although no responsible Protestant theology would seek to prescribe the modes of educational practice, it would speak with the promise of some value to general directives and goals in this area. This would be true especially of that theological approach which had both sound historical foundations and rigorous philosophical intentions.

No theology or philosophy of education which is true to Protestant insights and concerns would, of course, be able to overlook the significant current controversies concerning the "separation of church and state" and the role of public schools in American education. A defense of the traditional Protestant position is important not only because that position is frequently challenged today but also because it needs to be clarified and supported on firm principles derived from both theological roots and democratic experience. The Puritan and Reformation traditions, from which this position has been derived, insisted upon a co-ordinate responsibility among the primary institutions in a democratic commonwealth, the state, the school or university, and the church. Each responsible under God for its work within a definable area of the common life of society, the three orders were also conceived of as being responsible *for* one another, not *to* one another. Hence, the concern that the school or university be faithful to its essential tasks would be shared by both the state and the church. Such a defense of the school or university would, in turn, be centered in a willingness to serve and to be critical of education. Thus, there is no general praise of public schools (any more than there would be blind praise of church colleges); neither would there be the contention that whatever may be wrong can be corrected by sufficient numbers of qualified teachers, adequate buildings, or useful equipment—deficiencies which can be met with larger expenditures of public money alone. A Protestant position, informed theologically and by pluralistic democratic experience, would be more radical in its defense and its criticisms. To elaborate this important perspective would be a timely contribution to some current debates on education, and it would at the same time fill out and make specific application of this historic position.

To Revitalize Efforts in Higher Education

The tremendous expansions that are taking place in the college and university world, as well as the crucial place which is to be assigned to these institutions with respect to the future, demand a revitalizing of the work of the church in this area.

This is, moreover, an area where the experience of Christianity has been longest and deepest in the whole range of formal educational institutions. To undertake renewal here involves many of the problems already discussed, including the re-education of the laity and the importance of working on a secular frontier. Thus the Church is driven to ask old but deep questions: What is there in Christianity that calls for its association with, yet its critical distance from, education? Why must the church be present where education is going on, and yet have its presence be one of discernment? Why must men and women be sent to their cultural tasks and, at the same time, placed on guard against the ultimacy they demand? What is the character of the academic excellence which is worthy of Christianity? Must church-related colleges meet secular standards of academic excellence? What is required of Christianity to assure it? And, why should Christians in the private or tax-supported university defend its autonomy, its right to be a university, and indeed its need to be only this as its responsibility under God?

Such questions as these suggest the range of thought and reflection which are needed in any larger and more penetrating effort of Christianity on the higher-education frontier. Many denominations have already carried forward as much expansion of their own work as resources permit, and yet higher education continues to expand. If the number of their college and university pastors cannot be sizeably enlarged and the physical facilities they build cannot be expanded, then perhaps the major future effort must be devoted to other approaches. A small residential faith-and-life community, devoted to the training of the laity, is one approach that is getting more emphasis. Another is the regional center of study and work to which are brought the students, teachers, or educational administrators of a number of institutions for their training in theology for the laity and for the carrying out of their Christian vocations. In order to move with the tide, it may be considered essential for the church to train a "creative minority" for positions in the regular affairs of many community colleges, state colleges, or other branches of larger universities. One approach might be that of training a layman who has a specialized competency in higher education. After a brief theological training, he would be supported by the church as he takes up residence in a new college or university community and makes himself and his skills available until such a time as he receives an academic appointment. Once this has happened, the church is released from its burden and can set about the training of another. Such a form of "university ministry," though revolutionary at first glance, would bring that ministry into the very centers of institutions, and it would be especially effective in those institutions in their most formative years of development. With respect to its own related institutions, the churches may find the need to develop structures that guarantee still more autonomy and independence, while they as parent denominations serve them primarily by advancing them toward a type of secular maturity which places them on a par with all others.

The real future frontier for Christianity may well be the colleges and the universities, where the mind-set of each new generation of leaders is established. But if this proves to be true, as it seems to be, then some of the most important developments sought in the renewal of the church, in the manifestation of its unity, and in the involvement of its laity are even more urgently to be furthered than they would otherwise need to be. Insofar as the Church is concerned with the penetration of culture by going into the world, there is certainly no more significant enterprise available to it than higher education. The university has often been said to stand on the frontier of culture. This may well be the case in that the university, like the genetic mechanism of an organism, transmits to each new generation the basic characteristics of mind, the fundamental quality of values, which are handed on. Universities are resistant to mutations, too, but the pressures upon them in rapidly changing societies throughout the world are so great today that in the midst of a technical civilization their heritage may be bypassed and their present form may become indistinguishable from the technical institute. To help universities remain true to themselves and their own best traditions may be the very task which is falling not only upon them, but upon the Church as well. The Church's help may come in the form of defending the approaches to the gates of open and humane learning, of exalting the role of the mind and its inquiries, and of setting all men under the commands of truth and honesty and integrity.

To Be Devoted Wholly to the Mission of Education in Christian Faith

Everything that has been said underscores the central importance of the educational mission of Christianity. In the midst of the great needs of the world, the task of the Church is fundamentally evangelism and its supreme mission is to bring men to Jesus Christ and to learn of him the meaning of his Lordship. This evangelization of the world, whether at home or abroad, must take the measure of the dynamic forces which are shaping our time, molding the minds and the spirits of men, and serving as instruments in God's drama of human salvation. And though only the Holy Spirit can appoint and anoint the chosen for the labors of the Kingdom, and God alone can give the increase (we humans being blasphemous when we expect to raise up saints for the Church), yet the mandate of the gospel, the example of our Teacher and Lord, and the experience of the centuries have made it abundantly clear that God expects his people to think and to work in the world, to seek out and nurture and commission his witnesses among the people. This calls for a total sense of Christian vocation for all those who would serve Christ, and it calls especially for carrying through the special tasks in the life of the church which involve education.

In the light of all that has been cited—the complexity of human need and the inexhaustible potential in the awakening impulses of our time—the developing of leadership is the great task. Christianity has had laid upon it the inescapable commission to bring the treasure of its faith, as received and responsibly handled, to the world—and, in particular, to do the following: (a) to recruit, guide, and inspire the best young people for leadership as laymen and ministers, at home and abroad; (b) to offer theological and practical training for Christian ministries commensurate with the age they will serve; (c) to nurture children intensively in the Christian faith through the home and the church; (d) to make manifest and attractive the standards of mature religion and true learning in institutions of higher education; (e) to educate and train laymen and laywomen and to increase their involvement in responsible leadership in the whole range of the church's work; and (f) to provide in-service training, even to the point of basic reorientation, for pastors and other leaders in the church who are often baffled by the perplexing demands of our time.

Humanly speaking, the enlisting, training, and supporting of strong leadership may well be the factor without which all else we have lifted up will be relatively impotent. At the same time, the securing and nurture of such leadership will depend upon our effectiveness as churches in relation to all the other areas of need.

The church's mandate of God is educational. To serve well on that frontier is to reinforce all others.

GRAYDON E. McCLELLAN

The Ministry

IT is embarrassing for any observer to have to list the "new frontiers" of Christian ministry for American Protestantism, simply because the frontiers are anything but "new." Yet the embarrassment is not judgmental of the observer's acumen so much as of the church's vision. For years her prophets have beckoned, scolded, and cajoled, but the church has taken only timid and token steps to mount an effective city ministry; to integrate racially her membership and leadership; to enlist her congregations for aggressive mission; or to express the professed unity of the church in unified mission and ministry. Therefore these areas of endeavor still remain the "new frontiers" into which the church must yet move with decision.

RECOLONIZING AMERICA'S GREAT CITIES

American Protestantism that sought in the nineteenth century to win the world through its foreign missions movement is threatened today with losing America through its urban retreat. The threat becomes more than academic when one learns, for example, that in this country's largest city, New York, the United Presbyterian Church had had some 300 congregations in three of the five boroughs but had only 62 in 1961. Or that the "Methodist Church, the largest Protestant denomination in the country, is dying out in the cities," according to a report in the *New York Times*, March 15, 1959. The most enterprising, or at least clever, work of the non-Roman

communions in the inner city has been the closing or merging
of congregations. Our best leadership has been expended in
a strange rear-guard action that has left our diminishing
churches nervous aliens in someone else's territory, remnants
of imperialism in a dismembered empire. It can be left to
Gibson Winter [1] and G. Paul Musselman [2] to describe and
document Protestantism's flight from the city. We begin in
this chapter with the fact that although God's redemptive love
was dramatically offered to a city populace from a cross that
had been dragged through city streets, we nonetheless are not
at home witnessing to that love in the modern city. We don't
belong. These teeming millions are not our kind. We don't
like their litter, their rudeness, their profanity, their thoughtless
laughter and shouting on a hot night. We are offended by
sputum on sidewalks and urine in subway tunnels. We are
shocked at the drunk who walks wavy chalk lines in crowded
streets; the dope addict who darts out of some TV script to do
quick, senseless violence and then fades again into disturbing
anonymity; the juvenile gang who erupt in marauding protest
against this same anonymity and commit stupid carnage before
the police can be mobilized. All the middle-class mores that we
equate with godliness are outraged, and we abandon the city as
a place to live and, by implication, as a place to minister. For-
getting our commission to witness to all the world, "beginning
in [the city] Jerusalem," and embracing as though sacred the
secular logic that says, "Of *course* you can't bring up your children in the big city!" we strip our few remaining congregations
of their leadership potential, abandon the cosmopolitan masses
to ward politicians, welfare workers, Roman Catholic priests,
labor leaders, and a few Protestant ministers we secretly regard
as "odd ball," and flee to the suburbs. As for most of our pastors,

[1] In *The Suburban Captivity of the Churches* (New York: Doubleday
& Co., Inc., 1961).
[2] In *The Church on the Urban Frontier* (Greenwich, Conn.: Seabury
Press, Inc., 1960).

they follow the migration, for we have taught them well the discomfiture of city litter, smells, and violence. Besides, we expect success of their ministries, and what success can there be in any but a few of the city churches?

Protestants have a new justification for flight: the Jews and the Roman Catholics are so numerous in our great cities that one has to move out so that his children won't grow up belonging to a minority culture. The shameful thing about this "minority culture" computation is the fact that we probably are counting only *white* Protestants. And further, who says that we must be in the majority? We have always expected the Jews and the Roman Catholics to persist on a minority basis. Is our belief that much weaker that we cannot rear a new generation for the church except where there is a majority to conform to? Must we run out on God, with our children as our excuses, when he is calling us to the mission of the militant minority?

Whether we flee or dig in will soon be an academic question anyway, for suburbia is rapidly being swallowed up into the great strip cities. Our children will have to learn to dig in; we should begin to provide a heritage that will sustain them.

Protestantism's first task in the city, then, is *learning to be obedient*. Commissioned by our Lord to "be my witnesses in Jerusalem" first of all, we tiptoe out of Jerusalem and make a great flourish of evangelizing the rest of the world, especially suburbia, child of the middle-class culture our churches did so much to create. We are at home there, not because suburbia has taken on the mind of the church but because it has warmly embraced the religious culture we love and much of the social etiquette we delight in. Suburban life is denatured of most of the harsh embarrassments with which the city habitually offends the church, yet it is clearly sufficiently pagan to be certified as a legitimate mission field. Therefore, we pastors drive ourselves to gratified exhaustion in these environs, fondly perpetuating the myth that the American churches are stronger than ever. All the time we are digging a ditch for Protestantism to fall into, for we are only perpetuating in the suburbs a philosophy and practice of ministry, the religious-club chaplaincy, that already has failed decisively in the city—in the city, which promises to absorb the suburbs with remarkable disdain for the culture and etiquette that we have so carefully embroidered.

Protestantism's second task in the city is *learning to be at home*. The most impressive advance made by the churches in the inner city is not their successfully integrated congregations but their growing corps of first-rate pastors who have chosen the inner city as their permanent mission and whose families have joined them in making blighted urban neighborhoods their real homes. This is the beginning. But this is not to say that we are yet at home in the city. Far from it. It will take congregations which have already made the effort another fifteen years to be truly an accepted and effective part of inner city life, and Protestantism in general a full twenty-five years—*if* we mount an earnest attack on the problem in a manner comparable to the nineteenth-century foreign mission thrust.

PRACTICING A CHRISTIAN ANTHROPOLOGY

As this morning's newspaper documents America's failure in race relations, so the average church's membership roll, a color chart in black and white, documents Protestantism's failure at inclusiveness. We need not belabor this point. It is abundantly evident that we skillfully teach the world our theology of brotherhood, until social, economic, and political groups seriously apply the idea, then tremble, fumble, and become ecclesiastical neurotics in trying to be inclusive congregations under integrated staff leadership. We are not at home with our ethic. Thoroughly imbued with our fraternity-lodge-service club oriented concept of a racially stratified social life (even though we earnestly discuss annually the mission-study book on brotherhood), we don't know what to do with our Lord, inveterate fraternizer that he is. We even become secretly hurt at his refusal to stay embalmed in the first century, or enshrined in our devotional hymns and leaded windows. Why does he keep inviting the Negroes over to our church? Not just one or two, but whole neighborhoods?

I wish to suggest that the American church's persistent addiction to an un-Christian anthropology will begin to yield only when a theologically rooted liturgical revival begins in our congregations. It is impressive that renewal of the church in our time is so often accompanied by liturgical renewal—the Iona Movement, the House Church movement, Abbé Michoneaus' work in Paris, and the mission of the East Harlem Protestant Parish in New York, to mention a few examples. In the worship of so many congregations the whole experience makes the worshipers overly conscious of one another and of the person of the preacher before making them sufficiently conscious of God. Even the setting suggests only a more hushed gathering of the same old club group. And the worship does little to shatter our "cream of the community" mood. We are of the feather of birds who belong together, and the nicely phrased liturgical chitchat of our pastor or the stilted, rutted, liturgical gothic of our priest chiefly confirms the fact. There is little of thunder, wonder, and incarnation here. We are allowed to forget that the church is first of all a worshiping (not a fellowshiping) community of believers who are overwhelmed into a common sense of humility by the magnitude of God's love and by the utter unselectivity of his grace. Our worship should leave us instinctive brother to the drunk who might conceivably find his way into the pew beside us, to say nothing of our sober, colored brother who would less conceivably be sitting there. Instead, it allows us to retain certain reservations and recoil regarding serious integration.

Protestant worship is too pallid and unimaginative. It lacks the majesty of eternity, the cadenced rhythm of created life, the jarring impact of man's colossal moral failure, and the incomparable graciousness of God's redemptive acts. Depending upon the denomination and/or the pastor, it seems either to be avoiding tradition or to be exalting tradition, rather than using it as an inspiration for creating fresh, contemporary (not sentimental) worship forms. To experience worship at its relevant best, one need only to share in an East Harlem Protestant Parish communion service, for example, finding himself drawn irresistibly out of his social cocoon and into a warm, raceless community as he stands about the Lord's table, tears off a piece of bread, and hands the loaf on to his neighbor. Here is a service where even the announcement period reflects the idea of an earthy, recoilless fellowship rooted in a common redemption. It is the result of a group study of traditional liturgy coupled with a continued search for simple, readily understood, symbolic acts and expressions that will relate the worship to the zigzag life of East Harlem.

Worship could and should be a powerful force for bringing in the day of brotherhood, but pastors will have to lead their people into creative and co-operative quests, making them students at one and the same time of aging liturgies and contemporary community thought and word patterns. They should be joined by contemporary musicians and artists who will learn the chaste discipline essential to Christian worship and then discover fresh ways of expressing God's glory to modern man, at the same time catching up in creative forms the rhythm, pathos, and aspiration of modern life. A little tinkering with existing liturgies, a little sopping up of drippy sentimentalism, or a little tacking on of choice selections here and there, will not do. Most of our worship is fundamentally dull, inglorious, irrelevant, and lacking adequate abrasives. We have a major job to do, so that our worship will school our emotions in brotherly conduct, even as Bible reading and preaching school our minds.

Almost as important as liturgical renewal to the practice of a Christian anthropology is the development of integrated staffs. Not until our "Anglo-Saxon" congregations spontaneously include Negro and Spanish-American ministers as pastors to whom they bring their babies for baptism, their family problems for counsel, and their sons and daughters for marriage, will the church be living a Christian concept of man. Negro and Puerto Rican children in the church school, two colored faces in the choir, and one in the deacon's meeting will not do it. As it now stands, 99 per cent of our "Anglo" congregations do not even think of having nonwhite or Latin-American pastors, and fewer than that give it a second thought, *unless* they face the alternatives of closing their doors or becoming inclusive.

Dioceses, conferences, associations, classes, and presbyteries need to set about deliberately and firmly to teach their congregations that ethnic origin is not a proper element in the image of a proper ministry. This is not so easy as we might wish—not because of congregational prejudice alone, but also because pastors come out of minority backgrounds with a whole skein of liabilities, from birth straight up through seminary education, to handicap their ministries, on a professional basis alone, in qualifying for responsible posts. Nevertheless, there are first-rate pastors to be found who have risen above these handicaps, and nearly any judicatory executive could name at least one to a congregation seeking to be obedient.

THE MINISTRY OF THE LAITY

The "great laymen's movement" of American Protestantism evidences an unease in the churches, but represents no real surge of power. It points up the inevitable restiveness of Protestant laymen whose birthright ministry is carried on by ordained deputies, but it will dead-end in frustration because it is an unconscious rebellion against the clergy rather than the flower of a new partnership between pastors and people.

It is the pastors who are to blame. They have thought too much in terms of keeping laymen busy (when they themselves increasingly deplore the "busy" work of the pastorate), of "using more laymen" (when they themselves despise being used), and of "holding up the hands of the pastor," when they themselves care little for the role of assisting someone else's pastorate. The individualistic image of a stipendiary chaplain to a private religious club who, by mastering the arts of unction and inspiration, can enlarge the club and further his own career, must be smashed. The Church needs a tough new breed of servant-minded pastors who are willing to lose their lives in building up the ministries of their people; pastors who give themselves to enlisting, nurturing, training, and directing the laity in the most significant ministry of all—the ministry outside the church building, to the world. Here is an overseeing of ministry, requiring a pastor to be a bishop to a whole community of ministers and calling for an entirely new mind-set on the part of pastors. A large number of us need retooling for this role, and not all our seminaries are prepared to help us. It is imperative that we read the rich material on the place of the layman in Christian ministry now appearing in many quarters; that we converse with the young theologians who are insisting upon new concepts of ministry; and that we renovate our own practices of ministry in the light of the new insights gained thereby.

THE SUBURBAN CHURCH'S VOCATION

It is somewhat the fashion of the day to excoriate the suburban church for its luxuriant irrelevancy flowering out of its magnificent institutionalism. The excoriation is amply justified, but it must not become an easy and snide habit that blinds us to the resources for mission and ministry to be found in that same church. It is true that a strong, active congregation fits so well into suburbia's image of suburbia that such a congregation can easily find itself more expressive of suburbia than of the kingdom of God. Impressed by its public acceptance and by its genuine influence for good in family life, it too easily passes over its giant-size failure to involve its people in the world-rending struggle for social justice so characteristic of our day. Indeed, the church often seems to be baptizing suburbia's bulwarking of herself against the world with a gospel divested of all anger and offense. ("Long ago," said a prominent California pastor to a group of his colleagues, "I learned never to preach on anything controversial.")

Nonetheless, the suburban church has a vocation to leadership which is one of Protestantism's prime resources for mission and ministry. It is a church that has entrée to its people to a remarkable degree—and to an education-oriented people who are a great reservoir of leadership for church and society. It is a church with a significant financial stewardship. If the suburban church can be taught to disengage itself from the cozy culture of its surroundings and be led back into the atomic age where nothing stays nailed down, particularly racial, social, political, and national categories, it can become the power center of a resurgent Christianity.

But first suburban ministry must be brought up to date. The pastors are so busy with their fantastically active congregations, so much in demand among a people highly prepared to accept their pastoral care, that they are not inclined to listen to the prophets of our time regarding the irrelevance of the church's ministry. Sincere men who want to know how to be available to more people, they are looking not for irrelevant talk about irrelevancy but for techniques to improve and enlarge their ministrations so that they can reach out to the people whom they are now neglecting. A whole body of critical thought about the ministry has come into being in our time, but it has too largely passed by many of these men. They need an immersion in this material, with the help of denominational and seminary leadership, to be supplemented by dialogue with the more creative of their own colleagues, as well as with the urban pastors whose ministries are so much affected by what suburban pastors do or refrain from doing. Successful suburbia must be helped to see that it is not the great wave of the future but possibly a last flourish of a doomed cult of middle-class respectability. The pastors are the only community leaders with the necessary potential of independence to do the job. Suburban congregations must be brought back time after time to the harsh realities of a world against which they have been successfully ghettoed but which will likely engulf their children. They need to be made aware, for example, of the awful determination of the world that has already been born to crush the exclusive and excluding patterns of life to be found in their clubs, schools, real estate, and even their churches.

Having updated their understanding of ministry and identified themselves with the full life of man, these pastors need then to concentrate on the following: enlisting, educating, and training the people for believer-priesthood; producing enlightened Christian leadership for secular life and for the church; collecting financial resources for the church's general mission; and building bridges between the crowded cities and the more gracious residential life of suburbia so that minorities no longer have to elbow their way sullenly into this setting.

DISTRICT JUDICATORY, THE PRIMARY UNIT

American Protestantism as now deployed is no match for this urban and tension-torn age—not merely because of the dismemberment of its corporateness by denominationalism, but also because of the fragmentation of its mission by congregationalism. With society organized as it is into *district* political, labor, business, and professional associations that often include hundreds of "parishes" or neighborhoods, Protestant Christianity will have to develop a strategy that makes the conference, the association, the classis, the diocese, the presbytery, the district (or whatever the judicatory is called) the primary unit of mission. Protestantism predicates its strategy of ministry on the sacrosanct idea that the local congregation is its primary unit of mission, and the judicatory hardly dares suggest a larger over-all strategy. As a result, whole inner city areas are abandoned, crucial churches beside university campuses are permitted ultra-conservative ministries, and probing experimental ministries that seek more revelant forms of mission are kept in the "home missions" category, definitely stamped as less than first-class by the ecclesiastical aristocracy, namely, the installed pastors of local congregations.

Congregations alone do not have the resources, the leadership, the perspective, the relationships to warrant their carrying so heavy a responsibility for mission strategy, and to continue to leave basic decisions and chief initiative to them is equivalent to rejecting the army unit for a collection of guerrilla bands.

Yet it must be seen that to lift up the judicatory as the primary unit of mission does not downgrade the congregation. Rather, it heightens the significance of a congregation's work by making it a part of a larger endeavor. And, since practically all Protestant polities involve representation in the judicatory from the congregations, the shift in strategy would increase the importance of this representative participation in policy and strategy decisions. Being a commissioner to the judicatory would no longer be a perfunctory matter easily sloughed off but a large responsibility one dared not neglect.

With the judicatory planning and executing mission, its patterns of ministry would not be so rigidly tied to traditional pastoral charges but could more readily embrace—along with the more numerous organized congregations, industrial, prison, hospital, and campus chaplaincies—missions to estranged artists and intellectuals, and worker-minister missions to such other radically estranged segments of industrial society as the racketeer-oppressed dock workers.

If the judicatory is to be the primary unit of mission, a change must occur in the concept of the judicatory itself. The judicatory must become a learning and sharing group. Most district ecclesiastical bodies meet chiefly for organizational and promotional business, whereas in early Protestantism such bodies as presbyteries followed the interesting practice of meeting regularly to hear and criticize one another's preaching and theology. This practice, though slightly terrorizing as a suggestion for our time, nonetheless recognized the fact that presbytery was not a conglomerate of individual ministries but a *group* ministry in which the work of all was affected by the work of each. You had a stake in the soundness of my theology, and my ministry was acted upon by the quality of your preaching. We were in this together, and we were not merely self-continuing pastors thrown into orbit by our certifying agency, the presbytery.

There is a real need for the judicatory to bring its ministers together regularly as a part of its stated meetings, and its lay officers on occasion, not alone for business and promotional sessions, but also for vigorous theological and sociological encounters wherein the insights of current studies and experiments would be examined for what they have to say to the group ministry of that particular judicatory.

In the case of the larger metropolitan ecclesiastical units involved in the very difficult inner-city ministry, consideration should be given to the establishment at the heart of the judicatory's life of a center of learning, sharing and serving, where its ministers and lay officers could meet regularly and be related to a resident group of interns, in-service trainees (ordained ministers with three or four years of pastoral experience), and worker-ministers living under a community worship, study, and service discipline. Under such an arrangement the whole judicatory would be related to the whole of its mission; assigned ministers would both teach and learn from interns and trainees; probing experimental ministries would emanate out of the midst of the judicatory life and thought rather than somehow appear out on the periphery as a result of the special machinations of a national board; lay officers would grow in mission with the pastors; and the ministry of the local church would be in continuing communication with the mission of the judicatory.

CHURCH UNION ON A JUDICATORY LEVEL

Recently I heard a town-and-country specialist spell out the sin of divided Protestantism as illustrated by an oversupply of undernourished churches in towns and small cities competing with one another because their denominations have not yet found the path to union. As the executive of a city presbytery, I face every day the heartbreak of a fragmented and fading Protestantism which, in union, could marshall tremendous resources for dynamic mission, but which in division wastefully shuffles its forces in wondrously unrelated attacks on a ponderous foe. It is the judicatory that pays the heaviest price for the churches' divisions, and it is the judicatory that is required to wait until union is engineered on the national level. One wonders, however, if a rebellion among the judicatory executives (a breed not ordinarily given to rebellion!) would not startle awake a somnolent Protestantism maddeningly unaware of the provinces its outdated schisms are losing for the Kingdom's cause. If a bishop or two could be infected along with the executive secretaries, presidents, and general presbyters, the rebellion could have the makings of a first-class war!

In a less incendiary vein, let me say that it could very well be that the executives of district ecclesiastical units are the next group who ought to be in serious conversation regarding church union. Of course they as a group are men who have a personal stake in maintaining our divisions, but they also are the group most sharply aware of the fatal nature of division. Their jobs force a certain pragmatism upon them, and the Holy Spirit could use their pragmatism to speak to the churches regarding union. Such executives, therefore, should not confine their meetings to comity discussions and united campaigns (both of which *assume* the maintenance of division), but should begin conversations of appraisal out of which to address pleas of urgency to the top-level conversationalists and to the general church constituency.

PERSONNEL NEEDS

What is to be said about the personnel needs for these new frontiers of Christian ministry?

A new breed of church leaders has already been called for. Men and women must be enlisted in terms of a more flexible concept of ministry, readily adjustable to the demands for new patterns of work. Scholars who will not shun the rough-and-tumble of the political wars, if need be, these leaders will have to be able to read on the trot (speed-reading courses are a must for today's applicant for seminary training!). They should have the finest theological education, but they will need periodic terms of continuing education to compensate for their necessarily intense involvement in community life (and I am not referring to attending lodges and service clubs!). Some of them will need to be willing to do secular work in order to make breakthroughs into segments of society estranged from the church. Many of them will have to forget the traditional role of preaching (which role, incidentally, ought to be upgraded in most congregations), and devote their lives to house meetings, study groups, unstructured conversations, and the like.

What about the numbers needed? Are we facing a great shortage of ministers? I was asked this question more often than any other as Executive Director of the Department of the Ministry of the National Council of Churches. Free-lance writers kept asking me to document dramatically the shortage that they wanted to write about. I always was a disappointment to them, for I had to say that for the most part, the shortage was overrated. I had to say further that many churches are adding staff, rather than enlisting and educating laymen for *their* ministry. There are young people in several denominations looking for pastorates four and five months after graduation from seminary as this is being written. The *shortage* is in adequately educated and soundly equipped pastors, according to one denominational commission, and this is judgmental of incumbents every bit as much as of candidates. Nonetheless, some of the denominations do have more vacancies (for which they can provide salaries) than they can fill with the present supply of candidates, and others see a shortage coming up in the next ten years. As a result, excellent vocational guidance-recruitment programs have been or are being set up in several communions to increase the supply of candidates. This work needs more understanding and support from the budget makers.

The most serious shortage of ministers, however, lies in the area of ministry that is being left undone—the chaplaincies, the experimental ministries, the outreach through house meetings, and so on, for which we have scarcely begun to enlist. There is a highly important task of enlisting for a ministry that is not yet fully defined but which the enlistees themselves must be invited to help discover to the church. The churches have not yet addressed themselves to this sort of enlistment, and they may thus be failing to reach the most creative spirits available to them.

NORMAN GOODALL

World Evangelism

When we consider the recent extension of the Church and the divine and human resources available, we dare to believe it possible that before the present generation has passed away, the Gospel should be preached to almost all the inhabitants of the world in such a way as to make clear to them the issue of faith or disbelief in Jesus Christ.

THESE words have not been culled from some nineteenth-century oration redolent of the kind of optimism which has since been shattered by two world wars. They come from a statement issued two years after the war of 1939-1945. Their setting is a document called "Christian Witness in a Revolutionary World," issued by the International Missionary Council after its meeting in Whitby, Ontario. The word "revolutionary" was taken seriously in this pronouncement. The meeting had been held against the background—to quote another phrase from its report—"of a world torn and scarred by intolerable suffering and sorrow, a world at one only in its agonies and perplexities." But those who conferred together at this time were in no doubt about the nature of the Church's primary task or the spirit in which it should be pursued. The gospel is to be preached to all men . . . "in such a way as to make clear to them the issue of faith or disbelief in Jesus Christ." And for such a task Christians could dare to believe that the divine and human resources available were sufficient.

This volume is written out of faith in the sufficiency of the divine resources. It is not the purpose of this chapter to restate the grounds for this conviction but, rather, to consider those

138

human resources—their nature and use—which it is the business of Christians to offer to Him who alone can ensure their effectiveness and determine the time and manner of the task's completion.

When the Whitby meeting spoke of "the present extension of the Church" it had vividly in mind the fact of the "younger churches." Seldom had the term "younger" seemed less appropriate. "Honourable old age is not that which standeth in length of time, neither is its measure given by number of years." The force of this word from The Wisdom of Solomon was brought home to the Whitby meeting by the caliber of delegates from the indigenous churches of Asia and Africa, Latin America and the Caribbean, and the Pacific Islands, and by the witness of these churches amidst the hazards of war. It was clear that they represented not only the front line of the Christian mission but also its home base. Henceforth this fact must be reckoned with in all missionary thinking and planning.

NINETEENTH-CENTURY ASSUMPTIONS

It is doubtful that the full significance of this new fact has yet been grasped. Perhaps its implications are least realized among the faithful supporters of foreign missions in the congregations and parishes of the Western churches. It is sometimes said that the missionary enterprise of the twentieth century is largely being sustained on nineteenth-century assumptions. There is much truth in this, and the position is the more serious because it is in the devotion of thousands of anonymous church members—their interest, their generosity, and their prayers—that the deepest roots of the missionary movement lie. Yet, in general, "foreign missions" continue to suggest to earnest and generous supporters a kind of *noblesse oblige* of the Christian West. There is concern for those who are without the gospel, a genuine evangelical fervor, a sense of moral obligation that the "haves" should share with the "have-nots." There is pride in "our missionary" and jubilation when a younger church-man occasionally appears on a "deputation platform" as an encouraging evidence of what may result from all this devotion and fidelity. But far more rarely does there exist in a local con-gregation in the West a vivid and responsible awareness of what it means for Western churches to be partners in obedience with churches in other lands.

This tardiness in making the necessary adjustment, psycho-logically and spiritually, to a changed situation is not merely a matter of East-West attitudes, still less is it determined only by color-consciousness. One of the great chapters in modern Christian history is the missionary outreach of the indigenous island churches in Samoa. For more than a century these Poly-nesian "aristocrats of the Pacific" (as Robert Louis Stevenson called them) have sent contingents of missionaries to other islands in the South Seas, especially to Papua and New Guinea. They have their own martyr roll of pioneers who have been faithful unto death, and no gatherings at their home base in Samoa evoke more jubilation than the great annual "missionary rally" when their "own" missionaries—Samoans—thrill vast con-gregations with their deputation addresses. Early in 1961 a highly significant conference of churches and missions in the Pacific was held in Samoa, and the delegations included some outstand-ing Papuan Christian leaders. Some of the Samoans at this gathering, watching the Papuans in action as equal participants in the conference business, were astonished. "We never thought they were like this," they said. These Polynesians were main-taining their twentieth-century missionary enterprise on nine-teenth-century assumptions.

The remedy for this is not found when, as sometimes hap-pens, the shock of surprise produces an image that is equally distorted from another angle. "The younger churches have ar-rived; therefore the day of missions is over." This ignores both present realities in the world situation and abiding verities in the Christian life. The presence of indigenous churches in former mission fields, bearing authentic signs of Christian maturity, does not mean that the evangelistic task is completed, even when the distinction is recognized between "making clear the issue of faith or disbelief in Jesus Christ" and confessing the faith.

Statistics alone bring their stark reminder here. India, for example, presents heartening evidence of large and strong churches with great achievements to their credit. Yet the Christian community in India (nominal and real) is little more than two per cent of the whole. In Japan—where it is sometimes boasted that Christians include the best-educated elements in the population —the Christian community is one per cent of the whole. In Nigeria, the figure is three per cent; in Indonesia, four. Moreover, when such words as maturity, achievement, and leadership are given their fullest possible weight in reference to the indigenous churches in these lands, there remain stubborn and challenging facts concerning their poverty, their weaknesses in ministerial training and resources and, not least, the nature of their adversaries, which lay the most urgent imperatives upon the churches of the West to fulfill, by increasing, their share in the partnership. No one can study the reports issued in recent years by the International Missionary Council on the training of the ministry in Asia, Africa, and Latin America, or the same Council's "Studies in the Life of the Younger Churches," without being burdened by sobering conclusions and stirred to new endeavor.

LOST COIN OR LOST SHEEP?

But even such factors as these are secondary to the mandate of the gospel, the meaning of its fulfillment, and the character of a missionary church. Until the final consummation of God's purpose for this world, the Great Commission rests upon the

Church in all its parts. "Into all the world" remains the foremost marching order of every church in every land, and there is no discharge in this war. The terrain shifts, the forces are realigned, new contingents appear, new enemies attack. Whether in East or West, where the Church exists, the battle is on: it is for the several members of the one People of Christ to find their right relationship to one another and to accept the varying responsibilities of partnership, not primarily as younger or older, but as obedient children of the faith, equally privileged to be allowed of God to be put in trust with the gospel, equally responsible for seeing the world as their parish.

Though some of the most exacting consequences of this realignment in missionary thinking fall upon the historic missionary agencies of the West and their supporters, many within the indigenous churches of Africa and Asia need adjustment to a change of outlook no less revolutionary. The long habit of dependence, the expectation of always receiving, and preoccupation with the business of "running the church" quench the missionary ardor all too easily, or even prevent it from making itself felt. "Our pastor has no time to go out after the lost sheep; he's too busy looking for the lost coin." Though this remark of an African layman may well be applied to other countries, as a commentary on a younger church situation it is the more serious. It may be urged that where vision and zeal are present, institutional problems should not hinder evangelical obedience.

Nevertheless, in many parts of the world the lost-coin problem has assumed crippling dimensions. Over a long period the International Missionary Council was responsible for a series of expert studies, under the guidance of J. Merle Davis, in the economic foundations of the churches, particularly in Asia. These studies are now outdated in their details, but not in the conclusions which were built up on a vast accumulation of evidence. Among other things it was made clear that there was little hope of the churches in non-Western lands becoming "stabilized in their environment," economic and social, so long as the ministry was thought of primarily in terms of a whole-time profession, as well as a vocation, maintained on a financial basis commensurate even with the lower standards ruling in other professions. Still less could the churches in Africa and Asia be expected to shoulder, as they achieved autonomy, the type of institutional work mainly associated with Western missionary activity. In spite of many changes in the total economic picture, more recent experience has confirmed judgments of this kind. Too many churches and their ministers are locked within the problems of institutional maintenance instead of being at liberty to put first their evangelical and missionary obedience.

PARTNERSHIP—EAST AND WEST

The nature of the ministry and the sources of its maintenance, the place of great institutions—educational, medical and so on —in the life and essential responsibilities of a church, the channels and terms of financial assistance between churches in an affluent society and those in an underdeveloped country, and the right pattern of relationships between fellow workers of different races and cultures in a common task—these are among the problems, not theoretical but urgently practical, which are clamoring for solution on the basis of a genuine partnership between East and West. Much is happening in the approach to this partnership and in the understanding and fulfillment of it. This has been facilitated by the kind of service rendered through the International Missionary Council and the relationships which are developing within the World Council of Churches and other expressions of the ecumenical movement. But the rethinking and readjustment are still in their early stages, and further progress in these matters has an urgent relevance to the discharge of the church's mission in our time.

All this constitutes an important part of the setting in which

the missionary of today and tomorrow has to find his vocation
and be trained for it. Two dangers emerge here which are preva-
lent mainly in Western lands. One is the retreat from overseas
missionary service. This is sometimes due to the mistaken assumption, already referred to, that the day of missions is over.
It may also be due to the daunting character of some of the
problems involved and to the example of disillusioned missionaries who have found the frustrations too much for them. At the
other extreme there is the dangerous temptation to ignore most
of the problems posed by the term partnership and on the
ground—valid in itself—of the vast need of unevangelized
peoples, to revert to nineteenth-century missionary practice as
well as its assumptions.

Since the end of the Second World War there has been an
enormous increase, especially in the United States of America,
in the number of missionaries who have gone overseas with
apparently little awareness of, or regard for, the churches already established in the countries where they begin their work.
In general, these missionaries are not those of what are sometimes called (when labels are unfortunately required) the "major
denominations" or "historic churches": they represent a wide
and diversified range of "evangelical" missions, often undenom-
inational in their basis or related, in varying degrees, to a single
supporting congregation. Their spirit is that of the pioneer, and
in their proclamation of the gospel there is often a disregard of
the bearing of church order on Christian fellowship: sometimes
it is contended that the former is inimical to the latter. More
often than not these folk can count on generous support and
ample means for their work and they have little difficulty in
finding scope for their service even if this is among members or
adherents of existing churches who, in the judgment of the new
missionary, have still to experience a full evangelical conversion
and the gift of faith. These words are written with serious recognition of the deep significance of this element in the missionary
situation today. In many places it constitutes a vital, as well as

a large and increasing, factor in the total movement toward world-wide evangelization. It further bears characteristics (and *charismata*) which often constitute a challenge to the missionary fidelity of both the historic and the younger churches. Nevertheless this kind of missionary service too often bypasses problems and needs which are a fundamental part of the Christian scene today. In effect if not in intention, it becomes a reversion to nineteenth-century "patriarchialism" in missionary outlook and practice.

If the two dangers just described are to be avoided there is needed a great and increasing number of men and women who will find their vocation and equip themselves for it as missionary partners of Asian and African Christians, working within the indigenous churches and accepting all the disciplines and spiritual demands of the new situation.

In this connection it is usual to urge that far more specialist missionaries instead of general practitioners are required. It is true that the needs of this kind are many and urgent; agriculturalists, educationists with advanced degrees, scholars or potential scholars who can man the theological colleges or become experts in the encounter with representatives of other faiths, linguists, writers, and so on, are all called for. Yet it is a mistake to argue that only specialists of this caliber are required. The real situation in many of the indigenous churches—a situation recognized by more and more of the leaders of these churches—provides room and urgent need for all-round men and women whose best gift to the partnership is themselves—their personal experience of Christ, their ability to give a reason for the faith that is in them and to speak convincingly and persuasively of the Name.

Most of all, there is needed the dedication of a humble mind and willing hands to whatever task—especially the more obscure ones—will help the Church in another land to discharge its own missionary obligation more effectively and faithfully. At the heart of the training of missionaries of this character, there

is the need for the deep disciplined nurture of the spirit—an
education in the life of prayer, in the meaning of worship, and
in that discipleship which is receptive to gifts which issue in
humility and grace in human relationships and in an unending
capacity for caring. These are searching demands; and when it
is remembered that the context in which such dedication is
called for can nowadays provide little that is conducive to the
"romantic" picture of the missionary, the demand is all the
greater, though it may be more truly Christian.

To place renewed emphasis on the need for this quality of
disciplined life and of mature Christian experience may sound
at variance with much that has been said in recent years about
the necessity for the training of missionaries in contemporary
technical skills. These differing needs, however, should not constitute an either-or. The important point to recognize is that if
the primary concern is world evangelism, the technical and specialist equipment will avail little unless there are behind it persons of the quality here indicated. And it cannot be too strongly
urged that in country after country, despite all the revolutionary
changes which have to be reckoned with in formulating missionary policy, the basic and most urgent need—and one that
is far from being fully met (as is evidenced by the frequent plea
of the churches in Asia as well as by the vacancy lists of the
historic missionary agencies)—is still for men and women who
will bring this quality of life and this conception of service to
partnership-in-mission between older and younger churches and
do so without necessarily setting limits in advance to the term
of their service.

LAY MISSIONARIES

Though the scale and character of the unfinished task requires
that priority must be given to missionary service of this order,
there has of late years been a rediscovery of the place in the

mission of the Church of Christian men and women who spend part of their lives in a land other than their own in industry, commerce, and government service. These are sometimes referred to as "nonprofessional missionaries." This is not the happiest of titles, but it points to a role the significance of which may not be less than that of the whole-time Christian worker sent abroad by the missionary agency of a church. Of course, the influence, for good or ill, of citizens of a professedly Christian country resident in a non-Christian land is not a matter of recent recognition. One of the greatest pioneer missionaries in South India deplored, more than a century-and-a-half ago, "the baleful influence of the Europeans" which, in his judgment, made Christian missionary work impossible where they resided. The grounds for this complaint unfortunately did not disappear with the passing of the nineteenth century.

On the other hand, since the days when, for example, missionary work was greatly furthered by Christian officials in the East India Company, the strength which such men could lend to the Christian cause has been no less appreciated. The new emphasis which is making itself felt today, however, goes further than this; it envisages men and women deliberately seeking "secular" employment in a land other than their own in order to strengthen the Christian witness in that land. Professional men and women —teachers, doctors, and nurses—people with technical skills and business competence, may of set purpose choose employment overseas with what is fundamentally a Christian missionary intent, that is, the desire so to live and work that "the issue of faith or disbelief in Jesus Christ" may be made clear. This does not simply mean that in addition to his daily employment the professional or business man will give his support to the local church and perhaps engage in lay preaching. It involves the recognition that the critical point of Christian witness is in the Monday-to-Saturday secular environment, in the daily relationships of society and its business, at the places where men and women are confronted by everyday human needs and problems.

This conception of a new type of missionary, not employed by a mission board or a church, is part of a further realization that the Church's principal agency for world evangelism (in terms of its human instruments) lies in the Christian laity. A generation ago the phrase "liberating the lay forces of Christianity" caught the imagination of many. The concern and insight behind it was not wholly dissimilar from what is here under discussion, though its point of reference tended to be the kind of lay service which Christian men and women could render in the church. Today the new, or renewed, perception of what might be possible focuses much more upon this need to effect a genuinely Christian and redemptive impact upon the secular order itself, within the structures, standards, and relationships of man-in-society. Powerful expression was given to this a few years ago by a group of Asian Christian leaders meeting at Kuala Lumpur in the inaugural assembly of the East Asia Christian Conference. "The Gospel," they said,

> . . . is a Gospel of redemption of the whole human race and of the whole created world. By his death and resurrection Jesus Christ has reconciled "all things to himself." His purpose is not to withdraw individual spirits one by one from their involvement with material things and human communities in order to set them in a purely "spiritual" relation to himself. Rather his goal is "to unite all things in him." . . . Our discussions as Christians about economics, politics, and society are therefore conversations about Jesus Christ, that is to say, an attempt of faith to discern him in the social change of our nations, and to discover what it means to respond to his call in relation to these changes.

By the very character of this task, it has to be discharged "outside" the church and by the laymen whose daily responsibilities and relationships are at the place of greatest challenge and most needed commitment.

This is not, of course, to absolve the Christian ministry or the church in its own life as a community from responsibility. Church and ministry have their own involvement in the same situation. But the spearhead of the Christian impact is constituted by the laity. If this were taken as seriously as it ought to be, and with the urgency it demands, it would call for much reshaping of "church activities," based on a new understanding of the Church's task in nurturing and ministering to a laity sent forth on a redemptive mission of this range.

A great deal of fresh thinking and brave experiment is being provoked today by this view of evangelism as being concerned with man-in-his-environment, with the redemption of the corporate structures of human life as well as with man in his individual need of personal integrity and inward peace. Such developments as the Iona Community in Scotland, the Evangelical Academies in Germany, the Church and World Institute in Holland, the Ecumenical Institute at Bossey, and scores of "frontier" movements working under varying names and in many lands, all reflect the same vision and purpose. In many local congregations and parishes, a similar alertness is in evidence, and there is increasing interest in and demand for the help of the various departments of the World Council of Churches which are concerned with the same understanding of the wholeness of the Christian mission. Yet it has to be recognized that all this adds up to a contribution infinitesimally small in relation to the state of the world today, to the nature and scale of the problems of contemporary society and to the resources of a Christian community which is not increasing at the speed of the population growth.

THE SCANDAL OF DISUNITY

In such a situation the question of the relation of the "available human resources" to one another and their alignment in face of a common task assumes fresh urgency. The deepest incentives to Christian unity spring not from the size of the task, or even from the urgent needs of the world: they derive from the one Gospel, the one Redemption and the one Spirit, through the work of the one Christ who is not divided. Yet need and task light up from another angle the imperative of unity. On the one hand, there is the inescapable fact of the scandal of disunity. There is an island in the South Pacific which, for at least a century, has been the home of a little population almost one hundred per cent Christian in profession. Until a few years ago its circuit of village churches constituted one Church; there was no denominational competition. A personal link with the churches overseas was provided by one missionary from England, but all the village churches were served by an indigenous ministry and this one homogeneous church had sent out missionaries of its own to other parts of the Pacific. Since 1945, however, five or six new denominations, or "separatist" churches, have come into existence on this island as a result of the arrival of new foreign missionaries from the West, all independent of one another, all winning their converts from the historic churches of the island, and all claiming to have done this as an expression of their zeal for world-wide evangelization. When charity, tolerance, and humility have made the fullest possible allowance for the zeal of others, and for the acknowledged need of every historic church for constant reformation and renewal, there remains here a spectacle which can only be regarded, in the strictest sense of the word, as a scandal—a stumbling block. This particular instance is exceptional in its setting and in its vivid portrayal of what mission-in-disunity can mean; but the scandal is not peculiar to this island nor can its effects ever be insulated.

TWO CONCEPTIONS

The scandal which disunity occasions is, however, only one consequence of the failure to perceive that Christ redeems us into his one Church and calls us to witness as one obedient people. There are, for example, those consequences which impair efficiency at critical points in the Church's witness to the world. When the Whitby meeting of the International Missionary Council spoke with confidence about the resources now available for world evangelism, it included within its reckoning such factors as the spread of education, the rapid growth in literacy and of mass media of communication, especially developments in broadcasting. There can be no adequate use of these resources simply on a denominational basis. Apart from other considerations, relationships with governments are involved in any activity in some of these fields, and in these relationships divided approaches—still more, competitive approaches—are harmful as well as wasteful. But there are deprivations which touch something deeper than efficiency so long as unity-in-mission tarries. There is an inescapable impoverishment of the churches' understanding of their mission, with consequent weakness, spiritual and practical. This chapter has contained allusions to two conceptions of evangelism which are generally set in opposition to one another. One is reflected in the statement of the East Asia Christian Conference concerning the redemption "of the whole created world" and of an evangelism which includes "an attempt of faith to discern Him in the social change of our nations." The other regards evangelism as exclusively concerned with Christ's redeeming work in the soul of the individual, with redemption *from* this world rather than redemption *within* a social and temporal order which is itself an object of Christ's reconciling work.

There are, of course, long-standing theological differences here. Because of these—and for other reasons rooted in history —the separations, in practice and organization, between those who represent these differences tend to grow sharper. Yet the need for a real meeting between these two main positions is urgent, for the deepest of reasons. The gospel of the Incarnation cannot be presented to the world in the wholeness of its reconciling range if it fails to articulate in act and word the redeeming work of Him in whom all things cohere—the whole temporal process, the meaning of history, and the search for the right ordering of human relationships within these dimensions of time and space. Yet the gospel is also mutilated if it does not speak redemptively to man in his age-long inner predicament as well as in his outer relationships, declaring the one and only remedy for sin and the assurance and expectation of a kingdom which will endure when the fashion of this world has passed away. It is impossible to express too strongly the need for a meeting of these two main conceptions of evangelism, at a theological depth and in language which will speak to the mind of the age, and with a spiritual potency matched with the deepest needs of men because it is a word of grace, a gospel articulated in spirit and in power.

A word of grace . . . spirit and power. The search for Christian unity—especially as this is conceived within the ecumenical movement—does not spring from a desire for organizational tidiness or institutional uniformity and rigidity; nor does it envisage unity in terms which spell the end of variety. It is concerned that all who confess the one Lord shall live in a relationship to one another which will truly and fully reflect their unity with Christ and their common dependence on him and on the wisdom and power which his Spirit alone makes available. It is the search for the right relationship to grace, that grace of God which makes and sustains the Church and is given for the salvation of the world. For, first and last, in all thought of evangelism, whether within a parish of a few hundred souls or within a world which is the Christian's parish, there should never be any blurring of the fact that the evangelizing act is of God, not man. Christ's obedient people put themselves into his hands for his evangelizing purposes. They proclaim him and his saving Word; they bear witness to him; they serve in his name, through those manifold acts of service within society which take them across all frontiers, new and old. But all this is secondary; it is subservient to the will and grace of him who sent not his Son into the world to condemn the world but that the world through him might be saved. It is when this grace is released that the crucial moment in evangelism comes. When it is given, the gospel operates with power that can no longer be measured by the vessels that contain it—the size of the Christian forces, the techniques employed, or the strategic skill of the human instruments. The movement moves by grace, with power and consequences immeasurable.

THE HEART OF CHRISTIANITY

This takes us to the heart of Christianity and to the most distinctive Word which the Church has to offer to an unreconciled world. The Evangel is not primarily a word *about* something, not even about the condition of man or the state of society and its needs; nor is it primarily a word *about* the nature of the universe or the purpose of the temporal order with the unfolding marvels of the physical world: it is a word *to* all these things, within them, transforming them, directing them, reconciling them to the purpose for which all life was created and fulfilling that purpose in them and through them. It is God's Word of power. It is the power to make bad men good, the power to cast out devils and deal with the mystery of evil, the power to illumine the mind with truth and to nerve the will for right action. It is the power behind all other power, the power which will master while it liberates, so that humanity's knowledge and use of the unlocked secrets of the universe will be not for destruction but for the glory of God and the serving of his children until the process of history and the fabric of this world give place to the City which hath the foundations, whose builder and maker is God.

JOSEPH M. KITAGAWA

Other Religions

THERE is today a general confusion and ambivalence among Christians, especially in the West, in regard to the problem of understanding other religions. Even those who are fairly well versed in the contents of the Scriptures and in the history of the church are often totally uninformed or greatly misinformed about the realities in religions outside their own. Though many of them come in contact with Jewish friends or neighbors, they are inclined to dismiss Judaism simply as a contemporary form of the religion of the Old Testament. Until quite recently, Western education for the most part did not bother with the histories and cultures of non-Western peoples, to say nothing of their religions. To many Westerners, therefore, Islam, Hinduism, or Buddhism seemed to be as remote as, for example, the ancient Egyptian or Sumerian religions. Every once in a while, returned missionaries spoke of the customs and beliefs of peoples whom they tried to proselytize, but more often than not they painted gloomy pictures of other religions in order to promote missionary interests among the churches at home. Understandably, most Christians in the West had very little opportunity to learn anything about other religions. Many of them, to be sure, had heard of Mahatma Gandhi, who raised questions in the minds of some Christians, because they found in him not only utter dedication to truth and justice but also a saintly character. But then, many Westerners thought of him primarily as the political leader who almost singlehandedly had led the nonviolent resistance movement of the Indian masses against the mighty power of the British empire, and even those who thought of him as a religious man regarded Gandhi as being a Christian in all but name.

The situation has changed radically since the end of World War II. The postwar world situation has propelled many hitherto unknown leaders of Asian and African peoples to the forefront of international affairs, so that the names of Nehru, U Nu, Nasser, and Ben Gurion have become familiar to the West. These men not only play significant roles in making important decisions regarding the problems of the world, but also represent the hopes and aspirations of peoples in Asia and Africa who have been nurtured by their own religious and cultural traditions that are now being revitalized. Significantly, this development coincides with a vogue in the West for Eastern art, culture, and religions, as evidenced by the feverish publication of books in Western languages on the *Upanishads, Bhagavad Gita, Qur'an, Tao Te Ching, Wisdom of Confucius, Dhammapada,* and Zen Buddhism. These two factors—the resurgence of religions in Asia and Africa and the penetration of Eastern religious and cultural influences into Europe and America—have caught many Christians off balance today, for they had not been prepared for this unexpected turn of events.

THE PRESENT SITUATION

Since the end of World War II the problem of ecumenicity has become an urgent issue for Christendom. This does not mean, however, that the questions concerning relationships with other faiths have been overlooked. In fact, a number of theologians and missionary thinkers have attempted to re-examine these issues. With the combined efforts of the International Missionary Council and the World Council of Churches, Christian study centers for other faiths have been established in various parts of the world. These centers not only offer facilities to Christians for engaging in research concerning the other religions, but they also provide opportunities for Christians to meet and confer with the leaders and adherents of other faiths. It is encouraging to note that already some of the scholars of the younger churches, together with Western Christians, though still very few in number, have begun to take seriously the study of non-Christian religions and cultures.

Equally important is the postwar Westerners' general attitude toward things Eastern that marks a great change from the usual prewar attitude. Toynbee observes that although the West has exercised the predominant power over the rest of the world for the past four or five hundred years, recent events indicate that the East-West relationship has been altered. "The West's alarm and anger at recent acts of Russian and Chinese aggression at the West's expense are evidence that, for us Westerners, it is today still a strange experience to be suffering at the hands of the world what the world has been suffering at Western hands for a number of centuries past." [1]

Many Westerners, to be sure, realize intellectually that a new world order is in the making and that they have to understand the dynamics of peoples and events in non-Western parts of the world. And yet, Westerners for the most part are not prepared emotionally to encounter the "strangeness" of other peoples and cultures; as Professor Eliade astutely observes, Westerners in their encounter with Easterners tend to depend on the more Westernized representatives of Eastern peoples or enter into relations with the East only in such external spheres as economics and politics. He goes so far as to say, "The Western world has not yet, or not generally, met with authentic representatives of the 'real' non-Western traditions." [2] This is especially true respecting the religions of non-Western peoples.

One may ask, then, how it is possible for Westerners, especially Western Christians, to understand the nature and ethics

[1] Arnold Toynbee, *The World and the West* (New York: Oxford University Press, 1953), p. 4.
[2] Mircea Eliade, *Myths, Dreams and Mysteries*, Philip Mairet, tr. (New York: Harper & Brothers, 1960), p. 8-9.

of other religions. This indeed is a complex problem. Even in the present oversimplified discussion, we are made to realize that there is no single correct approach to non-Christian religions. Moreover, there are different kinds and levels of understanding of other religions, depending on the motives and perspectives of those who deal with this problem.

Christians historically have approached other faiths from the single perspective of the Christian world mission, and have thus calculated their concern for non-Christians on the basis of making converts. Even the study of other religions has been undertaken with this motive. "Because as Christians," says Professor Perry, "we are under mandate to proclaim the gospel to and make disciples of all peoples, we readily confess that our motive for studying their religion is ulterior or missionary." [3] Such an approach might enable a Christian to understand the nature of the Christian gospel in order to be sure of its relation to other faiths, but would throw very little light on the realities of other religions. Many of the so-called missionary scholars, who concern themselves with other religions, are in effect preoccupied with the Christian understanding of soteriology, that is, whether God's redemption is confined within the Christian community or not. It is true that this question cannot be bypassed altogether by any professing Christian. However, there are other kinds and levels of understanding involved in regard to other religions; so that starting with or being preoccupied with theological inquiry into soteriology alone fails to do justice to the task of understanding non-Christian religions. Ideally, it may be argued that theology is able "to produce that attitude of freedom of the spirit and of impartial understanding, combined with a criticism and evaluation transcending all imprisonment in preconceived ideas and principles as ultimate standards of preference." [4]

---

[3] Edmund Perry, *The Gospel in Dispute* (New York: Doubleday & Co., 1958), p. 84.

[4] Hendrik Kraemer, *Religion and the Christian Faith* (Philadelphia: The Westminster Press, 1956), p. 53.

Practically, however, all too hasty evaluation and judgment of other faiths, based on a rigid understanding of Christian theology, coupled with misguided passion and wishful thinking, tend to blind one's perception and capacity for understanding.

In a sense, the contemporary resurgence of Eastern religions and their apologetic self-assertion may be understood as part of a reaction against the exaggerated assertion of Christians about the religious and cultural universality and finality of their faith. It is well for us to recall that Christian expansion in Asia and Africa during the nineteenth and early-twentieth centuries coincided with the colonial expansion of Western nations in those parts of the world. In those days the political, economic, and military strength of the West was such that to Westerners Eastern civilization appeared to be stagnant, ready to crumble before the mighty power of the West. It was hard for most Westerners to imagine that "in Eastern civilization there is inherent a power that is no less remarkable than that of the West because it operates in a subtler and less conspicuous manner." [5] Likewise, many Western missionaries took it for granted that Eastern religions were disintegrating from within, so that they assumed the "cultural" as well as "religious" superiority of Christianity.

Confronted with the relentless advance of Western civilization and religion, adherents of Eastern religions tended to accept the "cultural" superiority of Christianity, but not its "religious" superiority, for they believed that their own traditional religions were sufficient to meet the spiritual needs of Eastern peoples. As Dewick states, "So long as their continued existence was not threatened, they showed little inclination to assert their own superiority and were often quite ready to express admiration for the teachings of Christ." [6] Many Eastern

[5] William S. Haas, *The Destiny of the Mind—East and West* (London: Faber & Faber, 1956), pp. 57-58.

[6] E. C. Dewick, *The Christian Attitude to Other Religions* (Cambridge: Cambridge University Press, 1953), p. 14.

religious leaders hoped, naïvely to be sure, that by incorporating some of the Western forms and categories, and modernizing and purifying their traditional cults and practices, their religions would be received by Christianity in a partnership of genuine interreligious co-operation. In this hope and aspiration they were bound to be disappointed, for Christianity continued to claim not only "cultural" but also "religious" superiority over all other religions. Also, Eastern religious leaders began to realize that in the acceptance of Western ways and logic, Eastern religions devaluated their own norms of belief and practice. For instance, Dr. D. T. Suzuki remarks that whereas, formerly, Buddhists welcomed the Western approach to the study of their religion, they are now resorting to the dialectic of Buddhism, rejecting the Western approach and methodology. "There is a growing conviction among the Buddhists that their philosophy does not require the support of Western logic, especially modern science." [7] This, be it noted, is not a unique development in Buddhism alone. Elsewhere, "there is manifest in the Eastern world today, along with the general national revitalization, a movement toward a heightening of religious group consciousness, embodying itself in movements for reform, reorganization, propaganda, consolidation, and concerted opposition to Christian missions." [8]

What is significant today is that, just as many Christians approach other religions from the standpoint of Christian faith, articulate Eastern thinkers try to understand and evaluate all religions, including Christianity, from the perspectives of their distinctive faiths. For example, Dr. Radhakrishnan asserts that the fundamental teaching of Christianity is not knowledge of and faith in Jesus as a historic person; to him, Christianity is the continuation of the perennial religion of the human race.

[7] Quoted in A. Eustace Haydon, ed., *Modern Trends in World-Religions* (Chicago: The University of Chicago Press, 1934), p. 38.

[8] Kraemer, *The Christian Message in a Non-Christian World* (Grand Rapids, Mich.: Kregel Publications, 1961).

Seen from such a Hindu theological perspective, Gautama the
Buddha as well as Jesus the Christ are "God-men," or the manifestations of the Spirit through human media. Accordingly, the
Son—the second person of the Trinity—is "man universalized,"
whereas "Jesus Christ is God individualized." [9] Also, according
to Radhakrishnan, this belief is not a monopoly of Christianity.
"God-men are the precursors of the truly human. What is possible for a Gautama or a Jesus is possible for every human being.
The nature of man receives its fulfillment in them. They are
our elder brothers." [10] In a similar vein, Suzuki interprets the
creation story from the perspective of Zen Buddhism. He states:

> When God saw the light which came out of his com-
> mand, he said, "It is good." This appreciation on the part
> of God is the first awakening of consciousness in the world:
> in fact the beginning of the world itself. The mere separa-
> tion of light and darkness does not demonstrate the begin-
> ning. The world starts only when there is a mind which
> appreciates, *viz.*, a mind critically conscious of itself. This
> is also the eating of "the fruit of the tree which is in the
> midst of the garden." The eating means "knowing good
> and evil," appraising the light and darkness, and in this
> appraisal, in this knowledge, there is the secret of living by
> Zen.[11]

Elsewhere Suzuki comments that Yahweh's disclosure of his
own identity—"I am that I am"—is the most profound of utterances. "This is the same as Christ's saying, 'I am,' that is, he
is eternity itself, while Abraham is in time, therefore, he 'was'
and not 'is.' Those who live in the light of eternity are and are
never subjected to the becoming of 'was' and 'will be.'" [12]

[9] Sarvepalli Radhakrishnan, *Recovery of Faith* (New York: Harper &
Brothers, 1955), p. 187.
[10] *Ibid.*, p. 179.
[11] D. T. Suzuki, *Living by Zen* (Los Angeles: Perkins Oriental Books,
1949), p. 13.
[12] D. T. Suzuki, *Mysticism, Christian and Buddhist* (New York: Harper
& Brothers, 1957), p. 112.

Reading these comments upon Christianity by non-Christian thinkers, Christians should not hastily conclude that these men have become partially Christianized, nor should Christians be disturbed by the presentation of a distorted understanding of the meaning of Christian faith. What these Eastern thinkers are doing is looking at Christianity through the eyes of their own faiths. They do not at the same time say that Christians should not approach other religions through the perspective of Christian faith [13]; they insist, however, that they too have every right to interpret Christianity from their own perspectives and to make theological judgments upon it. Thus, Radhakrishnan characterizes the original teaching of Jesus as a typical Eastern spirituality, emphasizing intuitive realization, a nondogmatic attitude, the nonaggressive virtues, and a universalistic ethics. He considers that Western Christianity has distorted the original ethos of Christianity by placing "the emphasis on definite creeds and absolute dogmatism, with its consequences of intolerance, exclusiveness, and confusion of piety with patriotism." [14] On the other hand, Sayyid Qutb considers Christianity as an individualistic and negative faith. "When it was embraced by Europe owing to specific historic circumstances, and when it proved incompetent to keep pace with life as it developed then, Christianity confined itself to worship and to matters of individual conscience, ceasing to have any control over the practical affairs of life...." [15]

To those Christians who hold that only they have a divine commission to witness for their faith, at the expense of other

[13] Cf. J. N. Farquhar, *The Crown of Hinduism* (1913); K. L. Reichelt, *Truth and Tradition in Chinese Buddhism* (1934); George Appleton, *Glad Encounter* (1959), and *On the Eightfold Path—Christian Presence Amid Buddhism* (New York: Oxford University Press, 1961); Kenneth Cragg, *The Call of the Minaret* (New York: Oxford University Press, 1956), and *Sandals at the Mosque—Christian Presence Amid Islam* (New York: Oxford University Press, 1959).

[14] Sarvepalli Radhakrishnan, *East and West in Religion* (London: George Allen & Unwin, 1933), p. 58.

[15] Quoted in Cragg, *The Call of the Minaret, op. cit.,* p. 247.

religions and without recognizing the same privilege for others, these statements by the adherents of non-Christian faiths may come as a shock. In much the same way that some Westerners forget that "the world has been suffering at Western hands for a number of centuries past," some Christians who resent the non-Christian criticism of Christianity forget that this is what Christians all these years have been doing respecting other religions. The crucial issue today, however, is not so much *whether or not* adherents of particular religions have the right to witness for their faiths as *how* they ought to do it. This is not to deny the importance of the contents and integrity of the faiths involved. As Pandit Nehru remarked recently, "Your manner of saying it—the mood you create, the kind of rapport you establish—all these are the most vital part of communication and have a great deal to do with the response you get." [16] This emphasis should not be interpreted as a preoccupation with the techniques or gimmicks of communications; what Nehru stresses is the basic attitude toward others who may or may not share the same views. Today, when the claims of Christianity confront both the rational and emotional rebuttals and countercharges of non-Christians, Christians are compelled to re-examine their basic attitudes toward other faiths and the people who adhere to them, for it will have a great deal to do with the response of others toward Christianity for years to come.

THE PROSPECTS

In any area of life, one's attitude toward others is integrally related to one's attitude toward oneself; the Christian attitude toward other faiths must also be seen in this light. We must bear in mind, however, that one's own faith and the faiths of

[16] Quoted in Norman Cousins, "Talk with the PM," *Saturday Review*, May 27, 1961, p. 13.

others require different kinds of understanding, even though the two cannot be separated. Utopians may equate the two, and confuse, for example, the comparative study of religions with theology. On the other hand, many Christians try to probe into the meaning of Christian faith alone and then attempt to communicate it to others, as though communication were a one-way street. How to maintain the necessary tension, while not losing sight of the internal relations, between the attempt to understand Christian faith and the effort to understand other faiths, is indeed a difficult problem in our time.

"In the past," says Adolph Keller, "Christian faith meant a certainty about life and its future, an assurance which gave a meaning to its continuous changes, an inner security which was a firm foundation from which the moving kaleidoscope of a whole world could be observed and judged." [17] Today, even convinced Christians are blinking and rubbing their eyes in a world that is changing and moving too rapidly for their comfort. Their image of a secure world has been destroyed; they have become sojourners in the world that is increasingly "alien" to them. Caught in this dilemma, some Christians try to retire to the citadel of faith of their Fathers. For example, in a recent article, Dr. Cawley tells of his encounter with a Jewish scholar. "In your opinion," asked Cawley, "will the time come, near or remote, when the Jew will become a Christian?" To this his Jewish friend replied: "The Jew will become Christian when the Christian becomes Christian." In citing this experience, Cawley exhorts Christians to return to the unshakable Pauline faith in Christ: "Paul won his earlier day for Christ, for the simple reason that Christ held all there was in Paul, and shone his deathless light through him. That same principle of faith, of life, and of light wins today wherever it may be." [18]

[17] Adolph Keller, *Christian Europe Today* (New York: Harper & Brothers, 1942), p. 4.
[18] F. Cawley, "Christ's Finality: A Lost Vision?" *Christianity Today,* Vol. 15, April 24, 1961, p. 17.

Inspiring though Cawley's affirmation of faith is, his proposed solution fails to face the reality of the situation, for the difficulty with Asian religions that challenge Christianity today, as Tillich points out, "is not so much that they reject the Christian answer *as answer*, as that their human nature is formed in such a way that they do not ask the questions to which the gospel gives the answer. To them the Christian answer is not an answer, because they have not asked the question to which Christianity is supposed to give the answer." [19] This is the very problem that vexes Christianity today and will continue to do so tomorrow.

In today's world, where there is more than one religion that claims the truth as its own, the choice of attitude is limited. One may hold that different religions are fundamentally the same, as advocated by some of the extreme Christian liberals, some Buddhists and by Neo-Vedantists. Or one can stress, as indeed many adherents of different religions do, the exclusive value and unique meaning in a particular religious system. To the former the uniqueness of each religion is its disgrace, while to the latter universality implies the surrender of truth. Both of these fail to take adequate account of the dialectic relationship involved in the universal and particular dimensions of religions.

It must readily be admitted that in our divided world a common-sense appeal for mankind's unity cannot be dismissed as sheer sentimentality. The liberals in every religious tradition have made great contributions to understanding by emphasizing the common bond of humanity, crossing religious lines; this is a necessary emphasis that cannot be forgotten. However, in their eagerness to stress the universal aspect of religions, enthusiasts tend to ignore the tenacity and importance of differences that exist among the religions. These "doctrinaire liberals," in their adherence to a one-dimensional truth about the universal

---

[19] Paul Tillich, *Theology of Culture*, Robert C. Kimball, ed. (New York: Oxford University Press, 1959), pp. 204-205.

features of religions, naïvely assume that advocating this point of view will automatically bring about harmony and mutual understanding among the diverse religions. As Kraemer points out, some of the more aggressive advocates of universality of religions can be "exclusivists in a concealed way," in the name of inclusiveness, by claiming that interfaith relations are possible only when all religions drop at the outset their uniqueness and accept solely "the tenet of the one, universal religion, hidden in all religions" as the normative concept.[20]

On the other hand, advocates of the absoluteness of one faith face difficult problems as well. For example, if a Christian holds that all other faiths are "counterfeits" of the true religion and thus should be eliminated or displaced, he cannot help denying, unwittingly to be sure, God's freedom and the doctrine of creation. If he concludes that only the Christian apprehension of the truth is correct, without rejecting the availability of the Divine to others, he cannot escape "monolatry," which implies the sort of relativism that he tried to avoid in the first place. In either case, extreme exclusivists oversimplify the problem of understanding of their own faith as well as the faiths of others. Actually, very few Christians have ever claimed that the Christian understanding of God is absolutely correct. Following Paul's testimony—"now we see in a mirror dimly . . . now I know in part. . . ." (I Corinthians 13:12)—most Christians would acknowledge that their manner of knowing, understanding, and even their mode of believing, are under the judgment of the redeeming God. One faces still greater problems in attempting to understand other faiths because of their unfamiliarity and because of one's own ignorance, together with mental and psychic attitudes that have been conditioned by particular experiences. "And when one has the will to overcome these barriers," says Professor Meland, "there usually follows an

[20] Hendrik Kraemer, *World Cultures and World Religions* (Philadelphia: The Westminster Press, 1960), p. 364, footnote 1.

overindulgent sense of identification and tolerance that both falsifies and sentimentalizes the factors involved." [21]

In rejecting extreme universalism and particularism, some Christian missionary thinkers are again emphasizing the historic motif of "fulfillment." Those who take this principle seriously stress the necessity of entering the religious life of non-Christians appreciatively and sympathetically, believing, however, that the religious quests of non-Christians will have to be answered in Christ. In the words of Canon Warren: "Our first task in approaching another people, another culture, another religion, is to take off our shoes, for the place we are approaching is holy. Else we may find ourselves treading on men's dreams. More serious still, we may forget that God was here before our arrival." [22] Dr. Cragg goes so far as to say that the church "exists to give, not to get; to preach, not to strive; to welcome, not to proselytize." [23] His chief concern, in regard to Muslims, is "the restoration to Muslims of the Christ Whom they have missed." [24] Such an attitude toward other faiths marks a great change from the attitude of many missionaries in the last century.

However conciliatory the fulfillment motif may seem, this principle alone will not resolve the intricate question of the relationship of Christianity to other faiths. To be sure, Cragg is interested not in "taking back cathedrals from mosques, but giving back the Christ." [25] But Muslims know that accepting Christ, in the way Cragg advocates, results in their ceasing to be Muslims. Likewise, despite Dr. Appleton's sympathetic interpretation of Theravada Buddhism, Buddhists would not accept

---

[21] Bernard E. Meland, "The Christian Encounter with the Faiths of Men," *The Resurgent Religions of Asia and the Christian Mission* (Chicago: University of Chicago Press, mimeo., 1959), p. 10.

[22] Max Warren, "General Introduction," in *Sandals at the Mosque* by Kenneth Cragg (New York: Oxford University Press, 1959), pp. 9-10.

[23] *Ibid.*, p. 142.

[24] Cragg, *The Call of the Minaret*, *op. cit.*, p. 246.

[25] *Ibid.*, pp. 256-257.

his judgment that Buddhism is a magnificent preparation for the final vision but stops short, and that Christ alone leads men "through the veil of the temples to the presence of God himself." [26]

The irony of our time is that both Christians and non-Christians are making affirmations of faith by means of the fulfillment motif. When both sides know, or think they know, the ultimate answers, their encounter often degenerates into exchanges of platitudes or "the dialogue of the deaf" (*le dialogue des sourds*), to use Dominique Pier's phrase. Bishop V. G. Shearburn of Rangoon aptly commented that "Christians and Buddhists have talked *at* each other in Burma, but they have not learned how to talk *to* each other as yet." [27] Kraemer, too, feels that a real dialogue among religions is bound to come in the future but that it has not taken place to date. What is implied by such a dialogue is not the giving up of the uniqueness of each religion. All genuine religions cannot help witnessing for their own vision of ultimate reality, and inevitably each religion tries to relate its faith to other religions from its own perspective. This means, then, that Christianity, like other religions, must try to be true to its own faith and also to its missionary task. However, Christians must recognize that there is a path that leads them to participation in the religious quest of those outside the Christian community if they take both the universal and particular aspects of religion seriously. In other words, Christians have an obligation to enter into genuine conversation or dialogue with adherents of other faiths, not for the sake of Christian missionary outreach, but for the sake of understanding their own faith. To put it another way, the attempt of Christians to probe into the meaning of their own faith is not possible without a profound understanding of the religious quest and meaning of non-Western and non-Christian peoples and

[26] Appleton, *op. cit.*, p. 139.
[27] Mentioned in a personal conversation with the writer in 1959.

cultures. The same principle applies to adherents of other faiths as well.

It must be made abundantly clear, at this point, that the coming dialogue among great religions will not solve all the religious problems of the world. Such a dialogue is not meant to be a religious counterpart of the Rotary Club. In fact, as Professor Takeuchi remarks, "Where there is an enhanced possibility of mutual appreciation there is also the increased risk of misunderstanding." [28] Admittedly, those who participate in the coming dialogue will learn something from one another, and the chances are that their understanding of their own faiths will undergo changes. Those who feel that they have nothing to learn from others will have very little to contribute to such a dialogue. Though the problems in the coming dialogue are still a matter of conjecture, we can suggest some principles that are prerequisites for those who take this path seriously.

A MEANINGFUL ENCOUNTER

First, those who engage in the dialogue of religions must be willing to follow the principle that each religion is "an autonomous expression of religious thought and experience, which must be viewed in and through itself and its own principles and standards." [29] This does not mean that each religion is so unique that it has no possibility of relating itself to other religions. Morphologically at least, all religions manifest features in common, as expressions of man's experience of the Sacred, however differently the Sacred is apprehended and interpreted. To be sure, each religious faith provides a world of meaning that is self-evident to its adherents, to a degree that outsiders

[28] Quoted by Canon Warren in "General Introduction" to Appleton, *op. cit.*, p. 12.

[29] A. R. Hamilton Gibb, *Mohammedanism, An Historical Survey* (New York: Oxford University Press, 1953), p. vii.

cannot share at the very depth of a tradition other than their own.

However, a dialogue implies that the meaning of the faith of one religious tradition is comprehensible, to a certain extent at any rate, to outsiders; hence there is an implied rejection of a thoroughgoing *Apartheid* principle in the religious domain. This realization demands that doctrines, cults, and institutions, as well as the modes of regulating human behavior and interpersonal relations in a particular religious tradition, must be viewed in their own context. This is easier said than done. For example, it is all too easy for an outsider to miss the "intention" of another religious tradition. Thus, though acknowledging the existence of a certain element of world and life affirmation in the *Upanishads* and elsewhere, Schweitzer concludes that "world and life negation occupies a predominant position" in the Indian religious tradition.[30] Many other writers, viewing Hinduism from this perspective, interpret the concept of *māyā* simply as "illusion" and conclude that Hinduism is a faith of world-negating asceticism. However, the "intention" of this concept of *māyā* in the sacred tradition of India, as seen in the *Bhagavad Gita*, is not that men should be urged to renounce the world and history. As Eliade rightly insists, the meaning of *māyā* is a warning against the idolatry of history: "that the state of ignorance and illusion is not that of *living* in History, but of *believing in* its ontological reality." [31] Those who engage in a dialogue cannot help becoming aware of the shortcomings of all religious traditions in carrying out their "intention." This being the case, one must not fall victim to the common temptation of comparing the worst in other religions with the best in one's own. Rather, as Sir Hamilton admonishes us, "while the practice of every religion to some extent falls short of its own highest ideals, the exposition of an outside observer should

[30] Albert Schweitzer, *Indian Thought and Its Development*, Mrs. Charles E. B. Russell, tr. (New York: Henry Holt & Co., 1936), p. 3.
[31] Eliade, *Myths, Dreams and Mysteries, op. cit.,* p. 242.

lay more stress upon the ideals which it strives to realize than upon the failings of our common humanity." [32]

Second, there must be a recognition on the part of the participants in the dialogue that each religion has its own history and that each religion views history from its particular perspective. This means, on the one hand, that Buddhism and Christianity, for instance, are not to be understood solely in terms of the teachings of Gautama and of Jesus, respectively; and, on the other hand, it must be acknowledged that one's mode of apprehending the meaning of history, to say nothing of the history of salvation, is conditioned by a particular religious and cultural tradition to a greater extent than is readily admitted. The recognition of this double-edged principle spares one from making an overeasy comparison of the type that leads to the distorted conclusion that what appears to be similar in different historic contexts or in different religious and cultural traditions has the same meaning. There is no such thing as completely objective historical data, for all data are to some extent interpreted data. This implies, then, that the horizontal dimension of history cannot be understood without reference to the vertical dimension of values in every tradition. This is another way of saying that there is no vantage point from which one can observe all religions objectively. Rather, this concept of dialogue implies participation and an effort to come to some level of mutual understanding through mutual participation. Realization of this fact places special burdens on the scholars of all religious traditions, for as Professor W. C. Smith succinctly points out, "In addition to their academic standards they may adopt as a new criterion the capacity to construct religious statements that will be intelligible and cogent in at least two different traditions simultaneously." [33]

Third, a dialogue of religions presupposes that the meaning

---

[32] Gibb, *op. cit.*, p. vii.
[33] Wilfred Cantwell Smith, *Islam in Modern History* (Princeton, N.J.: Princeton University Press, 1957), p. vi.

of a religion can be understood only if it is studied as something religious. "To try to grasp the essence of such a phenomenon by means of physiology, psychology, sociology, economics, linguistics, art, or any other study is false; it misses the one unique and irreducible element in it—the element of the sacred." [34] Kraemer is equally emphatic in stating that those who are involved in religious dialogue "should be themselves sincerely religious and, above all, have a readiness to take a candidly self-critical view of the empirical reality of their own religions." [35] Without such a self-critical attitude, the appreciation of other traditions, and a sensitivity to the religious meaning of religion, his own as well as others, one should not even attempt to engage in the dialogue of religions.

Fourth, in a religious dialogue overemphasis on and preoccupation with doctrines and dogmas should be avoided. A religion is not primarily a system of doctrines, coherently constructed for the purposes of an interfaith debating society; a religion is a "community" with its beliefs, laws, customs, and traditions, penetrating not only what is usually associated with the "religious" domains but also the "profane" realms of communal and individual life. For example, to understand the Sermon on the Mount is not the same thing as understanding Christianity. At the same time, any description of a religion based solely on observable factors is quite misleading; "it would be like the description of a man founded only upon his public behavior and leaving out of account his secret passions, his nostalgias, his existential contradictions and the whole universe of his imagination, which are more essential to him than the ready-made opinions that he utters." [36]

These are but a few examples of the most obvious principles involved in the coming dialogue of the great religions. It must

---

[34] Mircea Iliade, *Patterns in Comparative Religion,* Rosemary Sheed, tr. (New York: Sheed & Ward, Inc., 1958), p. xi.

[35] Kraemer, *World Cultures and World Religions, op. cit.,* p. 356.

[36] Eliade, *Myths, Dreams and Mysteries, op. cit.,* p. 107.

be pointed out that although this article has been addressed
primarily to Christians in the West, and thus has placed emphasis upon the dialogue between Christians in the West and
the adherents of Eastern religions, this is only one aspect in the
religious world situation. We should not overlook the fact that
Christians in Asia and Africa have already become deeply involved in the dialogue of religions in an existential way. It is
simply a fact that many Asian and African Christians, born and
reared in Christian communities in traditionally non-Christian
cultures, have experienced and are experiencing serious social,
psychological, and religious tensions, especially in the face of
the recent reassertions of Eastern religions and the whirlwinds
of nationalism. As the Indian Christians admit: "Having never
been in the habit of concerning itself with contemporary social
affairs, and therefore not having been educated to relate its
message to contemporary events ... [the younger church] stands
today as an ineffective spectator of the contemporary scene." [37]
Happily, the picture is improving today with an increasing
number of Asian and African Christians taking an active part
in the social and political affairs of their own lands as well as
participating in a self-conscious dialogue with fellow nationals
of other faiths. Whether or not there is adequate mutual understanding between the Christians in the West and Christians
in Asia and Africa is a related but distinctive problem that
cannot be discussed here.

In his recent book, Dr. Kraemer posits the difference between
the pragmatic and the fundamental aims of the dialogue among
religions. The pragmatic aim, according to him, is the prelim-
inary step, which is that of "removing mutual misunderstand-
ings and serving common human responsibilities." All too often
advocates of interreligious co-operation stop here without moving on to work toward a fundamental aim, which is an "open
exchange of witness and experience, cross-questioning and listen-

[37] *The Indian Journal of Theology*, I, 2, November, 1952, p. 48.

ing." [38] Serious adherents of all religions ought to recognize the necessity of working toward this lofty aim. Whether we like it or not, diverse religions will continue to develop according to their own dynamics, crisscrossing on the face of the earth. Facing such a prospect in the future, Christians have yet to learn to probe simultaneously into the meaning of Christian faith while sharing in the religious quests of those outside the Christian community.

There are, no doubt, some Christians who might fear that participation in a dialogue of religions is a betrayal of their Christian commitment to proclaim the gospel. But the proclamation of the gospel is not meant to be a one-way street; it requires both listening and witnessing. Only through constant dialogue and sharing in the serious religious quests of peoples of diverse religious and cultural backgrounds can Christians come closer to the mystery of their own faith, which is rooted both in particularity and universality. Admittedly there is no clear formula or blueprint for the coming dialogue of religions. We can only say at this point, echoing the statement of Gamaliel, made nearly 2,000 years ago, that "if this plan or this undertaking is of men, it will fail; but if it is of God, you will not be able to overthrow them" (Acts 5:38-39).

[38] Kraemer, *World Culture and World Religions, op. cit.*, p. 356.

JOHN C. BENNETT

Church and State

THERE is no pattern of church-state relationships that can fully solve the problems that arise from their different foundations and purposes or from their mutual involvement. A state is largely tied to the interests of a particular nation and it has the task of serving the common good from the point of view of that nation. A state as the political structure of a nation formed in part by the Christian tradition has precious moral resources for political life and for the culture; but it tends to use those resources for the consolidation of its own power and for the sanctioning of its limited purposes. The church should be a watchman to remind the state that it stands under the judgment of the God of all states and nations. At best, its institutions are provisional, and its policies in relation to other states are inevitably warped by too great concentration on national interest—usually a very limited view of national interest.

It is easy for us in the United States to see the weaknesses of the traditional church-state patterns. We are astonished at the ways in which established churches in other nations are controlled by the state, so that even their chief shepherds are appointed by the state and their ways of worship are subject to the veto of the state. We stand aghast when we read of the Byzantine form of Caesaro-papism which leaves the church a mere shadow of itself. And we are no more happy when we read of aggressive forms of clericalism which may for a time control the state for the purposes of the church. In contrast to these patterns, no one of which could be initiated today, the American pattern of separation of church and state seems to be a great emancipation for both church and state. I believe it to be such an emancipation, but the formula of separation hides the reality of mutual involvement which is the source of many tensions. Indeed, we may say that since church and state are concerned for the welfare of the same community, the formula of separation is not a solution, but a new way of posing the problem. At present in the United States tensions between church and state are complicated by the fact that they often take the form of tensions between particular churches concerning the meaning of "separation."

THE IMPACT OF HISTORICAL CHANGES

Everywhere the relations between church and state are conditioned by two pervasive historical changes. One of these is the growth of secularism and the other is the extension of the role and effective authority of the state. The latter is not so new as the present forms of secularism; the English Tudors, for example, had a strong state and knew how to use it to control the church, and there are totalitarian dictatorships today in nations which never knew anything but a political despotism that allowed little freedom to the church. However, these modern totalitarian states have more efficient instruments of control than former despotisms. Also, we must emphasize the fact that democratic states have greatly extended their functions in recent years, especially in relation to education and economic institutions. I shall deal briefly with each of these changes.

Secularism is the organization of life without any transcendental reference, without taking seriously the traditions of the historic religions. We should be careful not to confuse secularism with the emphasis upon the secular, with the recognition of the relative autonomy of the sciences and the arts and of political and economic and social forms. These are not unrelated to the purpose and rule of God, but they cannot be

true to their own nature if they are under the authority of
theologians or of ecclesiastical institutions. Often the word
"secular" as used of the state means that the state is neutral
as between religions, and even between all religions and those
who reject them, but it need not mean that the state is seeking
to inculcate a secularist philosophy. The Communist state does
exactly that, and some neutral states promote secularism by
inadvertence.

There is far more explicit secularism on the European continent than in North America. The great emphasis upon religion, upon a revival of religious interest, in this country seems
to belie generalizations about the prevalence of secularism. This
is not explicitly a "post-Christian" country, much less so than
several countries that still have established churches. The "death
of God" is not often proclaimed among us. Instead, religious
institutions flourish and religion is an important aspect of social
life. It is quite unfair to say that this American attachment to
the churches and to the traditional faiths is mere lip service
and that religion is chiefly the means of cementing the community of organization men. But it is certainly true that a large
part of the religion of our flourishing churches is extremely
vague and very little illumined or disciplined by the theological
traditions. There is an embarrassing conflict between the theological convictions which have become alive in theological
schools and the impulses of popular religion. Our religious
traditions have in large measure ceased to give form to the
culture. There is a residue of Christian ethics in the minds of
nations that have belonged to Christendom, and for this we
may be grateful. It is still an extraordinary opportunity for the
church in this country that the people are within earshot and
are in some measure prepared by their history to respond to
aspects of the gospel.

After we have made allowance for the degrees of vitality and
authenticity in the churches, and after we have given thanks
for the impulses of the Christian conscience which remain, we

must note the radical difference in the intellectual frame of reference in our society from that in an unbroken Christian culture. We may think that in terms of moral achievement the Christian culture was largely illusory, and yet until the eighteenth century people derived essential materials for their thought and especially, as it seems now, for their controversies, from Christian theology. Religious authorities and sanctions, the fear of Hell, and the hope of Heaven were taken seriously by the makers of culture to an extent that now seems remarkable. The normative relations between church and state in such a situation were naturally quite different from what they are today.

When we think of the extension of the role and power of the state, it is natural to think first of the totalitarian states. In those states we see in full development the forms of control by the state over culture made possible by modern technology. They also have ideological orthodoxies to be instilled in the population, and these orthodoxies in the case of communism and fascism are radically opposed to Christian faith. They have inclusive social purposes and the hope of realizing those purposes in a new society, a hope that gives incentive for maximum use of the instruments of control.

The modern totalitarian states have regularly domesticated the churches or, failing that, have been in continuous conflict with them. Often they have employed the "divide and rule" technique and have built up one church that was politically subservient against another that continued to resist. Totalitarian states have found churches that are aware of their vocation as churches one of the chief obstacles to totalitarian control over the culture. This was true of Hitler's Germany, in which both Protestant and Catholic resistance continued until the end. It is true now in Catholic Poland and in Protestant East Germany.

In the other Communist countries patterns have varied from country to country depending upon such factors as the strength of the church and the traditional forms of church life. The

Russian Orthodox Church and the official Protestant leadership in Czecho-Slovakia and Hungary seem to the critical outsider to have conceded too much to the state in order to maintain their external life as churches. After decades of persecution and impoverishment, the Russian Orthodox Church, which has accommodated itself politically to the regime, has won a measure of external prosperity and of opportunity to function as a church within limits that its tradition has made not too difficult to accept. The churchmen in the non-Communist countries are irked when they hear churchmen in Russia or China or Hungary or Czecho-Slovakia echo the propaganda of their government. Even sophisticated Protestant theologians in Hungary and Czecho-Slovakia have been too uncritical of Communist tyranny and have gone far to provide a theological rationalization for it by their emphasis upon their own social repentance for the past without preparing Christians for social repentance in the present. There is room here for our criticism.[1] I think that as decades pass in which Christians have to live behind walls of censorship in Communist countries, and also in which real ambiguities in the "free world" grow in size as they are seen from the other side, we must be very restrained in our criticism of the integrity of these Christians under totalitarian pressure. Whatever their failures of moral perception and of political judgment, their churches do preserve within Marxist societies the sources of Christian life which may have greater influence on the culture in the future.

I have dealt with the effects of totalitarianism in the state upon the life of the church, but the extension of the power of the state is present everywhere. A complicated interdependent technological society requires a great deal of initiative by the state if it is to protect the weak against the strong and if the national resources are to be used for the benefit of the community as a whole. Private enterprise, for example, is not able to

[1] Charles C. West, *Communism and the Theologians* (Philadelphia: The Westminster Press, 1959), pp. 73-77.

build enough low-income houses, and by itself it cannot bring about the desperately needed renewal of our cities. It cannot by itself provide social security or make medical care available to all the people. By itself it cannot provide an adequate system of transportation. And no one wants at this stage to leave education to private enterprise, even though it is important that there be no state monopoly of education.

Such action by the state as I am suggesting is not a halfway house to totalitarianism. Indeed, totalitarian movements flourish when these problems are neglected and people suffer from unemployment and needless poverty. It is striking that in the corporate teaching connected with the World Council of Churches and in the encyclicals of the Popes, especially in the recent encyclical by Pope John, there is almost complete agreement about the need of a mixed economy with a considerable element of what Pope John calls "socialization." [2]

After these things have been said about the extension of the role and power of the state, it is essential to emphasize its instrumental character and its limits. The state exists for the community and not the community for the state. The church by its very existence, by its worship and its teaching, should remind the state of its limits, for the state is tempted to make itself into god. The primary function of the church in relation to any state is to warn against all such perversions and to keep those who represent the state aware that they live under the purpose and judgment of God.[3] These developments in the modern state create new conflicts between church and state, new problems in drawing the line between the activities that are appropriate to each. The key issue in this country has to do

[2] Pius XI had said in Quadragesimo Anno, 115: "If these changes continue, it may well come about that gradually the tenets of mitigated socialism will no longer be different from the program of those who seek to reform human society according to Christian principles."

[3] (See Oxford Conference Official Report [Baltimore: Willett & Clark, 1937]. Report of section on Church and State includes a paragraph on "Duties of the Church to the State," pp. 70-71.)

with education, where both church and state have a stake in training the minds and forming the character of the people.

ASPECTS OF RELIGIOUS PLURALISM

In the United States the most determinative factor for church-state relations is not explicit secularism but religious pluralism. This has been the case since the founding of the Republic. The original provision for separation of church and state was chiefly the result of the claims of the many churches, some of which were established in the Colonies. But today this pluralism takes a new form, because it is not the differences between Protestant denominations of which we think when we speak of pluralism; it is the much deeper differences between Protestants, Catholics, and Jews. Strong commitment to one's own faith is compatible with toleration of and respect for other faiths, and indeed such mutual acceptance by various religious communities may actually be a gain for all of them. When Christian commitment is accompanied by openness and charity toward those who adhere to a different faith, by respect for their consciences, it is much more nearly true to itself than when it is bitter and intolerant against those who differ.

The tendency of most Christians, both Protestant and Catholic, until the seventeenth century, to believe in using the police power of the state against one another on grounds of heresy was an appalling blight on the life of the churches. I doubt if there is any change in the churches that has been more pervasive than the movement away from "the forcing of consciences" which once was generally accepted. This has been a tremendous gain. Yet there can be no doubt that this gain was possible partly because many people have come to care less about their distinctive religious convictions. Religious pluralism has been made easier by the growth of religious indifference, and by something else which often characterizes the thinkers and leaders of the churches: a wider area of uncertainty and of flexibility in the sphere of doctrine. In the great controversies of the period of the Reformation one is impressed by the confidence on all sides that the teaching of the Bible was plain. Today the great emphasis upon symbolic rather than literal interpretations of doctrine, upon the location of revelation in persons or events, rather than in intellectual formulations, supports this flexibility. I do not suggest that those who do hold quite rigid doctrinal beliefs without even a margin of skepticism cannot respect their neighbors who differ from them in a pluralistic society. But it may be that the pluralistic society would not be there to train the more rigid theological dogmatists in civil tolerance if it were not for the contribution of the broader and more liberal minds in the churches.

To understand the difference between our pluralistic society and societies before the eighteenth century, we must realize that it was rare for either Catholics or Protestants to believe, until the eighteenth century, that a nation could have enough unity to be stable and healthy as a nation if it contained the adherents of more than one religion. This was not merely a matter of religious conviction on the part of the statesmen; it was often far more their prudential judgment as to what is socially desirable. It seems fantastic to us that the beginning of religious toleration was the permission for heretics to emigrate to a neighboring nation or principality, but it was a great step forward to encourage the exile rather than the burning of heretics. If we allow our imagination to contrast this situation with the religious pluralism that we take for granted, we can begin to realize what a change has come over both churches and states within three centuries.

Religious pluralism is the condition of most modern nations, but in the United States pluralism takes a form that is unusual. I wonder if there is any other nation in which three great religious communities have as much inner strength and as much strategic social power as is the case in the United States. The unfortunate development of a "balanced ticket" in politics, especially in the large industrial states, is a symbol of this power. One should add that secularism does not necessarily reduce the social power of a religious community or institution! The election of a Catholic as President after decades of controversy over this issue is certainly a symbol of our religious pluralism. However much we may recognize the determinative character of the Protestant factors in our national history, Protestants have had to learn that this is not a Protestant nation. Also, we have had to learn that the dictum of the courts that we are a Christian nation can no longer be affirmed. Instead, the Supreme Court in the Zorach case said that we are a "religious people." The very important part played by the Jewish community makes it inappropriate to use Christian symbols as a community, though these symbols are still associated with the state in countries that are more influenced by explicit secularism than the United States. I shall deal later with the problem of the apparent establishment of "religion in general" that may be unintentionally implied in the Zorach decision.

One fortunate aspect of our religious pluralism is that our three religious communities have a biblical foundation; they have the Old Testament with its prophetic faith and ethic in common. Whatever differences there are between the central teachings of Protestants, Catholics, and Jews, these differences are minimal in the sphere of social ethics. Also, all three faiths remind the state of its limits under God. The overlapping between the three faiths as they express in maximum terms their distinctive convictions about the judgment and mercy of God should be a major source of guidance for the nation. This is the ultimate corrective for the idolatry of nation or state.

All discussions of the relations between church and state in the United States take for granted the constitutional system of "separation." There are differences of opinion about the meaning of separation, but in contrast to historic forms of the union of church and state these differences are marginal.

We can presuppose general agreement among most of our religious groups on three meanings of separation. All churches in America believe that the church should be free from control by the state in its own institutional life. Our churches would struggle against any overt interference with their teachings on political and social questions.

Second, all churches agree that no religious body in the nation should be allowed to use the power of the state to bring pressure upon any citizens because of their religious beliefs or practices. There are marginal problems here, as, for example, when the state requires all parents to have their children vaccinated. This is objectionable to Christian Scientists, but it is not imposed because of the influence of any religious bodies on the state; it is a simple health measure. Some Christians do want the state to permit practices in the public schools or in the community which are offensive to Jews. However, often this is more a lack of sophistication about what is offensive than a determination to use the state for the sake of a majority religious faith at the expense of a minority. There is also the desire of many religious people to have the state sponsor minimal forms of religious observance which are offensive to those citizens who reject all traditional forms of religion. I shall deal with this problem later.

A third presupposition that is accepted by all the churches is that churches should be self-supporting, both because this is just in a pluralistic society and because it is vastly better for the churches themselves than for them to depend on the state for support. Roman Catholics who may differ from most Protestants and Jews on the question of public support for church schools agree wholeheartedly that self-support has been good for the Roman Catholic Church in the United States. Indeed, Roman Catholics have every reason to accept the American constitutional system of separation, however much there may be debate on some applications of the principle of separation, for that church has had more freedom to be itself and it has had more stimulus to expand and probably more opportunity to influence new developments in the culture than in most of the nations which have the traditional forms of the Catholic state.

INTERPRETATIONS OF SEPARATION

If we grant this broad consensus in the churches, we must go on and make clear that there is a continual controversy concerning the interpretation of the meaning of separation between "strict constructionists" on the one hand and, on the other, those who take a more flexible view in order to make room for considerable co-operation between churches and the state and also to take account of changing situations which may make the strictest views inapplicable without serious injustice.

Roughly, opinion among religious groups seems to be divided in the following way. Roman Catholics generally hold the more flexible view. Jews quite as generally tend to be strict constructionists, and in this they make common cause with secularists of various kinds. Protestants are much divided, but the divisions are not very clear, and shift with different concrete issues. Generally Baptists are the most consistent representatives of the stricter view. There is a tendency for official Protestantism to hold that view, especially on school issues. And yet among Protestants there are many groups that in principle reject the strict view of separation.

Protestant opinions on this subject are usually developed in relation to Roman Catholicism. Fear of Roman Catholic power is the chief motive for Protestant endorsement of the stricter view. The Supreme Court decisions, especially those in the Everson, the McCollum, and the Zorach cases, have provided the chief frame of reference for the discussion of this subject in recent years, and the Supreme Court has in the main given support to the stricter view. Opinions in both the Everson and the McCollum cases made important use of the figure of "the wall of separation" between church and state, and both used a sentence that rules out all nonpreferential aid by the state to religious bodies. The Court said: "Neither [a state nor the Federal Government] can pass laws which aid one religion, aid all religions, or prefer one religion over another." No one in this country wants the state to give preferential aid to any religion, but there is much debate as to whether nonpreferential aid to all religions is or is not consistent with the First Amendment. The Court in the Zorach decision seemed to relent a little, and though it opposed any financial support to religions on any basis, nonpreferential or otherwise, it did say this: "When the State encourages religious instruction or co-operates with religious authorities by adjusting the schedule of public events to sectarian needs, it follows the best of our traditions." At least this suggests a different mood from that of the earlier decisions, which seemed to lean over backward to prevent even the most limited co-operation between church and state.

The complexity of the whole subject is illustrated by the fact that many who hold the strict view concerning the "establishment of religion" are willing to permit practices that seem inconsistent with it, and they do so because of the religious liberty clause in the First Amendment. The best example of this is the financial support of chaplains in the armed services by the government. The chaplaincy really embodies the principle of nonpreferential aid to churches, but it is not a matter of serious controversy because most people can see that it would be a denial of religious liberty to the personnel of the armed forces if religious ministry were not available to them.[4]

I believe that this emphasis upon positive religious liberty that is endangered by some actions of the state, so that these need to be counteracted by other actions of the state, has much wider application than to the chaplaincy, and opens the door

---

[4] Pfeffer, Leo, *Church, State and Freedom* (Boston: Beacon Press, 1953), p. 151. This is the best statement of the strictest view of separation. Pfeffer uses this argument to defend the chaplaincy.

in principle to some flexibility in the interpretation of the separation of church and state. When separation is understood only in terms of negative religious freedom or freedom from any possible religious pressures, one can easily defend the strictest view of separation. As soon as one takes seriously the concept of positive religious freedom, or what the First Amendment itself calls the "free exercise" of religion, the interpretation of separation as the negation of all co-operation of church and state and of all mutual involvement (as suggested by "the wall of separation") becomes untenable, and the door is open for experiments that seem dangerous to the strict constructionists.

"RELIGION IN GENERAL"

There are strong attacks from secular forces and from theologians themselves against what Peter Berger calls "the establishment of religion in general." [5] There are two forms of such establishment which must be carefully distinguished. One is the state's encouragement of all denominations, by means of tax exemption and by means of such special provisions as the military chaplaincy, to express their own distinctive forms of faith. The other is the nondenominational forms of religious expression which are associated with some of the activities of the state. This common-denominator religion, which is at most a vague theism, is more vulnerable to theological criticism than the state's nonpreferential encouragement of the various churches to be themselves. However, both these types of "establishment of religion in general" are criticized as unfair to citizens who reject all traditional religion. I shall discuss the question of nonpreferential aid to all religious bodies in the context of the education problem, but I shall comment here on

----

[5] *The Noise of Solemn Assemblies* (New York: Doubleday & Co., Inc., 1961), *passim*.

the criticisms of public expressions of a common-denominator religion.

There is much to be said in favor of the theological criticisms of this official religiousness. It often becomes little more than "faith in faith." Also there is a strong tendency to use religion to support national purposes and values, and to lose all the elements of judgment upon the nation which are present within the biblical faiths. Theological critics often cite Eisenhower's references to religion to prove their case, but I wonder if it is not possible to appeal from Eisenhower to Lincoln. Lincoln saw the nation in specific ways under the judgment of God. Should we say that the religious references in his Second Inaugural Address would now be inappropriate on such a public occasion? The official statements and symbolic acts which refer to God should receive their meaning from the teaching of churches and synagogues, and should not be abandoned as sentimental distortions of religion because churches and synagogues fail at this point. Transcendental aspects of faith, the prophetic judgment on the nation, should be implicit in the symbols for all who have a rudimentary knowledge of the traditions from which they come. I doubt if we should empty our public life of all references to God, for to do so would prepare the way for explicit idolatries. The implicit idolatries that may be involved in the misuse of religious symbols may in themselves be more confusing than the explicit idolatries, but they do point to their own correction as the explicit idolatries do not—or at least they can be made to do so by the churches and the synagogues. When we realize how precarious religious and moral insights are in any nation, I doubt if we should by a legal fiat inhibit all religious expressions in the context of the state.

The question of fairness to the secularist is quite a different matter. Certainly all vestiges of religious coercion should be removed—such vestiges as the denial of public office to those who have scruples about oaths that invoke the name of God. A religiously oriented community will usually cause an explicitly nonreligious or atheistic minority to feel some social pressure, but this has little to do with the actions or observances of the state. Churches should indeed try to avoid such pressure. They should teach their people that contrary responses to the ultimate mystery of existence are to be expected, that the churches themselves are often responsible for rebellion against religion because of their own ways of obscuring divine truth. There should be more than a grudging toleration of the critics of religion, because they have often brought a needed challenge to obscurantism and to an oppressive clericalism. But there is need here for mutual forbearance. Freedom *from* religion for the minority and freedom *for* religious expression for the majority are in some degree of conflict, and will require endlessly varied accommodations. But I do not see why a doctrinaire imposition upon the state of the negations of the minority is indicated. The practical effect of such negations is not likely to be neutrality, but an emptiness into which secular religions find their way.

APPLYING THE PRINCIPLES

I shall now deal with the two issues which are most frequently debated in this country. They are of great importance in themselves, and they illustrate the general principles which have been discussed.

The first of these issues is the extent to which churches should seek to influence the laws and the policies of the state. The idea of separation has not meant separation of the churches from public life, or even from politics in the broad sense. Most churches have sought to influence legislation and have kept a watchful eye on government in the areas of their greatest interests. The churches influenced by the Social Gospel have done this in their effort to bring about social and economic changes. They have been sharply criticized by social conservatives in the churches, but this criticism has been based more upon objections to the content of the proposed changes than on a consistent opposition in principle to the effort itself. The crusade for prohibition is the most familiar example of political action by churches and church groups of a conservative and pietistic type. At the time they often made common cause on this issue with the more liberal churchmen of many Protestant denominations. The churches have usually tried to avoid consistent identification with either one of the two major parties, and most of their political action has been on nonpartisan issues. Today conservative groups who reject the actions of the National Council of Churches are engaged in intensive efforts to influence government, especially on issues that involve their economic conservatism or their single-track and uncritical anticommunism.

There is little debate as to the responsibility of churches to give guidance to their own members on the moral aspects of public questions. They also attempt to give guidance to the electorate and to the government. Sometimes these two forms of action are difficult to distinguish, for guidance to their members becomes public knowledge. One of the best illustrations of this process was the famous letter in 1954 from the General Council of the Presbyterian Church (U.S.A.) to all churches in the denomination on the threats to civil liberties in the period of McCarthyism. This letter was published in full in the *New York Times* and received very wide publicity. This is one of the best procedures and, if employed with careful preparation on subjects about which there is competence in the churches, it can do much to bring a Christian judgment to bear upon public affairs.

The most important question that remains is where churches should set limits to their efforts to translate their distinctive religious convictions into law and public policy. Most readers of these words will probably agree that churches should seek to be the conscience of the nation, in order to make their ethical teachings effective in national life, but there is a very serious

danger in a religiously pluralistic society that the political conflicts of the nation may become religious conflicts. When this
happens, a nation is torn apart. This may indicate how important it is that our major faiths have so much in common in the
sphere of social ethics. We only have to look at the Hindu-
Moslem conflicts in India to see how the public life of a nation
can be bedeviled by religion. To a lesser extent, Protestant and
Catholic or Catholic and secularist conflicts over questions of
education in France and other European countries illustrate
the damage that is done when the passions of religion are combined with the passions of politics. I shall deal later with the
American form of this educational conflict, which may well do
great damage to this nation.

I think that it is a useful rule of thumb for a church to avoid
the attempt to enact into law those of its own distinctive moral
principles which are not shared by other churches, or which
cannot be defended in terms of broad principles of justice supported by a public conscience common to Catholics and Protestants and Jews and many high-minded secularists. The churches
should continuously attempt to raise the level of the moral consensus of the community. They should seek to make people
sensitive to moral issues where they are now blind or indif-
ferent. The prophetic and the educational responsibilities of
the churches have no limits. Any church has a right, and from
its own point of view, a duty to seek to persuade as much of
the public as possible concerning the claims of its distinctive
teaching.

But churches should recognize the limits of law as the means
for regulation of the day-by-day personal behavior of citizens.
If law is to have a chance of being observed, there must be a
pervasive public conscience that supports it. If the Protestant
churches had not gone so far in regard to liquor that they tried
in effect to make total abstinence the law of the land, they
might have done many things to curb the liquor traffic. For
example, laws forbidding the advertising of alcoholic beverages

might have been passed in the atmosphere of 1920, and they might have stuck. Perhaps a public monopoly of the manufacture and sale of liquor, to take the profit motive out of the enterprise, would have been a permanent reform, but it was opposed by churches that believed in principle in total abstinence. The Prohibition amendment was the greatest short-term legislative success of our Protestant churches, but it proved to be an abysmal long-term failure. Doubtless it was sabotaged by many antisocial forces but, even so, it could not have succeeded, because total abstinence as a moral law made no sense to large bodies of Americans. It meant that Puritan Protestants were trying to impose their moral convictions on Roman Catholics, Jews, and many Lutherans and Episcopalians, to say nothing of the nonreligious. Every church is capable of responding at some point to the effort to control the liquor traffic on grounds of public morality and social welfare, but many churches can never be convinced that the law should deprive all citizens of the legal opportunity to buy liquor.

One of the most encouraging developments in the relationship of American Catholics to the state is that their leaders are increasingly willing to admit that their church should not seek to make the Catholic view of birth control the law of the state. Actually the Roman Church is not trying to have laws such as those in Massachusetts and Connecticut enacted in other states. When pressed about the laws in those states, the answer of Catholic spokesmen is that they were enacted by Protestants and that the Catholics have merely tried to keep them on the books. What Catholics often say quietly about the error in attempting to make the sale of contraceptives illegal is likely to be said publicly with increasing frequency. Roman Catholics have every right to teach their own people not to use contraceptives. They have no right to use their strategic political power in some states to impose their moral code upon Protestants and Jews and many other citizens who as a matter of conscience reject that code. The same thing is true of divorce laws. The whole community has a stake in the health and stability of marriage and family life, but to enact laws that make divorce difficult beyond a certain point that may have to be discovered by experiment, is to make all kinds of circumvention of the law inevitable. Many non-Catholics sincerely believe that there are occasions when divorce is not only justifiable but even a moral duty, and they reject Catholic absolutism as cruelly sacrificing persons to an institution.

Something should be said here about the significance of the election of a Catholic as President. In the campaign President Kennedy emphasized the view that a man's religion is irrelevant when it comes to the choice of a President. He went so far in stressing this that he seemed to suggest that religion is a private affair unrelated to public life. If he meant this, he was wrong. The nature of a man's deepest commitments is of profound importance to his candidacy, but, as I have said before, there is so much in common between Catholics, Protestants, and Jews that it may not matter which of these faiths commands his allegiance. Also, as against those who would say that a person who stands outside all the traditional religious convictions should never be President, I think we should recognize that the complexities of the cultural situation and of the mysteries of human personality are such that a man who has no tie with any of the historic religious faiths may nevertheless have the integrity and the moral commitments and the spiritual perspectives that would make him a good President. We must not allow nominal and conventional religious affiliations to have more significance than the actual character and moral awareness of the individual candidate.

I think there are two things we can say now since the issue of a Catholic President has been settled. One is that President Kennedy has proved that a Catholic layman can stand up against pressures from his church, as he has done in regard to school legislation. Indeed, a strong case can be made for the view that a Catholic layman with a mind of his own on civil matters may be able to resist Catholic pressure more readily than a non-Catholic, who would be subject to the charge of bigotry and would be more vulnerable to political retaliation at the next election on the part of Catholic voters. The other comment is that the removal of the last symbol of disability for the large Catholic minority will surely be a gain for American pluralism. The fact that the first Catholic President has proved to be independent of clerical control has added greatly to the benefit in this development.

THE KEY QUESTION: EDUCATION

The second issue is the relationship between church, state, and education. This is the most serious area of conflict and debate at the present time. It is true that the consciousness of conflict is largely among churches, rather than between churches and representatives of the state. But the basic fact is that the state has moved massively into the field of education, where all churches have a stake whether they recognize it or not. The pluralistic character of the community means that the substance of education has to be free from the marks of all religious traditions as far as possible, and this creates the vacuum of which so much is said. Yet the vacuum does not remain empty, but becomes filled by a kind of secular religion of democracy. Even if there is no such positive filling of the vacuum, there is in education without any traditional religious content the inevitable suggestion that this content is irrelevant to life. This prepares the way by default for secularist attitudes. It is a real problem for all churches, but the Roman Catholic Church takes it most seriously and does most to provide a solution for its own adherents through the development of a nation-wide system of parochial schools. The current discussion about church and state is focused on the Catholic effort to get public support for parochial schools.

Before I deal with this most difficult question, I shall mention two educational procedures, which, though controversial, do not arouse the deepest conflict. One is the inclusion of religious subject matter in the curriculum without the attempt to indoctrinate. This should come naturally in the study of such subjects as history and literature and art. Also, there should be teaching about the various religious traditions in a spirit of appreciation and fairness. It would help to overcome the sense that religion is unimportant. Also, if done well, it would promote better mutual understanding. The difficulties in the way of this kind of teaching "about religion" have little or nothing to do with church-state problems. They come from the scarcity of teachers with the requisite objectivity, and from the fact that in some communities the feeling between religious groups may run so high that what is taught about any of the traditions would not be taken in a spirit of fairness. This is an area in which experiments must be encouraged. What is possible depends upon attitudes within communities, not upon interpretations of the First Amendment.

The other method to which I have referred is "released time" religious education. Here the principle involved seems to me to be crucial. The actual use of this opportunity in most communities may be open to criticism. There is a tendency among Protestants to regard released time as ineffectual, but this may be because they have not taken it seriously and have not emphasized it sufficiently to make it significant. The Supreme Court in the Zorach decision has given conditional permission for this method.

All these questions are overshadowed by the controversy concerning parochial schools. Direct aid to parochial schools would be clearly against the trend of the Supreme Court decisions from the Everson case in 1947 through the Zorach case in 1952. Yet I do not think that the most important objections to it are based upon a permanent and inevitable constitutional principle. There is a very defensible view of the meaning of separation of church and state that is consistent with nonpreferential aid to religious schools of all denominations. There is nothing un-Protestant or undemocratic about such nonpreferential aid. No denial of this can be deduced from the words in the First Amendment, though the Court has rejected it in its opposition to aid to "all religions."

I believe in emphasizing two reasons for opposing direct aid to parochial schools. One is that in fact such aid would be overwhelmingly aid to the Roman Catholic Church. It is only the Catholics who have a nation-wide system of parochial schools. Moreover, even if this difficulty were overcome by the establishing of other systems of parochial schools, the second argument against such aid would come into play. The establishment of several systems of schools, perhaps five or six, in most cities would seriously weaken all education. The resources of the community available for education would be dissipated. No schools would be adequate. Perhaps the Catholic schools would be the best, since Catholics with their orders of nuns can secure teachers on a subsistence basis. The public school would cease to be the unifying factor in the community, though this may be less necessary than it was a generation ago. The more serious result would be the almost certain weakening of all schools.

However, these considerations do not dispose of the issue. The fact that the Roman Catholics have five million children in parochial schools forces us to raise two questions. From the Catholic point of view there is a question of fairness, since Catholics bear the financial burden of maintaining their schools and do thereby reduce the costs of public education. The usual Protestant assumption is of a given system of public education with the Catholic schools as an intrusion. But actually in many communities the public schools are built with the understanding that the parochial schools will take care of a large part of the need for school space. Public schools in many places could not accommodate the Catholic children. The effect of this is that non-Catholics are saved taxes by the Catholic schools and the Catholics have a double financial burden. This is the problem as seen by Catholics. There is, moreover, another way of looking at it: it is in the interests of the whole community that the children in parochial schools get as good an education as the children in public schools. When the nation decides that all children must have improved instruction in science, or in any other field, it must include the parochial school children in this national educational purpose. It would be possible to set such high standards for all schools that without aid from the state, parochial schools would be forced out of existence, especially on the high-school level. But this would raise very serious problems of adjustment, and it would exacerbate the conflict between Catholics and non-Catholics in the community.

EXPLORING THE FUTURE

I conclude from this situation that we cannot force the logic of either of the main stereotyped positions to the bitter end. There will have to be a compromise, and I suggest that it should involve the following elements:

First, the distinction between public aid to children and public aid to schools or churches needs to be welcomed by Protestants and other non-Catholics as a constructive approach. I believe that Protestants should be less grudging in accepting this distinction, and should use their ingenuity to find ways of doing the best that is possible for the welfare of all children, regardless of the school they attend. This principle has already been used widely to defend auxiliary services for parochial school children such as transportation, medical care, school lunches, and nonreligious textbooks if they are the same books used by the public schools. *We must not forget that the parents of parochial school children help, as taxpayers, to pay for all these auxiliary services for their children. They should not be denied them merely because they do not need to make use of the whole public school system, for which they also help to pay.*

A second element in the compromise is found in the principle, already applied in other fields, that the state may pay for services it needs, even though such services may be rendered by institutions which are run by churches. This is accepted in the case of hospitals and orphanages, and makes it unnecessary for the state to duplicate all private facilities.[6] The usual objection to making use of this principle in education is that it would involve the use of taxation to cause citizens to pay for the teaching of a religion in which they do not believe. The fact that there cannot be general reciprocity in connection with schools because the Catholic system is by far the dominant one reinforces the objection. I think that selection of some nonreligious elements in the educational program of parochial schools, which might be supported on this basis, is an avenue that should be explored. As long as it is recognized that parochial schools provide the education required by the state, and not religious education alone, some adjustment here may be possible.

There is a third element in the compromise I am suggesting that may be an alternative to the second, or in various ways combined with it. There is a largely unexplored possibility of some units of education—language, mathematics, natural science—being provided to parochial school children at public expense *under the auspices of the public school.* This would require important concessions by the parochial school as well as by the public schools, but I submit that they are not impossible and would not involve payment by the state for religious education. One form of this suggestion is that there be part-time parochial schools with a kind of reverse of released time (sometimes called "shared time"), with the pupils going some days in the week to the public schools for part of their education. There would be enormous administrative difficulties in

6 See Pfeffer, p. 178: "As long as the sum paid to the denominational hospital does not exceed the amount the state would be required to expend to care for the patients unable to pay, the hospital is not really receiving government aid."

this, and it would increase the awareness of religious differences among children.

The general possibility I am suggesting is that children be related to both public schools and parochial schools. This might involve the public schools' lending equipment and teachers for nonreligious subjects to parochial schools, or the attendance by parochial school students part of the time at the public schools. Reflection on such possibilities as these might help us to get off dead center. One byproduct of this approach is that Catholics would have a stake in the public school system and would be less tempted to undercut it for the sake of parochial schools. Separation of church and state does not mean separation of the state from the children who attend parochial schools. (For additional discussion of this proposal, see Symposium on Shared Time, *Religious Education*, January-February, 1962.) Touchiness about giving indirect support to a church by enabling it to save on educational expenses ought to disappear if what is thus saved for the church is offset by the extent to which the church or its agencies still help to pay the community's education bill.

There is always tension between church and state arising from the fact that their purposes are not the same. Fortunately, these purposes may overlap to a considerable extent, but it is in the relations between nations that we most often see the contrasts. The Church is by its very nature universal. It cannot be identified with the interests of one nation as against the wider interests of humanity. The citizen of the United States who is a member of a church belongs to the world-wide Christian community, and in that context he comes to see his own life in relation to the love of God for all mankind. God has no favorites among nations. Yet within any nation there are strong pressures upon the churches to conform to a national pattern of life, and to the state's tendency to exaggerate its own interests.

We find that local churches are similarly under pressure to serve local prejudices and interests, as in the case of the patterns of racial segregation. It should be said that there is no conflict between the church and the national state on the race issue, but there are real conflicts between the church and particular American states which use their laws to protect the mores of communities against the federal law.

Today the chief conflict growing out of differences of purpose between churches and the national state must be seen in the policies of the nation in relation to the cold war. This is so big a subject that I shall do no more than indicate that it is, among other things, an important part of the church-state question. In particular I want to make clear that church-state issues are not all derived from American religious pluralism. There is almost a myopia in seeing these issues always in the context of Catholic-Protestant relations.

It is not sufficient to say that in the international context the issue is between the church and nationalism. Today American policy is closely tied to the interests of many nations, which have in common the desire to retain their freedom from domination by the Communist bloc. Yet it is true that when issues related to the cold war are debated in our American communities, they do become involved with a narrow nationalism. The conflict between much of the leadership of the Protestant churches and the staunch defenders of the House Committee on Un-American Activities who seek to have the moving picture "Operation Abolition" shown in churches is an example of what I mean. This may at times become a conflict between churches and some agencies of government, but it is usually a matter of resistance by churches to unofficial groups in the community. Also, these situations of conflict set members of the church against each other.

I believe we may be entering into a period in which the deepest conflict between the faith and ethics of the churches and the policies and actions of the state may be in connection with preparations for nuclear war. So far there is no clear pattern of opinion within the churches on this subject. If there should be nuclear war in the near future, I think it would seem both in and outside the churches to be a tragic social convulsion within which moral judgments would be difficult. But if time is given to us to face this issue over a long period, conflicts between church and state will develop. Both Protestants and Catholics should be able to find areas of agreement here. I do not see how the churches can be faithful without opposing military strategies aimed at the obliteration of populations. I know that the makers of policy in the state differ among themselves on this question now. No one can foresee what form the conflicts in this general area within the church and between the church and the state may take even a few years from now. There may be no neat church-state conflict, and yet within the sphere of the church there may be strong challenges to widely held views of military policy in nation and state.

A popular church as a whole has difficulty in detaching itself from the dominant trends in the nation. But if that church is not to become apostate, there must develop within it strong countervailing forces which will be in conflict with agencies of the state and with popular trends in the nation. If there is freedom for the Spirit within the church, these forces will be encouraged by a portion of the official leadership and by some elements of the church as institution. No one knows how much the church as institution may suffer, but it must expect to suffer. Churches can be prepared for such conflicts only by faithful attention to the distinctive revelation of God's will in Christ, and by loyal membership in the widest Christian community where the partial judgments of all national churches are corrected.

SAMUEL McCREA CAVERT

The Ecumenical Movement

TWENTY years ago William Temple described the ecumenical movement, in oft-quoted words, as "the great new fact of our era." Did the statement represent a prophetic insight or only a piece of wishful thinking? It is too soon to attempt a historical judgment, but some relevant observations may be made in the light of the third assembly of the World Council of Churches in New Delhi at the end of 1961.

That the Church has become a world-wide community is a well-recognized fact, but its world-wide character has never before been so visible as at New Delhi. The World Council now embraces one hundred and ninety-eight different Churches, of national or regional scope, in all six continents and the islands of the seas. The membership includes churches of the whole confessional spectrum, from Eastern Orthodox or Old Catholic at one end to Pentecostal or Quaker at the other. Even the Church of Rome was not entirely absent from New Delhi, for five of its priests were present as friendly observers.

Beyond question, the New Delhi assembly was the most widely representative ecclesiastical body, in both geographical sweep and historical variety, that has ever met. Some of the Churches, to be sure, are only tiny minorities in the midst of cultures dominated by other faiths, but at least it can be said that in our time the Christian church is universal to an extent never before realized.

THE CHALLENGE

The question, however, still has to be faced whether the Church that has become a world community is able to act as a world community. Does it have the inner coherence or the outer structure to enable it to *function* as one Body of Christ throughout the world? This question indicates the major frontier to which the Churches of the ecumenical movement have now come.

And it is at this point that the World Council of Churches has its primary significance. It is the instrument through which a Christian community that is now world-wide is trying to learn how to conduct its affairs in more than a national and denominational pattern. The assembly at New Delhi afforded clear evidence that in the period since its formation in 1948 the leaders of many, perhaps most, of the Churches have come to accept it as a vitally important phase of their own life. At Amsterdam in 1948 and even at Evanston in 1954 the delegates often seemed like spectators of a colorful event. At New Delhi they were active participants in a working body which knew it had to deal with serious matters that were their own responsibility. The interchurch aid and service to refugees, for example, which had originally been undertaken as emergency tasks, had become accepted as permanent parts of their own programs. The projects of ecumenical study and action, which had at first seemed side lines, began to appear as strategic contributions to the planning and policy making of the member Churches.

But can the Churches which are thus co-operating in certain common tasks also find a common voice of prophetic leadership in the complex social and international affairs of our time? Or will the temptation to "play it safe," which besets every movement after it has become well-organized and institutionalized, prove too strong?

The characteristic tendency of all institutions, whether political, social or ecclesiastical, is to become more conservative as they become more powerful. From this tendency the ecumenical movement can hardly be exempt. Moreover, the Churches included within it are so diverse in both their historical backgrounds and their contemporary social settings that it would be a near-miracle if they could move out into the world of secular affairs with anything like a common front. In some of the Churches a pietistic tradition still perpetuates a fatal separation between the "religious" and the "secular." In other Churches there is such a close association with the state that they find it almost impossible to take an independent position at variance with governmental policies. Still other Churches are such self-centered communities that they feel little concern for the world-at-large. In such a welter of differences in social outlook within the ecumenical movement can we really expect prophetic Christian leadership in relation to society?

To this question only time can give the answer. But the spirit of the New Delhi assembly was decidedly one of great concern for the character of the secular culture. There was no disposition of the Churches as there represented to become self-contained and absorbed in their own organizational interests. They were eager to find the ways of moving out together in relation to the great human struggle for a world of social justice, of interracial fellowship, and of international peace.

The best illustration of this is in race relations. Building on foundations laid at Evanston in 1954, spokesmen for the Churches at New Delhi could unite in saying that enforced segregation is contrary to the gospel and that "no one who believes in Jesus Christ may be excluded from any church on the grounds of his color or race."

The wrestling with this issue in the World Council of Churches between 1954 and 1961 resulted in the withdrawal of three South African Churches from its membership. From one angle this is sad evidence of division among the Churches in their social witness. The Dutch Reformed Churches of South

Africa have been so closely identified with Afrikaner nationalism and so unwilling to take a stand in opposition to its policies
that they could not accept the World Council's position, even
though some of their influential leaders were in agreement with
it. Whether the decision of these Churches to separate themselves from the ecumenical circle will be more than temporary
remains to be seen. In any case, the element of much greater
importance in the long run is the evident determination of the
World Council to deal boldly with urgent social issues even
if this causes serious tensions within its organizational structure.

But the question inevitably arises whether most of the social
and international problems of our time are not too complicated
to justify the efforts of Churches to deal with them in more
than the most general terms. Can an organization like the
World Council ever hope to achieve enough technical competence and expertness to be entitled to a judgment on such an
issue as the abolition of nuclear weapons or the liberation of
peoples from outside political control?

That there is no easy answer to this question is illustrated
by what happened at New Delhi when "an appeal to all governments and peoples" was presented to the assembly for its
consideration. Two distinguished and honored Christian laymen espoused opposing viewpoints as to what it is appropriate
for an ecumenical body to say on such controversial issues as
were involved in the "appeal." Professor Charles A. Coulson,
foremost British mathematician and scientist, insisted that it
should be limited to a plea for what is specifically "Christian"
in its substantive content, and therefore to a plea for greater
mutual trust and confidence among the peoples of the world.
President Nathan A. Pusey of Harvard University, on the other
hand, was strongly supported in the view that the Churches
must also go on to do the best they can, even if very inade-
quately, to apply the truths of the gospel to concrete situations
in which fateful decisions are being made.

It has to be admitted that when in the past a Church has spoken on complex public issues it has often meant hardly more than giving a religious sanction to a national viewpoint. It has not usually meant that insights derived independently from the Christian gospel have been brought to bear upon the situation. The Christian judgment has been unconsciously warped by the nationalistic bias to which every group is prone. Perhaps the World Council, however, may be able to provide a corrective to this tendency. The fact that it embraces within itself Christian leaders from many different nations may, in time, lead to a method of arriving at judgments in which the nationalistic biases are less determinative and in some measure transcended.

The final outcome of the effort of the Churches to find in the ecumenical movement a way of exerting a prophetic influence in the social and international order may be momentous. During much of its history the church has tended to be a unconscious guardian of the *status quo*, if not by its utterance, at least by its silence or indifference in the face of social wrongs. To conserve the values of the past is, indeed, an important social responsibility, but this can never be the only role of a church that is heir to the insights of the Hebrew prophets and of Jesus Christ. It has to be the defender of the oppressed, of the victims of injustice, and of the down-trodden whenever the dignity and rights of any children of God are denied by the forces of dominant authority and power.

But to do this wisely and effectively in this age of concentrated political and economic power calls for more than an occasional pulpit utterance or the fragmentary testimony of a denomination. It calls for a united witness by the world-wide Christian community. Is it possible for the Churches to acquire such a voice? Certainly not without paying the price of a continuous and intensive study both of the social significance of the gospel and of the contemporary problems of society. It is only through some such instrument as the World Council that there is any likely prospect that the Churches can move strongly across this baffling frontier.

MISSIONS

Another ecumenical frontier emerges in the new stage at which the missionary movement has arrived. When the International Missionary Council was integrated into the World Council of Churches at New Delhi, and the latter body established a Division of World Mission and Evangelism, it was much more than a matter of organizational administration. It is hardly too much to say that it marked the end of one missionary era and the beginning of another.

The underlying meaning of this fusion of the missionary and the ecumenical interests is that it is now the Church as a whole, not a missionary agency, which is to be thought of as responsible for the Christian world mission. The missionary task is no longer to be regarded as something that can be delegated to interested individuals or societies. The incorporation of the concerns of the International Missionary Council into the World Council of Churches is a visible symbol that the Church must take the missionary task into the center of its whole life.

It is also a symbol that the missionary task is to be approached in a more ecumenical perspective. The old distinction between "sending" Churches in the West and "receiving" Churches in Asia and Africa breaks down. All Churches are more clearly seen as partners, on a plane of complete mutuality, in the common responsibility of making Christ known, loved, and obeyed throughout the world. This is more than a theoretical principle. Some of the Churches of Asia—in Japan, Korea, India, the Philippines—in spite of their meager resources have actually begun to send missionaries to other lands. Moreover, the Western areas which were once thought of as Christendom are themselves seen as mission fields, needing the reinforcement of world-wide Christian influences in a great struggle between Christian faith and the forces of a godless secularism.

In the period of revolt against the imperialism and colonialism of the Western powers the missionary movement in Asia and Africa has been under a heavy psychological handicap. To peoples in the midst of surging nationalisms missions appeared like just another aspect of Western cultural domination. It is a great tribute to the "younger" Churches in those continents that they have not been swept off their feet by nationalistic excesses but have continued to welcome the co-operation of missionaries. The fact that the World Council is itself so young as not to have a history of association with Western expansionism puts it in a position of strategic opportunity in relation to the present missionary situation. So also does the further fact that Churches of West and East have come into the Council at the same time and on a basis of ecclesiastical equality.

The active role which the Churches of Asia and Africa are already taking in the leadership of the ecumenical movement is impressive. The number of Churches in these two continents which are now members of the World Council is twice as large as it was at the first assembly in 1948. Eleven of the Churches which became members at New Delhi were from the emergent nations of Africa. That the Churches of India could be hosts to the Assembly and carry the responsibility so effectively was a happy evidence of their competence. In the Assembly the representatives of the Asian Churches made noteworthy contributions, as in the able keynote addresses on "Witness" and "Service" by an Indian and a Japanese Christian, respectively.

The infusion of new insights and new aspects of cultural experience into the Christian community of the world may be pregnant with consequences which none can yet foresee. An intimation of the possibilities was given by the young Burmese pastor, U Ba Hmyin, at New Delhi. In describing the response of different peoples to the universal Christ he drew a striking parallel between Christianity as it takes deeper rootage in Asia today and the early Christian movement in its transition from the Jewish into the Greek culture. He said:

> "When Christian witnesses moved out of the world of Jewish thought and understanding into the wider world of Greek language, thought, and life, it was one of the most profound changes and crises of the Church. Greek thought, forms, language and modes of apprehension became part of the very life of the Church ... Now the question is: Is it possible to do in Asia what first-century Christians did in the Greek world?"

Another segment of the missionary horizon that is crucial for years ahead is where Christianity meets the non-Christian faiths. The resurgence of Buddhism, Hinduism, and Islam is a conspicuous phenomenon of the present reaction against domination of Oriental cultures by the West. In this situation the missionary movement has to find its way between a sterile syncretism of religious ideas and a stubborn unwillingness to recognize the values in non-Christian religions. That the Christian movement has not yet come to clarity on this issue was apparent at New Delhi. On no point was there more evidence of divergent approaches. Some were so concerned to guard against compromising the uniqueness of Christ that they resisted any reference to the spirit of God as at work in any way in non-Christian faiths. Others were equally concerned to make it clear that God "has not left himself without a witness" in any of the spiritual quests of mankind.

Here is a frontier on which more intensive Christian thought and study must be marshaled. One may venture the prediction that such thought and study will lead to a clearer consensus that to approach other religions with a genuine appreciation of their rich contributions to Oriental cultures is entirely consistent with the deep conviction that Jesus Christ is the Light of the World. The idea that other religious history may be a *praeparatio evangelica* for faith in Christ and discipleship to him is by no means modern, but we may be entering upon a fuller understanding of it.

A LIVELY HOPE

The most dramatic frontier of the ecumenical movement has been marked by the coming of the Russian Orthodox Church into the World Council. When the Council was officially established in 1948, the Russian Church rejected membership, alleging that the Council was "political" and "social" in its orientation instead of being devoted to spiritual and doctrinal concerns. In spite of this rejection the Council kept the door open. Thirteen years later the Russian Church reversed its decision and decided to apply for membership. Although there were some misgivings that this action was motivated at least in part by political considerations, the application was approved by the New Delhi assembly, with only three Churches voting in the negative and a few others abstaining from voting. At the same time three other Orthodox Churches within the Communist orbit—those of Roumania, Bulgaria, and Poland— were also received into membership.

What will this new development mean for the future of the ecumenical movement? One obvious result will be the strengthening of the Eastern Orthodox witness in the World Council. This may sharpen some of the theological discussions in the Council—for example, on the relation of Scripture and tradition. In general, the Council will probably give more attention in the future to the Catholic heritage of the early centuries. It may thereby become more truly ecumenical. We may expect that there will be a fuller recognition of the basic principle that in the pursuit of unity the Church must maintain both its Catholic and its Reformed character. On the one hand, those of the Protestant tradition will increasingly realize how deep is their indebtedness to the pre-Reformation Church. On the other

hand, it is reasonable to hope that those of the Catholic tradition will appreciate more fully how much all Christians owe
to the renewal initiated by the Reformation. The larger measure
of Orthodox participation should bring about a mutually enriching encounter between Eastern and Western Christianity.

The more immediate interest in the Russian Orthodox membership, however, has to do with its bearing upon the relation
of Christians on opposite sides of the Iron Curtain and upon
their functioning in the World Council. That the task of the
Council will become more difficult as the result of Russian
participation can hardly be doubted. As the range of its membership widens, the area of agreement on common activities
may tend to become narrower. Tensions in the Council will
almost certainly be stronger, at least for a time. The conflicting
political backgrounds of Russian and American Christians
might, for example, make it difficult to find a common basis
for supporting such an activity as service to refugees from Communist areas.

Might the program of the World Council even be reduced
to hardly more than consultation and conference and exchange
of views? This is a possibility that has to be faced. But it is a
calculated risk that the Council is right in accepting. To exclude
any body of Christians that reaches out for fellowship with
others because of recognition of a fundamental oneness in
Christ would be to surrender its ecumenical character.

Without debating the question whether the leadership of the
Russian Church was acting wholly from religious motives in
seeking this fellowship, at least two things can be said with
confidence. One is that the Russian Church has given convincing proof that in the face of terrific obstacles, and at times of
persecution, it has preserved the Christian faith and Christian
worship throughout the revolution, and therefore deserves the
gratitude of Christians everywhere. The other is that from the
standpoint of long-range Christian strategy nothing could be

worse than for the Christians of Russia to be kept isolated from Christians of the free world.

The overarching consideration is the unique opportunity which the ecumenical movement now has to give visible evidence that all Christian people, in whatever secular environments their lot is cast, have a common loyalty and a oneness that lie at a deeper level than any political factors. It is open to us to cherish the lively hope that the world-wide Christian movement may be able to transcend the political and economic divisions of the world to a greater extent than most people have believed to be possible. Nothing that has happened in our time has been such a potent witness that the Church of Christ is not tied to any national culture but has a life of its own as a community not wholly shaped by external social pressures.

What we are now experiencing may prove to be an impressive modern parallel to Paul's description of the power of Christ to reconcile separated peoples. The sharpest social conflict in his day was that which existed between Jew and Gentile. Yet he could declare that Christ had broken down "the dividing wall of hostility." Since Paul saw Christ as the great Reconciler, he saw the Church as the Community of Reconciliation. In the participation of Christians in the World Council from both sides of the present "dividing wall of hostility" the Church may again be able to provide a concrete illustration of the truth of what the Epistle to Diognetus said in the second century: "What the soul is in the body, that Christians are in the world; for the soul holds the body together and Christians hold the world together."

NONMEMBER CHURCHES

In spite of the rising tide of ecumenical interest indicated by the coming of twenty-three additional Churches, of national or regional dimension, into the World Council at New Delhi, it is still true that it embraces less than half of the Christians of the globe. The frontier that lies between the Churches of the ecumenical movement and the Churches which do not identify themselves with it is well marked, and in some cases very wide. How far are we justified in expecting the distance to be narrowed?

The most complete separation, of course, is that which lies between the Roman Catholic Church and the Churches which have found common ground in the World Council. During the first decade of the Council's existence there was little to indicate that the Church of Rome would ever pursue any other policy toward it than one of studied aloofness. At the time of both the Amsterdam assembly in 1948 and the Evanston assembly in 1954, the Roman Catholic authorities were not sufficiently concerned to send observers.

By the time of the New Delhi assembly, however, there were many signs of awakening interest. Roman Catholic scholars were writing books about the ecumenical movement, not in a polemical spirit but in an apparent desire to understand and to appraise its significance. An eminent American Jesuit, Father Gustav A. Weigel, could even describe it as "the most striking ecclesiological event since the sixteenth-century Reformation." The Vatican appointed a special Secretariat for Unity to represent it in matters of relationships with Christians in other bodies. At New Delhi the Church of Rome was represented by five unofficial observers, designated by hierarchical authority. Though they took no part in the discussions, their presence was gracious testimony to a friendly interest. It seems possible that Pope John XXIII may invite Protestant and Eastern Orthodox observers to attend, in turn, the Vatican Council which he is summoning in 1962.

None of these developments should be regarded as an indication that the Roman Catholic Church may become a member of the World Council of Churches or establish any official connection with it. The dogmatic insistence that the Church of Rome is the only true Church and that the Pope is the Vicar of Christ on earth makes this unthinkable. The Roman position, as papal encyclicals have announced again and again, is that the only way to unity is a return to the Roman obedience by those who have departed from it. For Rome to become a member of a Council of Churches would be to deny its own claim. An impasse is thus created for which there is no foreseeable solution. But there is good ground for believing that a new climate of more irenic relationships between Rome and those whom she now often refers to as "separated brethren" is developing, and could develop much further.

A considerable measure of real co-operation may also come to pass, provided it is not defined in formal ecclesiastical terms. Already Roman Catholic and Protestant scholars are working together in such fields as biblical studies and research with sufficient amity to exchange views and share results. In the field of Christian concern for social welfare there is often friendly conference among responsible leaders in both ecclesiastical groups at the national level. All of this is, in large part, a by-product of the ecumenical movement. The increasing unity within Protestant and Orthodox Churches is apparently leading the Roman Catholic Church to take a different attitude toward them, and also is giving them a better channel of communication with Rome.

By an interesting coincidence the same assembly of the World Council which was the first to receive observers from Roman Catholicism was also the first to welcome Pentecostal denominations into membership. This is a happy sign that the gulf between "main line" Protestantism and what are patronizingly referred to as "sects" is beginning to be bridged. Many North American Christians think of their Pentecostal neighbors as of negligible importance, but in South America they are one of the strongest Protestant groups in the Continent. More important than their increase in numbers in recent years is the theological question which they raise: whether their emphasis on the immediacy and potency of the Holy Spirit's activity, so characteristic of apostolic Christianity, is not a truth that needs to be rediscovered by all the Churches of today. If a growing participation of the Pentecostalists in the ecumenical movement should help to bring this about, and if the Pentecostalists in turn should gain a deeper appreciation of the Church in its corporate life as the Body of Christ, it would be a blessing on both sides.

The group which designates itself as "Evangelicals" has taken a reserved and cautious attitude toward the ecumenical movement in its organized expressions. Their chief criticism has been that the ecumenical movement is too "inclusive" and lacks an adequate doctrinal platform. More recently a less negative attitude has been developing, perhaps due in part to Billy Graham's personal contacts with ecumenical leaders. The facts that outstanding figures in biblical theology are active in ecumenical circles and that some of the most robust theological discussion of today is sponsored by the World Council may also have a modifying influence on the future attitude of Evangelicals.

The largest Protestant body which remains outside the ecumenical movement is the Southern Baptists. To appreciate their position one must bear in mind their emphatic insistence on the independence of the local church. This is a viewpoint which is shared by Baptists generally, but Southern Baptists hold it in the most thoroughgoing fashion. They are suspicious of any form of ecclesiastical authority and of any type of association that seems to them to look in that direction. They feel that they can bear their testimony more uncompromisingly if they "go it alone" and do not become involved in ecumenical relationships. They wonder whether the World Council might not become some sort of "superchurch" which would limit their freedom of action.

If Councils of Churches, local, national, world-wide, succeed in demonstrating increasingly in practice that their *raison d'être* is really to be the servant of the Churches, and that the kind of unity which they seek is consistent with liberty, there is little reason to doubt that the evangelistic and missionary zeal of the Southern Baptists will eventually flow into the ecumenical stream. A hopeful sign is that in many places Southern Baptist congregations are co-operating in local Councils of Churches.

"EVEN THOUGH WE DIFFER"

The growth of the ecumenical movement to its present stature raises the question of its ultimate goal. Whither is it headed? Does it fulfill its mission by drawing the member denominations into greater fellowship and co-operation? Or is its essential genius to prepare the way for a union of Churches in which the denominations will be superseded?

Within the ecumenical movement today there is no agreement as to how this question is to be answered. All can agree that the old pattern of competitive and exclusive denominationalism is wrong. But some are convinced that if the denominations become more and more co-operative in spirit and in practice, their continuing existence is justifiable as a method of insuring desirable freedom and diversity. Others are equally convinced that the denominational system is irreconcilable with the oneness of the Church as willed by its Lord.

Before any consensus can emerge we must have a clearer understanding of the nature of the union under discussion. For many people the word "union" conjures up a picture of highly centralized authority and administration in a monolithic structure organized from the top. A doggerel parody of a familiar hymn suggests what they assume to be involved in union:

> Like a corporation moves the Church of God;
> Brothers, we are treading where Henry Ford has trod.
> We are all mass-minded, one huge body we,
> Planning world salvation through the hierarchy.

This, of course, is a caricature of what the more thoughtful students of the unity of the Church are thinking about. Their concern is not with size or power or efficiency but with the deepest spiritual factors. Their desire is for the kind of Church which bears the most convincing witness to one Lord Jesus Christ. They cannot be satisfied with anything that makes this witness less clear to the world. And that is what the denominational system tends to do, for the denomination, as denomination, has come into existence because of some particular doctrinal position, some special interpretation of Scripture, some preferential form of church order, some theory of the sacraments—or perhaps because of some wholly secular pressure of race or class or political circumstance.

Those who are today agonizing over the disunity among Christians are further concerned that the Church should be in the world as the unique reconciling force which God intends it to be. It tries to proclaim to the world that the divisions which separate men can be transcended in a new kind of community that has its center in Christ. Yet the denominational system introduces one more kind of human separation into society and thus obscures the nature of the Church as the Community of Reconciliation.

If anyone feels that this is too radical a criticism of the denominational system, let him remember that in spite of the great advances in good will and co-operation there are still three ways in which some Churches are constantly withholding Christian fellowship from others. First, there are Churches which are not willing to transfer members, when they move to another place, to a church of another denomination. Second, there is no ministry that is recognized throughout the Christian community as a whole. Third, there is even the exclusion of devout members of one Church from the Holy Communion in another. If these three grievous separations within the family of Christ can be overcome, the claim that the denominational structure is not inconsistent with the unity of the Church might perhaps be justified. So long as these denominationally enforced separations continue, the denominational system cannot really be reconciled with the unity of the Church.

In the movement toward union the crux of the problem is whether we can learn how to develop a type of unity which preserves the values of Christian freedom and Christian diversity. Historical denominationalism has protected these values, though at a tremendous cost. But why should it be necessary to have a separate denomination in order to testify to each important Christian insight or type of Christian experience? Why, for example, should all the Christians who know the rich values of liturgical worship gather into one denomination and those who find spiritual nourishment in freer and more spontaneous forms gather into another? Why is there not ample room for both within one Church of Christ? If each group has a distinctive witness to bear, that witness can be borne better in fellowship with others than in isolation. And both groups need to remember Augustine's word: "Even though we differ, let us abide together, for charity is of God and is the true sign of His Church."

There is no reason why church union must necessarily involve a high degree of centralized administration. There must, of course, be some organ of conference and counsel and planning, but if there is a common tradition of loyalty to Christ, a common body of Christian convictions, and a deep sense of a common mission in the world, there can be an effective unity with a bare minimum of governmental controls.

Whether a united Church on a national scale will ever be practicable depends in large measure on the readiness to make room within it for a wide variety of differences and a ferment of new ideas. There can be no united Church if its members are to be like the ecclesiastic of whom Bishop Charles H. Brent once said that "the only kind of unity he can grasp is where everyone agrees with him." Unless there is a realization that a diversity of Christian insight and experience is valid and is to be welcomed within the united Church, unity will never be achieved, or if achieved would not last long.

The most far-reaching project of church union yet accomplished is that which has resulted in the Church of South India. Here for the first time the separation between Churches which cherish the historic episcopate and those which have not included it in their structure of the ministry has been bridged. In North India, in Pakistan, and in Ceylon plans for an even more inclusive Church are at the stage of official decision. If the Church of North India comes into being, it will embrace Anglicans, Presbyterians, Methodists, Baptists, and still others. The North Indian pattern differs from the South Indian chiefly in the method of unifying the ministries. In North India provision is made for this unification at the start, through a ceremony commissioning all the ministers of the several Churches for their wider ministry in the United Church. In this commissioning by prayer and the laying on of hands, bishops of the Anglican Church and officials of the other Churches both share.

If there is to be any general church union in the foreseeable future, it will probably follow this general pattern. It will almost certainly include provision for bishops. As a practical matter it is unreasonable to expect that Churches which have treasured episcopacy down the centuries (and they include a great majority of Christians of the world) should now give it up. Moreover, those who have not had episcopacy as a feature of their church order ought to be able to see in it a valuable symbol of the continuity of the church in history and its unity around the world.

This, however, cannot involve a requirement to accept the doctrine that the Church truly exists only where there is an unbroken succession of episcopal ordinations going back to the Apostles. Within the Anglican communion itself belief in the necessity for an "Apostolic Succession" through bishops is a controversial issue, and there is no reason why an internal problem of Anglicanism should be brought into a plan of general church union. Unless non-Anglicans are willing to have bishops and Anglicans are willing to leave room for different interpretations of the espicopal office, the prospect of church union will be limited to Churches outside the episcopal tradition.

In any case the issue of intercommunion remains as the source of an especially painful tension. In spite of pleas for patience in dealing with the issue from bishops and archbishops and theologians, there are signs of rising impatience—especially among Christian youth and the younger Churches. At the New Delhi assembly one of their spokesmen, Philip Potter, chairman of the World Student Christian Federation, dealt frankly with this subject. He spoke of the ecumenical fellowship which Christian youth are increasingly having in conferences, work camps, and other activities, and of their sense of frustration when they are then denied the opportunity of giving expression to their oneness in Christ in the Holy Communion.

Perhaps it is not irrelevant to our present ecclesiastical impasse over intercommunion to recall an incident in connection with the somewhat similar tension over the Kikuyu case of nearly fifty years ago as recorded by G. K. A. Bell in his biography of Randall Davidson. When missionaries in East Africa in 1913 met for a conference on their common responsibility for Christian witness and closed with an open service of Holy Communion held in a Presbyterian church and celebrated by an Anglican bishop, all agreed that it had been a moving spiritual experience. A little later, when protest arose in England, the Archbishop of Canterbury asked a commission to study and report on the issues at stake in the controversy. Someone with a sardonic sense of humor summarized his own understanding of the report in this comment: "The Commission comes to the conclusion that the service at Kikuyu was eminently pleasing to God and must on no account be repeated."

THE LOCAL CHURCH—THE KEY

The final observation that must be made about the ecumenical movement as it looks to the future has to do with its present top-heaviness. It might even be described, without serious exaggeration, as a head without a body. The active participants thus far have been chiefly national officials of the Churches, leaders in missionary and international service, and theological scholars. The rank and file of church members have hardly been aware of what was happening. Pastors generally, with notable exceptions, have thought of it as something of marginal concern to the local church. As Bishop Berggrav of Norway once remarked in his pungent way: "The ecumenical movement is like a locomotive, with steam up, all ready to go, but it is not hitched to the wagons."

So long as this condition prevails, there will inevitably be a considerable measure of instability in the ecumenical movement. Since the World Council is a Council of Churches, not an independent organization, its true significance is determined not in any "summit conference" but in the places where Christian people actually live and work and worship. As G. K. Chesterton says, "Nothing is real unless it is local." Until the parish church more clearly sees itself as directly involved in all the ecumenical issues of our time, the ecumenical movement will have an air of unreality about it. The local church is the most challenging ecumenical frontier.

PAUL ARTHUR SCHILPP

Philosophy

AS long as religion insists that belief in myths constitutes religion's very essence, it would seem that philosophy and religion, so far from co-operating with or mutually fertilizing each other, will have to drift further and further apart. What is more, this drift away from religion will not be limited just to (science and) philosophy, but will be true of an ever-increasing host of thoughtful persons.

If it is true, moreover—as Dean Samuel Howard Miller of Harvard's Divinity School insisted in his recent commencement address at Princeton Theological Seminary—that the churches are addressing themselves in a dead language to situations and issues that no longer exist,[1] then any philosophical thought *worthy of the name* can have little, if any, effect upon these churches.

Unfortunately, on the other side of this fence, much contemporary philosophy hardly is worthy of the name. Under the impact of philosophical "analysis" too much of today's philosophy has come to be linguistics, semantics, grammar, and lexicography, so that it too has very little applicability to the problems, situations, and issues which actually plague mankind.

It is my complaint, then, that *both* religion and philosophy have become sterile, dry, useless, and dead.

But, so far as philosophy is concerned, I have had my say on this subject.[2]

[1] See *Time*, June 16, 1961, p. 40.
[2] In my Presidential Address before the Western Division of the American Philosophical Association, "The Abdication of Philosophy," reprinted in the *Texas Quarterly*, Summer, 1960, pp. 1-20.

It is true that in the past, philosophy quite generally has fortified religion, particularly Christianity; and religion in turn has had a considerable influence on philosophy. This is so well known that it needs no demonstration here.

PHILOSOPHY'S CONTRIBUTION

But *what can philosophy do for religion (Christianity) today?*

Before it is possible to give a meaningful answer to this question, we must have at least a notion of what philosophy is. If we can agree on the minimum definition of philosophy as the process of rational thinking, this may be sufficient for our purposes here, for it will mean that we shall want to examine whether and to what extent rational thought is or could be applicable to Christianity today and in the near future.

If religious "faith" is defined in the famous answer of the Sunday school pupil who said, "Faith is believin' what you know ain't so," then the answer to our latest question is obvious. In that case rational thought has nothing to do with religion (Christianity). What is more, this attitude is by no means limited to immature and untutored church school pupils. The proposition, "I believe because it is absurd," has been in vogue among Christians and even, at times, among Christian scholars, for many centuries. It is not dead even yet. There are still too many sincere and well-meaning clergymen occupying pulpits who opine, because Paul used the phrase "the foolishness of preaching" (I Corinthians 1:21), that this qualifies them to preach "foolishness," and that because "the wisdom of the wise" is said to be brought to naught, the absence of wisdom is a first prerequisite for becoming a preacher. Thus a premium is still being placed on thoughtlessness and unreason. I know, of course, that these descriptions do not apply to our better preachers and to our more famous pulpits. But these latter scarcely constitute a majority. All too generally the impression still prevails that the

"Good News" is simply a matter of proclamation, which needs neither reason nor understanding. To that extent philosophy not merely has nothing to contribute to religion, but is actually felt as a handicap, an unwelcome intruder.

And for *foolish* religion philosophy is, indeed, just that: a handicap, a negative critic.

However, a book like this is not addressing itself to that kind of group anyway.

Unfortunately, on the other hand, Christianity, even at a much higher intellectual level, where reason is respected and thought is welcomed, still is encumbered by a veritable ballast of mythological notions which, in the very nature of the case, resist the rational processes of logical thought that constitute philosophy.

If the essence of Christianity were to be found in the two great so-called commandments of love of God and love of one's fellow man (which are actually principles rather than commandments, since love cannot be commanded), and in the enjoinders contained in the Sermon on the Mount (rightly called the Constitution of Christianity), then not only need there be no conflict between Christianity and philosophy, but also philosophy could very well become a valuable tool of such Christian thinking (and even living).

On the other hand, manifestations of "religion" which appear to depend on and to consist of little more than mythology presented as a series of articles of faith, the affirmation of which constitutes a membership card—such religion had better keep away from serious philosophy. To rational reflective thought, one claim to virgin birth is as much to be questioned as another, as long as all such claims are advanced as being beyond question. From the standpoint of rational critical thinking, the worship of Jesus as God is, in itself, no less idolatry than would be the worship of Moses as Yahweh or the worship of Muhammed as Allah. When what is really needed is to "let this mind be in you which was also in Christ Jesus," emphasis on a physical

be the best rational reflection of which the twentieth-century mind is capable. Accurate and precise logical thinking on the basis of a fair recognition and consideration of all the available relevant facts is still the best single tool open to man. At this point we can learn from the specialists in all areas, not least from those in science and philosophy.

One thing is sure: the materialistic-mechanistic philosophy as an *adequate* interpretation of the universe, which characterized the second half of the nineteenth century and much of the early part of the twentieth, and the most extreme representative of which was probably the German philosopher Ernst Haeckel (1834-1919), has become so generally discredited that outside of the Communist orbit and of America's physiological psychologists, it no longer comes in for serious scholarly consideration. It became untenable in philosophy because science itself, from which it had been taken over, found it inadequate. Organismic conceptions, like that in the philosophy of Alfred North Whitehead, have taken the place of the former mechanistic philosophies.

But this does not mean that, therefore, a spiritual interpretation of the universe suddenly became the vogue in philosophy. Far from it. The Logical Positivism (or, perhaps better, logical empiricism) which has largely come into vogue in recent years has been as far removed from any spiritual conception as was the former mechanistic materialism. It put in place of the material machine an absorbing and all-consuming interest in language, its structure, meaning, and use; so much so, in fact, that the persons, objects, events, and any other referents of language have, for the most part, been blissfully forgotten. It is as if language were only about itself. Semantics, surely, has its place; and "the clarification of concepts" (Moritz Schlick) and precision of language are certainly valuable, sometimes even necessary. But there are those of us who still believe that language, when all is said and done, is only a tool, however precise and delicate. A tool to be understood, perfected, and used for *other* purposes, not just for the joy and game of perfecting the tool.

It is obvious that preoccupation with language for its own sake has no room for religion. All religious concepts, as, indeed, all metaphysical ones, are for it just so much empty meaninglessness.

Despite this fact, I would be the last to say that logical empiricism and philosophical analysis have no contribution to make to religion. Their very emphasis and insistence upon clear and precise use of words could and should be a boon to any religion worthy of human adherence. Throwing around empty, meaningless terms, or even nonsense syllables, as, for example, is usually done in so-called pagan incantations (which, however, may not be so far removed from so-called Christian incantations either; as, for example, in the phrase, "in the name of Jesus we pray," which is reminiscent of the almost universal notion that to know the God's name and use it is more or less to force him to do our bidding!) is not, after all, a form of religious practice or behavior which rational reflection could condone or approve. The fact that it makes the people who use those phrases *feel* good, proves very little.

The clarification of concepts and semantics does have a legitimate and valuable use, therefore, even in religion, and the philosophy concerned with them is therefore not useless. Christianity could well afford to go to school to this kind of philosophy, at least for a little while.

But a Christianity which would take philosophical analysis as *its* philosophy would soon discover that it might have an admirably clear language and grammar, but no longer any religion.

This, however, depends, one supposes, upon what one means by religion anyway.

AN ETHICAL RELIGION?

Is it too much to assume that—to most serious and thoughtful religious persons in *any* religion—religion involves their highest commitment? If this be the case—and if we limit our definition of religion to *ethical* religions in order to avoid making our definition so sweeping and broad as to include all the mythologies of the most primitive societies—we may then define "ethical religion" as

> commitment to the highest, noblest, sublimest, and best that I can think, imagine, and understand; and a way of life commensurate with the greatness of that to which I have committed myself.

If it be objected that this, conceivably, might do as a definition of "ethical religion," but *not* of Christianity, one would be forced (by logic) to ask: Is Christianity, then, commitment to *less* than the "highest, noblest, sublimest, and best that one can think, imagine, or understand"? Or, perchance, is it supposed to be commitment to that which can neither be thought nor imagined nor understood? In either case it would stand self-condemned! For—again in the logical nature of the case—it is, obviously, impossible to "think, imagine, or understand" anything higher than the highest or nobler than the noblest or sublimer than the sublimest or better than the best! And what one can neither think nor imagine nor understand—again: obviously—can not enter into one's conscious experience at all.

Our definition of ethical religion, therefore, is either applicable to Christianity or else Christianity is either a commitment to less than the highest or not capable of rational understanding at all. If the latter, then—in the light of the minimum definition of philosophy we have accepted above—philosophy can have nothing to do with it; for philosophy is nothing if not rational thought. And if it is the former (that is to say, commitment to less than the highest), then Christianity would not be worthy of the best religious minds.

I suggest, therefore, that, *if* Christianity is an ethical religion at all, *and if* Christians are in any sense justified in assuming that their—Christian—commitment is the highest, noblest, and sublimest commitment of which they, individually and collectively, are capable, then our definition of ethical religion not only is but *must* be applicable to Christianity. But this does not imply that our definition may not also be applicable to other ethical religions as well.

COMMITMENT AND A WAY OF LIFE

We need next to call attention to the fact that the two major nouns in our definition of ethical religion are "commitment" and "way of life." Any real commitment is an act of will emotionally conditioned and motivated. And a way of life commensurate with one's commitment means translation into action, conduct, behavior. At both these points religion goes beyond philosophy. A man's philosophy *may*—and probably should—influence conduct and behavior; although, admittedly, it often does not seem to do so. In any case, such influence is not a necessity implied in the very nature of philosophy. But it *is* implied in ethical religion. True: rational thinking should lead to rational behavior; but rational behavior is not involved necessarily in rational thought.

Although philosophy would seem to involve a commitment to rational thinking, it does not involve—in terms of itself—any necessary commitment to ethical ideals, still less to "the highest, noblest, sublimest, and best that I can think, imagine, or understand." Philosophy is too much a matter of the intellect to be much of a matter of will and emotion. Even the commitment to rational thinking is felt more as a necessity of the intellect than as an act of will. Although it is probably quite

true that to the extent to which interest is involved in the philosopher's commitment to rational thinking, his commitment
is certainly not without emotional accompaniments. The rationally reflective necessity may still be a *felt* (!) necessity.

Be this as it may, a person's (ethical) religion involves both,
commitment as well as appropriate conduct; conduct appropriate, that is to say, to the nature of the commitment. The
sublimer the commitment the more is demanded of behavior.
Thus, again, the vital religion of an ethically committed person
is not—certainly not primarily—a matter of verbal assent to
articles of belief, but rather a matter of the magnificence of the
object(ive) of one's commitment and the resulting conduct
made inevitable by the grandeur of that commitment.

This is not to say that beliefs are unimportant. But they are
important precisely to the degree to which they do *not* represent merely intellectual assent to this, that, or the other doctrine, but constitute a faith which calls for action, conduct.
Beliefs which the believer himself can do nothing about—such
as assertions concerning historical happenings or not-happenings
in the long-distant past—are religiously insignificant: precisely
because they make and can make no difference in the respective
believer's behavior and life. What I truly have faith in is bound
to influence my conduct. Faith in man—as, indeed, faith in a
moral God—is inescapably going to be reflected in my behavior;
otherwise it is not faith but merely intellectual assent.

JESUS—THE LIGHT OF THE WORLD?

It does not, for example, do much good and makes less sense
to proclaim Jesus Christ as "the Light of the World" unless
the *kind* of illumination he provides is specified and made clear.
Thinking people the world over are quite tired of having dogmatic pronouncements shouted into their ears, pronouncements
the precise meaning of which never seems to be made clear.

Christianity, if it is to have any appeal to thinking minds, must at least be willing to specify which areas of life Jesus illuminates and why. One would think that it should be possible to do this. Darkness *does* cover the earth today; darkness and confusion. Our age may not be dark in the sense of the (probably mistakenly called) "Dark Ages"; but, in another sense, it is almost infinitely darker, and certainly much more confused, than they were. The possibility of total human annihilation hangs over us as something much more devastating than any Damocles sword. What light, if any, does or can the Nazarene shed into such darkness?

He illumines the secret recesses of the human heart and practices depth psychology long before the days of Freud, Jung, Adler, *et al.* He lays bare man's basic selfishness in the same breath in which he not merely teaches but in his own life's conduct demonstrates the heights of human selflessness, altruism and self-sacrifice of which man is capable. With almost one stroke he depicts both man's next-to-limitless depravity and his possible divine approximation to what it can mean to be a man! Both aspects of this disclosure are certainly illuminating. They keep us from rosy-hued views of human nature in the raw, and, at the same time, keep us from despairing either of man or of his future—*provided* he does not blow himself to smithereens.

It is interesting, moreover, to note that at both these points, Jesus strikes a chord which we find not merely reiterated but strongly emphasized in much of today's existentialist philosophy. *Angst, Sorge,* anxiety, care, are concepts stressed by almost every twentieth-century existentialist. The essential depravity of much of man's condition not merely comes in for a thorough airing, but—at least in *some* existentialists, as for example in Jean Paul Sartre—actually constitutes a major emphasis of the existentialist position. At the same time, most existentialist philosophers call upon man to rise to his "authentic being" and become in spirit and in truth what, as a man, he has it in his power to become: his authentic self!

Existentialist philosophers may not use traditional religious language; but the comparison here is inevitable, and the similarity of ideas would seem to be inescapable. This, then, is a point where a real and significant meeting of philosopher and Christian can take place.

THE SIN OF NATIONALISM

What is more, such light cast on human nature also sheds light on man's social, political, economic, and national and racial conduct. The selfish individual does not suddenly become unselfish in all his various social relationships and commitments. Rather, the same selfishness which prompts his actions in personal life dominates his social life as well: only more so.[3] The selfishness of nations, for example, is so universally accepted a fact that the phrase is never used: it is taken for granted. In fact, that is precisely what is *meant* by nationalism.

But in the nuclear and hydrogen age, nationalism is *the* sin against mankind (for reasons too obvious to need reiteration here), upon which sin too the light shed by the Nazarene falls in merciless fashion: for the dignity of every human being and the notion that every man is my brother just will not permit my looking on any man or nation as my "enemy." This is not softheaded sentimentalism nor obliviousness to the depth of degradation to which men or nations may sink. It is no blindness to what has—rightly—been called "radical evil." But it is the recognition of the fact that nations too are made up of human beings and that therefore, what is possible for human beings is, in any case, not impossible even for nations. It is possible, moreover, that mankind has now reached the point where what has long been called "the first law of life," namely

[3] As Reinhold Niebuhr showed all too powerfully, years ago, in his famous *Moral Man and Immoral Society* (New York: Charles Scribner's Sons, 1932).

self-preservation, makes of selfless altruism, even on the international and interracial levels, no longer either a virtue or a luxury but an absolute necessity, which veritably shouts: Co-operate or perish! Light thus shed is not unilluminating.

JESUS—THE HOPE OF THE WORLD?

Or let us take another concrete example. The theme of the Second World Council of Churches (Evanston, 1954) was: "Jesus Christ: the Hope of the World." Hope for what? The fact of the case is that despite all external attempts to gloss it over, the more than 150 Protestant denominations officially represented in the Council never did come to any agreement on the precise meaning of the official theme of the Council. Some insisted to the bitter end (and for some more reasonable representatives it was bitter, indeed—although most of even these carefully refrained from giving voice to their bitter disappointment) that the phrase ultimately could only mean that Jesus was the Christian's hope of salvation in another, that is to say, the next world.

It cannot be denied that the other-worldly character of even Protestant Christianity is far from dead. It is equally certain that, to just the degree of its other-worldly emphasis, the Christian church minimizes Jesus as the hope in *this* world. To the extent that this is the case, such a Christian emphasis fails to be first, last, and all the time an ethical commitment here and now. To this same extent it fails to speak intelligently to the philosophically trained mind. The latter may have no valid objection to an other-worldly *hope*, so long as such hope is recognized as hope and not as knowledge. But he does object to a proclamation of Jesus as "the Hope of the World" when it isn't our lived-in "world" which seems involved, but a future state which may or may not be a "world" at all! If Jesus is the hope of *this* world, then the thoughtful mind will insist that it be spelled out *why*, in what sense, in which human areas, and to what extent Jesus is that hope. In a world, for example, which —ever since the angels (that is, we) won the war for "freedom from fear" (one of the "Four Freedoms" of the "Atlantic Charter")—has been unable to sleep fearlessly a single night for dread of having all humanity annihilated by nuclear destruction, in such a world the intelligent man wants to know how, in this situation, Jesus is the hope of the world. If the would-be orthodox Christian replies that inasmuch as his kingdom is not of this world, Jesus is not concerned with the possible self-annihilation of the human race, the thoughtful modern man will say that in that case proclaiming Jesus as the hope of the world amounts to an unfortunate hoax.

THE FORCE OF LOVE

I do not think that the Christianity of the Christ is actually thus bankrupt, even in the fact of the presently existing world situation. Jesus' preaching of the superior force of love as over against the love of force and violence does seem to have very definite ethical applicability to today's world situation. The parable of the Good Samaritan does have meaning today—but only if we translate "Samaritan" into "Russian" or "Red Chinese." The enjoinder: "If someone strikes you on one cheek offer him the other cheek also" *is* an ethical precept applicable in any age and to any situation. But—as in the case of the Good Samaritan —it needs to be translated into the language required by the momentarily existing situation. In December, 1941, for example, that translation would have had to read: "If someone attacks you at Pearl Harbor, invite him into San Francisco Harbor also!" That is specific enough. It is drastic enough. It is radical —in the best sense of this word: it goes to the roots of the problem! It certainly is revolutionary. So revolutionary, in fact, that by comparison to it, the strictures of Marx's *Das Kapital* appear scarcely parlor-pink. But it *is* ethical. What is more: it is religious. It is even Christian! And it is *irr*ational only if we forget what a totally unexpected shock such an invitation would have given the Japanese. That would have been the very last thing for which they were prepared! No, it would not have resuscitated the 4,000 Americans killed on December 7, 1941. But it might very possibly have saved millions of *both* Americans *and* Japanese killed *after* Pearl Harbor. Would that not have been worth while?

I did *not* say that to have followed the Nazarene's precept in this instance would have been "politic," nor that the nation would have approved. On the contrary, I am quite sure that the American people would have demanded the immediate impeachment of any President who dared to do what I have suggested. But this proves only that America is not Christian. It does *not* prove that the principle would not have worked.

Christians are *supposed* to believe that "love turneth away wrath." Such faith is, at least to this writer, of the very essence of a supreme ethical commitment. But—aside from a few Quakers, a few Brethren, and a few Mennonites and FOR members—how many so-called Christians are there, in any of our major Christian churches, who actually do believe this and dare act on it? Unfortunately, the question answers itself. So that it isn't Jesus, but his self-proclaimed followers who, in their unwillingness to accept and abide by his principles, deny that Jesus is the hope of *this* world!

Under these circumstances, is it any wonder that today's philosophers, by and large, do not find it possible to take the vague Christianity of the hour very seriously?

Or, when they see white Baptists (or Episcopalians) jailing Negro and other white Baptists (or Episcopalians) just because the latter want to take seriously the ultimate dignity of every human being, regardless of color, sex, or creed—this somehow does not seem either rational or moral, let alone religious or Christian, to a thinking person of the twentieth century.

Thus one could go on with concrete illustrations in almost every area *ad infinitum*.

To the present writer the sad fact today is that—*if* ethical religion is man's supreme commitment—then neither Christianity nor Judaism are the religions of most professing American religionists today. What we have, for the most part, are "Sabbath-Jews" and "Sunday-Christians." Both days, in each case, are only one of seven! For more than six-and-a-half days we practice the philosophy of materialism and worship at the shrine of American nationalism. We want, we need, nay, we have to have things, contraptions, material objects, luxuries—without these we cannot do; and we are perfectly willing on Friday night or on Sunday to ask God's blessing upon these our material necessities. Our supreme devotion is not only *not* to God, and not even to man—but only to a relatively small segment of the human race, namely those who happen to live between the Atlantic and the Pacific Ocean and between the Rio Grande and the Great Lakes. The nation is not only our *real* God; it demands and gets our both supreme and unquestioning loyalty. In fact, to question it is treason!

If Christians do not take their own publicly professed—but actually unpracticed—religion seriously, why should philosophers? Which, one supposes, is another way of saying that if Christians want philosophers to take their religion seriously, they had better themselves begin to do so. Such a demand is, of course, nothing new. But it will have to be made over and over again, "world without end," inasmuch as the demand has hardly yet been heeded by more than a handful.

Contrary to the requirements for membership laid down by most orthodox Christian institutions, so far as this writer has been able to ascertain, the Nazarene himself laid down *only one test* for discipleship, when he said: "By this shall all men know that ye are my disciples, that ye love one another" (John 13:35). And: "By their fruits ye shall know them" (Matthew 7:16).

Suppose we apply these criteria to today's official Christendom. In doing so, let us remember that the criteria are *not* supplied by philosophers from out of their bag of philosophical concepts, but are taken right out of the very mouth of the founder of Christianity, at least insofar as the record we have in the New Testament is trustworthy! The so-called fruits of their "love for each other" are, perhaps, too well known to require detailed enumeration or analysis; such, for example, as the tortures of the crusaders, the Inquisition, the endless proliferation of denominations and sects, and their profound respect and love for each other, as shown, just for example, in the national election of 1960!

No, I fear today's institutional Christianity stands self-condemned by the one test its founder provided.

I am sorry about all this, truly sorry. For I am myself a product of this religion. It is not easy to come to such conclusions or to make such pronouncements. But, both as a philosopher *and* as a religionist, I am not merely interested in the truth, I am dedicated to the search for it. Was it not Jesus himself who said: "...the truth shall make you free"? My respect for truth requires that what I have been saying be said.

If these things be so, then philosophy can have little truck with the Christianity that *is*.

But the religion of Jesus, the principles of the Sermon on the Mount, the ideals of the two great (so-called) commandments —those are something else again. Here we come face to face with ethical concepts and ideas which are grounded, if not in the universe at large (to prove this might be beyond the finite powers of finite man), then at least in the nature of man and in his rational-moral-spiritual capacities.

If the universe is such that its evolutionary process has not merely made the appearance of a being endowed with rational, moral, and spiritual capacities possible—and this, fortunately, is no longer a debatable question if, indeed, it ever was!—but which offers a habitat where those capacities have an opportu-

nity to develop and increase to unknown and perhaps unknow-
able limits, then ethical principles and Christian ideals are
neither homeless here nor the mere Utopian dreaming of softheaded idealists. If, in the light of the fact that this earth "is
red in tooth and claw," it cannot be said that the Universe is
on the side of ethical religious commitment, it can at least be
asserted that neither is it opposed to such principles and growth.
What is more, so far as the *human* universe is concerned, it
seems fairly clear that human progress depends not merely upon
man's intellectual growth, but upon his moral and spiritual
advance every bit as much. If it is true, for example, as Charles
A. Beard pointed out, that "the cause of our moral confusion
lies in our contemptuous dismissal of ethics," then it is implied
that human progress itself is inescapably tied up with ethical
advance. Man's further religious development will depend *not*
upon the further proliferation of religious myths or (so-called)
orthodox beliefs, but upon the increasing infusion of ethical and
spiritual considerations and principles, all thoroughly grounded
if not in rational, then, in any case in not irrational concepts.
Reason, by itself, may never be an ultimate criterion. But for
a being that possesses a mind and has the capacity of using it,
unreason certainly is, even though only a negative one. Which
is another way of saying that no rational creature has any rational, moral, or spiritual right to believe anything which goes
counter to his best rational judgment—*in* Christianity or out.
Man's reason may be faulty, since man, after all, is only finite
and limited. But it is never so faulty as is *unreason*.

This does not mean that we are advocating a return to a new
rationalism. It does mean that we cannot afford to remain in
an age of credulous and soft irrationalism.

The Christianity (or, for that matter, any other religion) which
would have the right to appeal to the thinking man of today
and tomorrow will, first, have to rid itself of its irrational, mythi-
cal elements, and, second, have to appeal to the highest, noblest,
sublimest, and best ethical and spiritual judgments of which the

modern mind is capable. This is not to say that even the highest, noblest, sublimest and best which man may be able to think, imagine, or understand today will not have to yield to still higher thoughts and profounder understanding tomorrow . . . and tomorrow . . . and tomorrow. For man, at any time, is after all only finite, and his thoughts and understanding are therefore always limited and relative. But it is this very fact that leaves the door wide open—in religion as, indeed, in anything else—for endless human progress and advance.

A religion geared to such an ethical world view not only will have nothing to fear from philosophy (or science), but also will find in philosophy a helpful co-worker in the process of making this world a better place in which to live. *The* "Millennium" may not come by any sudden divine interference. But many increasingly more "millennial millennia may very well be created by a mankind espousing, proclaiming, and—most importantly!—living, in spirit and in truth, such a (Christian) religion.

The view here developed will be accused of being too humanistic to be Christian. I shall be charged with having left God out of consideration. To this charge I plead both guilty and not guilty. Guilty in the sense that I believe that *any* religion is *man's* religion (*not* God's) and that it is up to man to build a new and better world (or, if he insists, destroy himself and all his works); but not guilty in the sense that—if there is a God—then this is, after all, God's world, a world in which he allowed man to evolve: man with his rational-moral-spiritual capacities. Into such a being's hand He has laid man's own fate: for good or for ill. The adventurous God took an awesome chance in such a being's evolutionary creation, but one which was immensely worth the taking. Whether man will measure up to this great opportunity or, instead, destroy himself, who knows?

The challenge is ours. It only awaits man's reaction.

ROGER HAZELTON

Theology

IN many respects the subject of this chapter has been treated, or at any rate illustrated, in those which have preceded it. Theology in any cultural period, of course, involves thinking through the implications and consequences of the Christian faith for its own witness and mission in the world. Indeed, theology takes place precisely at the frontier between church and world, which after all is where Christians must give a reason for the hope that is in them. All theology is then frontier theology, whether its primary movement is one of defensive shrinkage or of aggressive encounter. The foregoing chapters have already given good and sufficient evidence of this fact.

Nevertheless, there may be considerable merit in directing attention now to what might be called the theological enterprise itself. For good or ill, theology is an academic discipline carried on largely by professional teachers. It has long been one of the branches into which humane learning is divided. Though no one would wish to restrict its meaning to the sort of thing which happens in classrooms and gets written down in textbooks, it would be decidedly unrealistic not to grant the predominantly academic and professional character of present-day theology. This may be in part regretted, but it can scarcely be denied.

This fact about theology has some real advantages which should not be overlooked. For one thing, it makes possible a large and growing measure of genuine theological community. As a way of thinking and working shared by many persons equipped with special aptitudes and kinds of training, theology embraces common problems, common methods, and a common technical language. Such community is far from perfect; it is constantly being threatened by religious and cultural disunity; but it does manage to exist, and there are signs that it is steadily increasing.

Another advantage in the academic and professional character of present-day theology concerns its frankly intellectual orientation and purpose. Theologians are not "idea men" whose efforts constitute a kind of propaganda ministry on behalf of actual Christianity, but scholars and interpreters to whom has been entrusted the communication of the truth of Christian faith. They are generally responsible church members as well, and naturally engaged in commending the grounds of their own allegiance to others; but the meanings and issues which are bound up with the study and teaching of theology are such as to throw theologians willy-nilly into the midst of the intellectual arena, with its claims and counterclaims to the possession of truth, its specialisms, and absolutisms.

Yet there are undoubted disadvantages, too, in the fact that most contemporary theologians are teachers of a subject called theology. The complaint is often voiced that theologians work in an atmosphere of calculated impracticality if not irrelevance, writing only for each other, and woefully out of touch with the ongoing life of their churches. One may properly point out that this charge is partly unjustified or that it can be explained by nontheological factors; but the gap in communication is there, it is unfortunate, and steps should be taken to bridge it. Church people regularly ask, "Why must theology be so difficult?" The fact that they do not ask this sort of question with reference to equally difficult studies like sociological research or mathematical physics may actually be a kind of backhanded tribute to theology; it may mean that theology, unlike these other subjects, has or ought to have an eminently practical and personal bearing upon Christian existence in the world.

A further disadvantage consists in the fact that when it is

thus conceived and carried on, theology represents the calling of Christian individuals rather than the vocation of the Church. Theologians should not merely be academic personnel, and certainly not in any sense an intellectual élite, if this carries with it any connotation of ivory-tower isolation or special privilege; they must do their thinking, as most of them now do it, on behalf of the whole Church and with reference to its widest and deepest concerns. The day for private speculative theologizing is clearly past. There is great need for the patient building of consensus, the frank encounter of traditions, the willing exposure to the unfamiliar and the hitherto-suspected viewpoint. This can only happen within the church-at-large and with its blessing, encouragement, and solid support.

The justification for theology, if any be required, is given in the following statement by Daniel D. Williams. "What theologians are doing," he writes, "is as necessary to human life as breathing. Man is the being who asks for the meaning of his own existence. He must know who he is and who God is, what justice is, what to hope for." [1] However functionalized and clericalized in the contemporary world, Christian theology represents an essential and enduring human quest. We shall see in the ensuing pages just how this search for the fundamental human relevance of theology is being prosecuted, and what its present posture and future possibilities may be said to be.

THE CURRENT CHALLENGE

Like any other sort of human endeavor, theology must be understood as a juncture of the old and the new. This is to say that it has both a conservative and a constructive function to perform. Today this twofold stance is particularly noticeable and also emphatically necessary. There are the gains from almost

[1] In *What Present-Day Theologians Are Thinking* (New York: Harper & Brothers, 1959), p. 174.

a generation of theological revival, often called neo-orthodoxy, still to be realized and consolidated. It must be admitted frankly that what goes on in local churches, on the North American continent at any rate, does not reflect the fact that we have been experiencing a veritable theological revolution over the past thirty years. Surely the sermon topics, services of worship, or group activities in the Protestant churches we know best give little evidence that something truly radical and reformative has been taking place in recent theology. There are outstanding exceptions, of course; and yet there almost seems to be a kind of bottleneck within our anomalous, amalgamated, activistic Protestantism that, notwithstanding years of seminary teaching, ecumenical encounter, study conferences, continues to repel the truth which theologians have been trying to point out to us.

This is all the more remarkable since recent theology has in fact been more closely and consciously related to the life and work of the Church than possibly at any time during the past two centuries. Such theology has by and large been "confessional" theology; its intent has been far more the proclamation than the accommodation of the central Christian doctrines; and its whole orientation has been toward the Church as a historic fellowship called into being through covenant with God, carrying forward the redeeming work of Christ within the present world, and living in expectation of the final consummation of his victory over sin, guilt, and death. Yet it must probably be concluded that what theologians have been calling "the Church" bears very little manifest resemblance to the organizations to which church members "belong." It is understandable that they should feel an obvious contradiction, or at any rate a decided irrelevance.

The way out of this apparent impasse is not for theologians to shrink and harden their confessional outlook, and certainly not to abandon it altogether. Some important lessons have been learned, some emphases and motifs established, which need nothing so much as to be communicated more tellingly and on

a wider Christian and cultural front. There is no way back to
the earlier, more self-assured and rationally acceptable viewpoint of theological "liberalism." To suppose that such an avenue was still open would merely add to the inevitable scandal
of the Christian faith the further and gratuitous offense of an
unrealistic utopianism. At least, neo-orthodoxy managed to
address itself to the sort of experience we know well; it spoke
from and to our situation of personal despair and cultural dis-
illusionment; and it is clear that this is still in large part our
condition. In a time of nuclear madness, something more is
required than commendations of the reasonableness of Christianity. The wisdom of God can hardly be dovetailed or made
continuous with the all-too-evident foolishness of men.

The great and durable merit of neo-orthodox theology (we
may as well adopt the label, inaccurate and misleading as in
many respects it is) consists in its dominant stress upon the
creative priority and saving initiative of God as disclosed in
Jesus Christ, and upon faith not as a problem-solving or security-
producing experience but rather as God's own gift, unmerited
and free. Thanks to this movement in theology, we now know
what the gospel is; there is little danger that we shall again confuse faith with works or God with religion; we have been recalled to the sources of our being as Christians living by the
grace and under the judgment of God. It is not likely that the
lessons taught by neo-orthodoxy, once learned, will be soon
forgotten.

Yet the posture of crisis cannot be prolonged indefinitely, in
theology or anywhere else, and the time has clearly come for
something more than bare reiteration. Now that the *kerygma*
has been given the chance to speak for itself, as it were, without
the well-intentioned but incongruous supports of earlier liberalism, it must not be allowed to remain sheer enigma. Implications need to be traced, and assumptions brought into the
open. What is valid in neo-orthodoxy, obviously, is precisely
that element of orthodox or right-believing faith to which it

called our attention so emphatically. What has to be discarded is its "neo" character—that is, the rather stylized traditionalism and schematic repetitiousness into which it has sometimes fallen.

This breaking-up process is already under way, and it has been initiated chiefly by thinkers influenced by the very perspective they seek to widen. Hence our immediate theological future, it would seem, does not belong to a resurgence of liberalism, even though some liberal features, especially in the realm of ethics, will almost certainly come into their own again. It would be wholly inaccurate to characterize this next period as a "great debate" between neo-orthodoxy and liberalism; in all probability neither of these will remain as live options for a Christian thinker who takes seriously both the conservative and the constructive task.

As theology takes place at the juncture of the old and new, "between the times," so it is always in motion and cannot wait for the church-at-large to catch up with it. The frontier on which it stands and exists is an expanding, ever-changing one. There is great need for translation of the central Christian doctrines into the vocabulary of daily human circumstance, and this requires apologetic gifts of a high order. But the need is greater still for exploration into the depths and heights of human existence aided by the light of these same doctrines, and this calls for a more daring, uninhibited kind of wisdom. Let us hope that in the next theological generation such wisdom may be released and encouraged more generously.

A REVELATION OF RELEVANCE

The situation in theology today may also be characterized in terms of the relationship between man and the gospel. We have been told rather often in the past decade or two that the word of God spoken in Christ meets and fits our human condition; it has not always been made clear just how and why it does so. Even when such an attempt has been made, it has customarily taken the form of dreary generalizations purporting to come from the gospel, almost invariably judgmental and imperative, calling for "response" on the part of man. The tenor of such pronouncements has been sweeping, abrupt, Germanic, with very little of either humor or compassion in them.

In keeping with the prevailing mood, theologians have made use of subhuman metaphors such as stimulus-and-response or vertical-and-horizontal for conveying the relationship of the gospel to man. Thus they have attempted to elucidate the truth in Barth's early dictum that "there is no way from man to God; there is only a way from God to man." This conception of revelation and redemption as a one-way street has in fact become distorted out of all resemblance to the gospel itself. Even the "I-Thou" motif is usually rendered in the terms of confrontation or sheer up-againstness. Man is encountered, brought up short, called to account by the gospel which always comes to him "from above downwards." In its light he stands revealed for what he is; he stands "in crisis" exposed and evacuated of all self-assurance; his utter obedience and once-for-all decision are demanded.

As a needed reaction to much in liberal theology, in particular its gradualism and optimism, this stress can be understood and approved. But as basic theological interpretation it leaves very much to be desired. Man and the gospel are made for each other. They belong together. This, too, is a part of the gospel. It becomes exceedingly difficult to make this clear within the restrictive and depersonalized categories of much neo-orthodox thinking. It is not merely a wish to say a good word for man, or to give him something to hope and work for, that motivates today the theological reaction to this neo-orthodox reaction; it is rather the suspicion that some implications of the gospel itself have not been faced, that part of the important truth of faith yet remains to be said.

Furthermore, it is the gospel that makes man man. It addresses him not as an assortment of functions or a player of social roles; it speaks to his true condition and represents "deep calling unto deep." This profoundly humanizing purpose of the gospel needs elucidation and defense. It cannot be conveyed through geometrical or mechanical symbols. Such an effort only makes plain anew that the letter kills, but the spirit gives life.

The word which expresses this newer concern in theology is "relevance." The gospel is about man and for man. It creates a new human situation, proclaiming what is true of every man and always because of what God has done for all men, and offering to all the gracious gift for which faith is the only condition. It does not depend upon our knowledge, belief, or assent that God has acted in Jesus Christ to save those who in love he created and sustains. Yet this gospel is entirely pertinent to man as he truly is, whatever he may pretend to be or imagine he is. Not only does it speak a word to his condition, telling and timely; it offers and invites him into newness of life, forgiveness of sins, and the blessedness of peace with God.

This concern with relevance is to be rather carefully contrasted with the recent theological interest in preserving the purity of the gospel. The two aims are not necessarily antithetical, but they are certainly different. What many of us are saying now is that relevance must take precedence over purity. The fear of contamination, of the admixture of alien ideas and categories, is altogether understandable in a period of new-found Christian self-consciousness and self-definition. Then thinkers must distinguish sharply between biblical and classical forms of thought, between Jerusalem and Athens, between faith and reason. But if one continues indefinitely in this game of line drawing and fence building, the cause of the gospel itself suffers. Now, instead, Christian theology must find ways of calling men to claim their rightful inheritance and to live on the promises of God.

Just before the turn of the present century P. T. Forsyth ventured to set the Spirit over against the Word as affording different vantage points for theological reflection. Although he

employed this distinction primarily to characterize different
types of church order, it can also be extended to the relationship
between man and the gospel. In his Word, God binds himself
to man, limits himself, tells man who he is. But in his Spirit,
God imparts himself, gives himself away, becomes internal to
man. Neither Spirit nor Word can stand alone, and in the last
analysis each illumines and completes the other. That is why
each belongs, theologically speaking, within the Godhead. The
deepening persuasion of present-day theology is that a pattern
of interpretation based chiefly upon God as Word must now be
corrected by fuller, more generous reference to God as Spirit.
In this way, it is felt, the true relevance of the gospel for the
human condition may be stated and shown, as in fact the good
news which God intended it to be.

ENCOMPASSING THE SECULAR

Again, the present theological moment may be seen in terms
of an exciting consensus which appears to be forming on the
nature of the church *vis-à-vis* the world. Thus far the consensus
has been taking place chiefly under ecumenical auspices in separate studies and conferences, although there are very solid evidences of the same kind of thinking in the systematic work of
Paul Tillich with its strongly apologetic interest, as also in
Barth's later work, particularly in his volumes on the doctrine
of creation.

The "church-against-the-world" emphasis of twenty or thirty
years back is now being radically questioned and superseded by
a far more positive appreciation of the secular and the cultural,
and on explicitly Christian grounds. Except for a few defensive
sectarian backwaters, this development is widespread. "Secularism" is no longer linked with "paganism" as defining the target
at which the gospel is to be "thrown like a stone." There is even
much consideration given to the meaning of such terms as

"Christian worldliness" or "sophistication." Clearly, this represents a drastically altered orientation and perspective.

Some words of Robert McAfee Brown set the newer mood and bear most cogently upon the matter:

> ... whatever else we are, we are men of the world, and do not cease to be men of the world when we become theologians ... the world is God's world. Because he has been pleased to act within it in a life and a death and a resurrection, we must be confident that having set his mark upon it, he may also be acting within it at many other places too. Since we have seen him at work in the world of Jesus Christ, we must be prepared to see him at work in other places in the world that Jesus Christ redeemed ... it is the world that God loved so much that he sent his only begotten Son into it. Our theology does not separate us from the world. It ties us more closely than ever to it.[2]

A statement like this is made not as a throwback to liberal theology but in extension and correction of neo-orthodox insights. There can be no question here of infidelity or treason to the plain word of God spoken in Christ. On the contrary, this kind of thinking takes with utter seriousness the substance of the doctrines of incarnation and atonement; it is through and through christological.

For Christian theology, to be sure, the world has a double meaning. It is not only the object of God's love but also the place where love is violated and denied, where faith is tempted and threatened, where we have tribulation. There can be no simple affirmation of the world which is not at the same time its negation. But this is not to be understood Buddhistically as any sort of refusal to become involved. The deeper Christian truth about the world is that, in spite of the principalities and powers which lord it over men, the world still belongs to God; far from being merely a neutral realm, it is the realm in which

<hr>

[2] In "Theology as an Act of Gratitude," *Union Seminary Quarterly Review*, December, 1960, p. 93.

response to God must be made, in which it is strictly impossible for man to be neutral toward God. The world has indeed already been redeemed, "in principle if not in fact," to borrow Reinhold Niebuhr's well-known phrase; and this is where our thinking about it must begin.

This changed conception of the world has its counterpart in a changed understanding of the Church. Theologians are now asking if there is not something profoundly secular and by no means simply "religious" about the gospel itself. Dietrich Bonhoeffer once described his theological task as "giving a non-religious interpretation to biblical ideas." For this and other similar remarks he has frequently been accused of being a liberal theologian—a charge which is clearly quite wide of the mark. Ever since Kierkegaard was rediscovered, the view of the Church as the divinely appointed repository and propagator of Christian truth has been under heavy attack in theological quarters. In particular, the Church as the institution for promoting "religion," as well as human religiousness itself, has come in for scathing criticism.

What is now being said more and more frequently and strongly is that the nature and the mission of the Church are one. The truth is not that the Church has a mission for the world, but that it is God's mission to the world. In this vein one may even claim that the Church is most itself when it is least itself—that is, when it is intent upon giving away its truth, identifying itself as did its Lord with the lot and likes of men. The true form of the Church, then, is precisely the form of the servant which was assumed by Jesus. We do not ask first what the Church is, and only then what it ought to do. As God himself is a missionary God, so the Church *is* mission—for it to be is to be sent, to lose its life, to serve mankind. And this, let it be cautioned, is neither a diluted humanitarianism nor a complacent evangelism. It is not an effort to "apply" the gospel, but rather to think in its light and to act with its help.

Among the more significant tokens of this changed conception of the Church is a far-reaching awareness of the place of the laity, that is, the *ministry* of the laity, in effecting redemptive contact between the Church and the world. At the ecumenical level, it has been insisted that the Church realizes its servant-form in the world not primarily by pronouncement, corporate action, or decision, but through the taking part of Christian men and women "incognito" in the common tasks of social life where the joy and the cost of their discipleship is made manifest and operative. "The place for the salt is in the soup," says Hans-Ruedi Weber, echoing Jesus' metaphor of the Christian life.

Theologically, this new awareness has tremendous implications for the understanding of the Church, as both a gathering and a scattering of the whole people of God (*laos*). It makes laity and ministry interchangeable terms, whatever may be the purely functional differences between ordained and nonordained church members. It stresses dialogue and alongsidedness with the world rather than the didactic stance. It asks whether there may not be a "style of life" which renders Christian conversation and penetration of the world possible. Again, the Church is seen as existing in and for the world; and it is made clear that in order not to be *of* the world the Christian must first of all be *in* it. The consequences of this view for the Protestant-Catholic dialogue are only now beginning to be explored, with chief attention being given to the matters of ordination and vocation. There is good reason to hope that future theology will follow up these significant clues with reference to baptism and the eucharist, relations between men and women, church order, and the lay apostolate.

THE FRONTIER OF DIVINE MYSTERY

The last type of theological tension or polarity to be mentioned here is that between mystery and meaning. This is by no means the peculiar concern of present-day theology. Christian thinkers have always been engaged in making meaningful the fundamentally mysterious substance of the truth of faith. But our present situation contains elements which render this task especially important and imperative. On the one hand, there is the widespread assumption that radical mystery is no longer needed as a category for interpreting man's being-in-the-world or, what amounts to the same thing, that it is merely a name for our current ignorance. At the same time, there is apparently general agreement that the criteria of meaning must be narrowed and sharpened, following the model of scientific thinking. Taken together, these add up to the persuasion that one must become very dubious indeed about so-called theological truth.

On the other hand, however, it is now plain as never before that mankind lives by nonliteral and even nonverbal symbols whose truth-value may be suspect but which nonetheless succeed in ordering and rendering experience. They may not yield verification, but do bring necessary and comprehensive clarification. Is it not gratuitous to deny "meaning" to those modes of personal and concrete apprehension like picture, poetry, and myth by which we do in fact express both positively and negatively what is meaningful in our existence?

Theology today, dominated largely by an existentialist philosophical base, has tended to take its stand against all the reductive attacks of the logical analysts. Yet even these latter have become more willing to grant a certain sort of meaning to theological statements. Theologians of the next generation will be forced to defend their conception of the truth of faith more cogently and persuasively, not simply by polemics against analytic reductionism and scientism, but by providing the grounds of a conversation with all men on the basis of generally shared experience and reflection. Ultimately, the truth that is in Christ must be of a piece with all other truth, else Christ would not be the very Logos or meaning of God respecting man's existence.

Whenever we ask or seek to answer theological questions we come up against the fact that we are trying to say something which cannot finally be said at all. We find that we have to put into words which make a pattern of intelligible meaning something which is at bottom so mysterious that every attempt to reduce it to self-evidence is at once self-defeating. The polarity which provokes all theological reflection is fundamentally that between the word of God, his speech to us about himself, and our own human words in all their impetuous frailty and brokenness. How does a theologian get to work in such a situation? Not by reveling in mystery or "throwing paradoxes at people's heads," as Tillich says; and certainly not by presuming to have the last, best word to say about God's mystery which surpasses knowledge. No, the theologian must say what this mystery does in fact mean, locating it and calling it by its right name, marking it and protecting it from the dissolving acids of scientism and rationalism. The task of theology is today what it has always been—that of limiting human meaning by the frontier of divine mystery. It is the work of making our own a reasonable understanding of what has first been given us through faith.

One requirement for entering upon this task is that theology must allow God to be heard, to speak for himself, as it were. Under no circumstances must theology be permitted to become a kind of Christian ideology, a form of club talk or shop talk about God's deed in Jesus Christ. The second requirement has to do with the kind of statements made about God's action in theology. They must be of such a sort that the mystery of God is built into them, so that they suggest far more than they can possibly say. It is no accident that the earliest word for "creed" was "symbol." Symbols have the avowed purpose of opening up dimensions of reality and truth which would otherwise remain hidden and cannot be grasped in any other way. They are truly adequate, even rationally adequate, to the extent to which they point beyond themselves and so communicate their own inadequacy. Perhaps it is paradoxical to say so, but the more transparent a symbol is to the transcendence that inspires it, the truer and more meaningful it is.

Theology is a rich complex of such symbols, each and all of them involved in translating mystery into meaning, but achieving this by means of fidelity or authenticity which discloses God's transcendent worth and power. (Immanence is as mysterious as transcendence!) Theologians may never rightly claim to have the last word to say concerning God, but they must always make sure that they have given God the opportunity to say the first word.

What is theology, then, in this or any age, but a manner of speaking about God which opens up and makes way for God's speaking to us? Its truth is not rational but reasonable, not blatantly paradoxical but profoundly personal. Therefore, as theology arises in doxology, so it must inevitably return to doxology. It is from first to last the intellectual praise of God.

Rev. A. Ettenhofer